De Anima, or About the Soul

De Anima, or About the Soul
Aristotle

Translated and Edited by Glen Coughlin

WILLIAM OF MOERBEKE
Translation Series

Stuart D. Warner, Series Director

ST. AUGUSTINE'S PRESS
South Bend, Indiana

Manufactured in the United States of America.

1 2 3 4 5 6   27 26 25 24 23 22

Library of Congress Control Number: 2021949683

hardback ISBN: 978-1-58731-200-7
paperback ISBN: 978-1-58731-201-4
epub ISBN: 978-1-58731-202-1

∞ The paper used in this publication meets the minimum
requirements of the American National Standard for Information Sciences –
Permanence of Paper for Printed Materials, ANSI Z39.48-1984.

St. Augustine's Press
www.staugustine.net

For Maureen

Contents

Introduction

> You would not find out the limits of soul,
> even by travelling every path, so deep is its
> account.

> Heraclitus, Fr. 45

Whereas the *Physics* of Aristotle lays the groundwork for the study of all nature,[1] the *De* Anima (or *On the Soul*) is the most fundamental work in one part of that study, biology, the study of the most developed of natural things.[2] This book is the first one in Aristotle's work on biology, the fifth in his natural science.[3] As the name indicates, its subject matter is "the soul." This already raises red flags.

How can there be a philosophical study of the soul? If it exists at all (and many would deny it), it is an object of faith, not of philosophy. Very few modern biologists, except those moved by faith, would ever posit a soul, and even fewer would follow Aristotle in speaking about the souls of plants.

The first problem is simply equivocation. "Soul" translates the Greek, "ψυχή;" it can also translate the Latin, "anima." Both words originally mean "breath." The word "soul" itself is more difficult to pin down, but it seems to come from Gothic and Old German words connected to words having to do with swiftness, motion, and strength. These etymologies, as etymologies are wont to do, point us to the basic experiences people must have had when first naming the things in question. Soul looks to have meant something like an inner force or something that moves within things that seem to have such inner principle, i.e., living things; the Greek and Latin point to an obvious sign (or, one might think, cause) of life in the most familiar of living things. Soul, then, seems to be understood simply as the principle of life. A thing is alive, so it has a soul. It may not have a soul which can be separated from the body, or it may. Perhaps some living

---

1   See Coughlin, 2005, pp. x–xv, 209–218.
2   Aristotle argues that the study of the soul belongs to natural science or natural philosophy in I.1, 403a16–28. He qualifies the claim at *Meta.* VI.1, 1025b34–1026a6.
3   In the order of doctrine (not necessarily of composition), the *Physics* would be the first work in natural philosophy, followed by the *De Caelo, De Generatione, Meteorologica*; after this comes the *De Anima, De Sensu et Sensato, De Memoria*, etc.

things have such souls and others do not (which is Aristotle's view). But what is common to all is that they are alive and so must have a principle of life within them. Whatever that is, whether fire particles, or the harmony of the parts of the body, or electrical impulses, or DNA, or an immortal spirit, it is called "soul."

All of which explains why one of the first things Aristotle says in this book is that we have great certainty or precision about the soul.[4] This seems a foolish claim when so many deny the existence of the soul. But they do not really; they only deny the existence of a soul as understood by some philosophical or religious tradition. They really mean that they do not believe in a separate spiritual thing inhabiting the body, or in an immortal part of human beings. If they were to understand the word "soul" as Aristotle does, they would say no such thing. They do not fail to recognize that they are alive, one hopes; consequently, they cannot be unsure about whether they have some principle of life, but rather about what it is. And this agrees entirely with what Aristotle is saying: The certainty about the soul to which Aristotle is referring is about the existence of the soul as a principle of life, not about what it is. In fact, he almost immediately goes on to say that there are serious difficulties in figuring out *what* the soul is.[5]

Well, then, if the soul is the principle of life, we must ask what life is. The fundamental notion of life seems to have to do with self-movement and sensation or knowledge.[6] If either of these are present, we think there is life. Definitions proposed by biologists are varied, but uniformly identify the living with what displays certain operations, such as growth, reproduction, sensation, irritability, homeostasis, metabolism, etc., or with what has at least some of these operations.[7] All these may be reduced to self-motion or to knowledge of some sort. Even homeostasis, which seems like a sort of state or condition, implies that the organism which remains in that state is actively producing that result. It is not a lack of activity but the work of maintaining a positive disposition for life.

The experiences and evidence upon which the modern scientist depends in his definitions and his arguments may be called "external:" They are known or verified by looking outside of ourselves, by looking, e.g., to measuring sticks and clocks and balances, reducing our observations to what is intelligible in terms of centimeters, seconds, and grams. If we cannot always manage that, we still want to be able to define in terms of things which are "objective," i.e., available to us not by introspection, but by observation of the exterior world. We want to see the evidence and we want it to be the sort of evidence that can be shared, so that others can look at what we are looking at and verify what we claim; that way, we can all have some confidence in the truth of the observations and can judge whatever claims are based on them.

4   I.1, 402a1–3.
5   I.1, 402a10–22.
6   I.2, 403b25–27
7   See, e.g., Harold, 2001, p. 232.

The difficulty with an exclusive dependence on exterior observation is patent: Even if we stick to such evidence, it is only available to us because we can sense it. However much it may be true that we can verify the observation that the internal temperature of a human being is, when he is healthy, more or less 98.6 degrees Fahrenheit, unless I experience seeing the thermometer, there will be no such verification. If I were so dogmatic as to reject that experience as unobjective, I am no longer qualified to be a scientist. Modern science, like every other discipline, presupposes certain experiences, in particular, sensations.

Not only is the experience of the observations and experiments of modern science necessary for the science to exist at all, it is also true that experience really has two sides: We experience the extra-mental reality of the object of study, but we also experience our experiencing of it. We are conscious of the fact that we are sensing and measuring and speaking to others about our results. Every healthy person is aware that he senses, thinks, moves, etc. Serious denial of this can only come from obstinacy or madness. Even if I claim that our perception of all these things is merely an epiphenomenon of some stimulation of the brain, I assume the existence of brains and their activities, which are only known to exist by these very sorts of experiences.

The communicability and "objectivity" of the experience sought for in the natural sciences is, besides, only attainable on one side: I can reproduce an experiment you perform and experience the sort of thing you experienced, but I can never experience your experience of your experiment. That is unrepeatable even for you – all you can do is remember it. Every experience is that of a single person at a single time, directly accessible to that person alone. Are we going to discount this experience because it is not external or measured or repeatable?

In fact, if I am to understand what it is to be alive, I must refer to my own experience of living. To know what it is to sense, even in the most superficial way, I have to experience it myself. Your doing so won't help, for I could never even judge that you sense at all without having myself sensed and compared the ways I respond to what I sense to the ways I see you respond to what I sense: We both jump when the thunder roars. Nor can I understand self-motion without the interior experience of being a self-mover. I cannot tell by external observation alone that a dog is moving himself. The fact that I see no other mover is hardly a reason – no one thinks that rocks fall down by moving themselves even though we don't see a mover in that case either. Much less can I tell simply by looking at the constituents of dogs or people, at their chemical makeup or measurable physical properties like volume or density or electrical charge. None of these reveal life and are, in fact, only seen as related in some way to life when I can correlate some internal experience to some external experience. In some cases, I do this without really thinking about it. I see my hands with my eyes using external experience, and I move them and feel things with them using an internal experience which no exterior experience could ever replace. Other times, I need to do a little more work to correlate the external and internal experiences. I need a reason to connect a scan revealing brain activity to certain activities of life, for example, seeing or remembering. Without the subject of such a scan reporting what he is internally experiencing while the scan reveals certain neural actions, we would never have any reason to connect the two, and if I did not myself have internal experience, I would not even know what he meant when he said he had experienced seeing color or remembering a distant past. The external experience, which is all the scientific observer has, could never by itself suffice for the understanding of the scan.

These two sides of experience, exterior and interior, are both necessary for the study of life, but in a different way than they are for, say, physics. In physics, one must experience the observations and this means one must both know the thing outside the mind in the natural world and must be oneself aware of that knowing. But the awareness of knowing is not itself another thing to be drawn upon as a datum of the science. If we are to study biology, however, we need to recognize life, and we do so by recognizing living operations. If we fail to do so, we will be like the man born blind who still studies optics: He may understand all the mathematics and even grasp the definitions of the variables and constants in his equations, but without the actual experience of color and light, he will simply not know what he is talking about. Similarly, living activities are not discernable by merely exterior experience. Modern biologists tend to find it hard to define their own field of study precisely because they insist on studying it as if it were physics or chemistry. It is not; it is a more specialized field with a different set of basic experiences to call upon. In particular, it calls upon self-reflection.

Just as our exterior experience should not be cut off from our interior experience, so neither should attention to our interior experience cut us off from exterior experience. In fact, we know that we move ourselves because by interior experience we know ourselves as movers and we know ourselves as being moved partly by the exterior experience that goes along with it. We recognize that we move our limbs and we feel our feet moving and stepping on the ground and, as we do so, know by sight that we are moving within our surroundings. Our interior experience matches our exterior experience; we put these together into one coherent experience of living. Having done so, we are able to recognize that other organisms react as we do to their environments. We see cats turn their eyes toward a bird, creep up on it, stalk it, and pounce. Each part of this process is something we recognize as belonging to a living thing because it is so like some things we ourselves do, and in doing, recognize that we are both mover and moved, sensing and desiring. Without this recognition of living operations in ourselves and others, there simply would be no such thing as biology. There would be no discernable subject, unless we arbitrarily name certain chemical or physical processes "life." But what we really mean by the word "life" is not those processes, but self-movement and sensation and knowing.

From the fact that we need to use internal experience to begin biology we must not draw the false conclusion that our initial knowledge is a sort of direct intuition of the soul, as if we were immediately aware of the soul in itself. Rather, we understand it only as a principle. We know our vital activities arise from ourselves, that we are principles of them, and also that they in some way remain within us or terminate within us. We thus know ourselves already as divided into a mover and a mobile, and we call the mover the soul. Our own experience isolates, in a way, our soul, but, for all that, we have no direct intuition of the soul and we still do not know what it is in itself.

None of this is intended to denigrate the modern biologists or their definitions. When the modern biologists define life, they do so in a way appropriate to their inquiries into life. They are interested in the chemical bases of life, in the physical structures that permit life, in replication of DNA as a mechanism for passing on traits, etc. All of this is laudable and even wonderful, and it would be silly to deny that without the strict empirical methods of the modern scientists, we would be a great deal more ignorant of life than we are. As in chemistry and physics, thinking about everyday observations is simply not up to the task when digging into the details of mechanisms and physical structures. But (restricting ourselves here to biology) those methods, though they reveal wonderful and unexpected truths, do not actually make sense when abstracted from our initial experience of life, depending as it does on both external and internal experience.

But one might object: If I am right, how can the modern biologists, if they insist on nothing but external experience, get anywhere at all in biology? It is probably better to say that they refuse interior experience in words but rely on it in fact. They do not reflect their own dependence on internal experience, but admit it tacitly in, e.g., their list of vital operations. How do they know that *these* are the sorts of activities they ought to list, when they themselves admit they cannot define life? I suggest it is because they really do recognize their own living activities as such and use that knowledge it in their thinking, but do so more or less unreflectively. It is hard to see how their investigations can be so very illuminating if they do not know what they are talking about at all. Even if they disagree with Aristotle or each other about the nature of life, that disagreement itself depends upon a more fundamental agreement about what life is. They cannot disagree about whether life is this or that if they do not even mean the same thing by "life." That central meaning, upon which all tacitly agree, is a very primitive, indeterminate, and natural beginning of the discussion of life. They, like everyone else, do in fact know what life is, vaguely and confusedly, but still very certainly. It is upon this primitive knowledge that Aristotle draws in writing the present work.[8]

A number of important consequences follow from the centrality of interior experience in the study of life. First of all, when we recognize ourselves as

---

8 There are also some few passages in the *De Anima* that have an unhappy reliance on the outdated physical theories of Aristotle, but there is much, and that the bulk and the most important part, that does not.

moving ourselves, we see ourselves as both a mover and a mobile, as divided into two parts.[9] This experience is likely the source of the universal notion of a "soul" separate from the body, the latter being the mobile, the former the mover. "For it is not unclear whether they [i.e., animals] are moved by something, but [rather it is unclear] how one must distinguish the mover and the moved in it."[10] We give whatever it is that permits us to move ourselves the name "soul," and, if so inclined, can then set out to find out what it might be. A sign that the soul is understood as a mover set over against a mobile, the body, is that Aristotle takes it in hand to prove that the study of the soul is part of natural philosophy and he does this by proving that the operations of the soul are in some degree bodily. It is as if he thinks one might doubt that the soul is something in any way bodily.[11] The soul is understood at first as a "principle of life," nothing more.

Insofar as we notice the division between the mover and the moved, we understand the mover in us to be causing a motion in us, and so we recognize a form of motion or change in which what is moved and its mover are not utterly separated, as they are, e.g., when a baseball bat hits a ball. While we move our bodies around in space, our "soul" moves us by moving our limbs, for example. We move ourselves around by causing motions within our bodies. A motion such as this, one which does not produce an effect in an exterior object, may be called "immanent."[12] Other sorts of motion (Aristotle will point out that they are not strictly speaking motions[13]) which do not produce any exterior effect may also be called immanent, then, motions such as sensing and thinking and desiring. For in each case, the activity in some way terminates within us. When we digest food, we either turn it into energy for our activities or into parts of our own bodies. When we sense, though the thing sensed be outside, the act of sensing is inside. The same is true of thinking, and here we can even be thinking of something interior, like our own thoughts and impressions. And desire is an act of desire even when unfulfilled, when it ends in unfulfilled longing, when it terminates without gaining its object. It is this immanence which makes vital operations vital and makes them so different from the activities of the inanimate. Moreover, they indicate a transcendence of mere matter simply because material as such is passive, but in the case of immanent activities, the organism is not merely passive, but *acts in itself*. The inanimate only moves when moved by another; it never has immanent or living activities.

9   *Phys.* VIII.5, 256b33–258a5.
10   *Phys.* VIII.4, 254b28–30.
11   I,1, 403a3–28.
12   Immanent is derived from Latin, "in" (in) and "manere" (to remain) and means to remain within or to be present within.
13   II.5 417a30–b12; *Meta.* IX.6, 1048b18–36.

This interior experience is the basis for our knowledge of ourselves not only as alive, but also as individual substances, unified beings. We know that we sense and that we think, and if so, we must be some one thing which is able to know both of these. The mere fact that we know that smelling is not thinking indicates that we are unified, for only something which at once knows both of two things can tell them apart.[14] We know that our body, too, is one with us. It is not united to us only as what is known is united to what knows it. We are not only aware of our bodies, we *are* our bodies in an essential way. The body is one in substance with the one who has an intellect and the powers of sense. Besides the immediate experience we have of being our bodies, we also see by exterior experience that as we grow from single cells to fully organized and operational bodies, we grow the organs needed for sensation and thought: eyes, ears, brains, etc. These organs are bodily things, parts of our own bodies. We are not bifurcated into body and mind or body and soul. Our experience of growing also proves our unity over time. I remember when I could not see over the kitchen counter, and I know that that child is the same person as the one who now has to look down into his grandson's face. Moreover, our ability to move our bodies is also found in the same subject as these other powers. We are the ones who move ourselves because we sense or know something we want and move towards it. And while we use our senses and intellects to direct our motions, we also also use our motions to better sense and think. We walk around a statue to get a more complete idea of it. Despite the division into mover and moved implicit in our ability to move ourselves, and the separation of the known and the knower which our cognitive abilities manifest, all these functions reside in the same person, the same individual substance.

Our focus on the unity of the experience of life manifests that the Cartesian dualistic split between *res cogitans* (thinking thing) and *res extensa* (extended thing) is not real. Descartes posited that the exterior world is one of extended bodies, and the interior world, the world of our selves, is one of thought, and that there was no overlap here. While he held that the soul, the unextended *res cogitans* controlled the body by way of the pineal gland, riding about in the body as a sailor in a ship, the body really was another thing, foreign to our purely spiritual nature.[15] But this is simply contrary to experience. My consciousness extends to the tips of my fingers. I am perfectly aware that I am a being which exist throughout the length and breadth of my body. The *res extensa* is not just an inert mass, but, in the case of some animals at least, a living and sensitive being. Extension cannot be opposed to consciousness, but at least some *res extensa* are actually *res cogitans*.

So we cannot be reduced to mere extension, to complex machines. Besides

---

14 See the discussion of common sense in III.2, 426b22–29.
15 *Meditationes de Prima Philosophia*, 6; (Descartes 1964, pp. 78, 86–87); see also *Les Passions de l'Ame* (Descartes 1967, pp. 120, 351–54).

what we have just said, the parts of a machine are one only by arrangement and order: They do not come together to form one being. Rather, each part retains its identity even as they are all incorporated into the whole machine. The parts of organisms, on the contrary, are what they are because they are parts of the whole. A hand cut off from the body is no longer a hand, except equivocally. We have the interior experience of being one being. This experience, again, is found most of all in our perceiving ourselves by way of sensation and intellection.

Now, there is no contradiction (though there may seem to be one) between being composed of parts and being one substance (as opposed to being one by order or composition or function). For example, the whole word "breakfast" is composed of words which are still discernable and still retain in combination something of their meanings when taken apart, but which come together to form a new whole with a new meaning. The parts of organisms are like this: They are distinct in their functions, their boundaries, their materials, but they are not actually separate beings each on their own; in fact, they are only what they are because of the unity they find in the whole organism.

While modern biology tends to see organisms as complex assemblages of accidentally united parts, there have been moves within modern biology towards accounting for the parts of organisms in terms of their wholes, notably by Franklin Harold, who promotes the ideas of "morphogenetic fields" and "emergent properties" in his discussions of cell anatomy.[16] He sees the problems that the parts only function insofar as they are parts, and that organization does not simply arise from the chemistry of the molecular constituents of cells. How can the cell organize itself, for example? It is constantly replacing parts and moving materials from where they are produced to where they are needed. How does it "know" how to do this? By an analogy to electromagnetic and gravitational fields, the suggestion is made that the cell as a whole has an integrity allowing the parts to work in concert, so that the whole is in some way before the parts. The field is "morphogenetic" because it generates the form, the μορφή. But the field is itself a whole with differentiated parts – if not, it explains nothing – and so it cannot be the ultimate explanation of the organization of the cell.

Still, Harold's *a priori* commitment to a materialist conception of life[17] seems to prevent him from seeing that the whole is not an assemblage of parts each of which retains its separate existence even while in the whole, so he continues to think of the cell as a machine nothing of which cannot be explained in terms of the chemistry and physics of the components. It may well be that chemistry and physics can explain everything in the organism but still not explain everything that needs explaining, as grammar can explain every sentence in Shakespeare but leave all the most important things unexplained. There are

16   Harold 2001, pp. 148–157.
17   Harold 2001, p. 65.

aspects to the organisms that are simply not the sorts of things which can be explained by reduction to the inanimate and reference to exterior experiences alone. It is only by reflecting on our interior experience that we can know that we are one being and not just an assemblage, however sophisticated, of independent parts, whether they be organs, cells, or proteins.

Besides failing to explain the unity of living things, a mechanical understanding of life also fails to illuminate in a fundamental way the two most obvious activities of life, self-motion and sensation or thinking (we need not distinguish the latter two here). The motions which we identify with life are all immanent activities, as we saw. The mechanical understanding is characterized by the idea that all activities are transitive. A acts on B and B is acted upon by A, but they are always thought of as separate beings, parts perhaps of some accidental whole, but never parts of one substance. The wholes made of these parts can never be self-movers because they are never selves. This comports, too, with the emphasis on exterior experience. Looking at things exclusively from the outside, we can see how the parts of organisms work on each other, but not that they are parts of something essentially one.

Not only are the relations of the parts of organisms and machines different, so is their relation to the "fuel" they consume. No machine does more than use fuel to move one part which moves another part placed outside of it. In contrast, animals and plants use "fuel" (i.e., food) to do this, but they also use food to rebuild those parts of themselves that are worn out, even those very parts which are involved in the process of digesting food, i.e., the stomach, intestines, etc.[18]

The way machines act for an end (as the notion of an artefact indicates they do) and the way organisms do also implies a deep separation between the two. For machines are tools which we design to achieve an end, but that end is never the good of the machine. The car you drive does not fulfill its own desires in being driven, it fulfills yours. Artefacts, in short, have their ends in something other than themselves, whereas organisms act and use their tools for their own sakes. The growth of a tree, the feeding of whale, the healing of a wound, the reproduction of every organism, are all cases in which the organism uses its built-in tools, its organs, for its own good. Mechanisms are certainly not opposed to finality, but their finality is inescapably ordered to something other than themselves.

Sensation, too, is not intelligible on a mechanical view. The biologist who wishes to understand sight, for example, cannot reduce it to parts of the body acting on other parts in the same way as inanimate things act on each other. The latter always act on something else, their activity never remains within them. Fire heats water, not itself. But sensation is an activity that remains in the organs of sensation. Yes, it has a passive element, insofar as the object of sense

18   Leon Kass 1999, pp. 27–29.

moves the sense power; still, the actual activity of sensing is not transitive because the eye does nothing to the thing seen. Were we to open up all the parts of the body needed for sensation to occur, we would never find, using external experience alone and a mechanistic model, a part that sensed. For such a part would have to have within it the thing it is aware of and that acts upon it, while not having it as its own form but still as the form of the other, of the agent, since that is what it is aware of: This is what knowing is.[19] This sort of activity is simply beyond the ability of *res extensa* as understood by the mechanical philosophers.[20]

We have no reason, then, to think, as did Descartes, that animals are mere machines with no consciousness nor, worse, that our own bodies are machines accidental or extrinsic or even opposed to our inner selves.[21] We are aware of what sensation and self-motion are because we have these activities *in* ourselves. There is no contradiction between being a body and being a conscious being. When I see the same sorts of external operations in animals (or, for that matter, in other human beings) I must grant that they too are alive, that what I see externally, they perform internally and, in the case of the higher animals at least, that they internally experience their vital activities. Denial of this would at least constitute a formidable objection to evolution, as there would then be a unbridgeable gap between our cognitive way of being and the animals' mere reactivity.[22]

Thus, the crime of anthropomorphism is too often cited. Projecting the human into the non-human, attributing to the non-human what only the human can have, is, of course, at best metaphor, perhaps sometimes helpful or even necessary metaphor, but no basis for science. Still, the projection onto the non-human of the characteristics which we humans have in common with the non-human, even if those characteristics are known only by way of introspection, is not only not unreasonable, it is necessary, a necessity without which there will be no science of biology at all. We have no choice if we are going to study life but to realize we are ourselves alive and that that datum is a unique and fruitful fact.[23]

Having seen what sort of experience is presupposed by this work, and a few consequences of that experience, we should note that the book also depends upon some previously determined doctrines from the earlier works in natural philosophy, especially the *Physics*. The distinction between mover and moved is

---

19   II.12, 424a17–24.
20   For a fuller account of the novel mode of alteration found in sensation and how it differs from the sorts of changes which the inanimate is capable of, cf. Appendix 4, *The Sensing Soul* .
21   *Le Monde, Traité de l'Homme* Descartes 1967, p. 120.
22   See Jonas 1966, pp. 53–58.
23   Ibid., p. 91.

fairly clear even without argument, but the *Physics* goes further to prove that the mover and the moved cannot be the same thing or the same part of the same thing.[24]

One way in which the claim is established is particularly interesting. Aristotle argues that a thing cannot move itself because it would have to be both in potency and in act in the same respect.[25] As agent, it must have what it gives, but as patient, it must not have what it receives. So a self-mover is a self-contradiction, unless we see it as divided into two parts, one in act, the other in potency. The pre-Socratics thought the soul must be in motion, as if what is in imperfect act[26] is required to produce imperfect act; but as Aristotle shows most fully in the *Metaphysics*, it is not imperfect act, i.e., motion, as such that is needed to cause motion, it is simply act – in fact, perfect act is all the better as an explanation.[27] Thus Aristotle claims that the soul is a cause in three ways, as end, as form, and, what is more pertinent here, as agent.[28] The distinction here is not between two parts of the body (though that may also be required for there to be self-motion[29]) but between the body which is in potency and the soul which is an act.[30]

The distinction of the four causes – matter, form, agent, and end – is also aassumed.[31] Of special importance is the distinction between form and matter, as it is in these terms that the soul will ultimately be defined.[32]

The *De Anima* assumes, too, that nature exists, as does the *Physics*,[33] and that it is a first principle of motion in a thing *per se*; that is, given a natural thing, that thing must have in it, just insofar as it is natural, a principle which is at the root (i.e., is a first principle) of all its motions and which belongs to the thing because of what it is, not accidentally, as a piece of marble falls down because it is a piece of marble, yet it is only accidental to its falling that it be a statue.[34] Living things are sources of their own motions because of the very kinds of beings they are, so they clearly have natures in this sense. In fact, one might say

24 *Phys.* VII.1, 241b24–242a15 (or 241b34–242a49 in the alternate text); *Phys.* VIII.5, 256b33–258a5. (The reader may wish to note that in my translation of the *Physics*, I put what is normally called the alternative text of *Phys.* VII.1–3 in the main body and placed a translation of the more commonly translated text after the translation of Book VIII. Cf. Coughlin 2005, pp. 144–50, 198–205.)
25 *Phys.* VIII.5, 257b6–12.
26 *Phys.* III.2, 201b32–33; *Meta.* IX.6, 1048b18–35.
27 *Meta.* XII.6, 1071b3–22.
28 II.4, 415b8–28.
29 *Phys.* VIII.4, 255a12–15.
30 II.1, 412a19–22, 27–28; b4–6; II.2, 414a12–19.
31 II.1, 412a9–10; II.4, 415a8–b28.
32 II.1–2.
33 *Phys.* II.1, 193a3–4.
34 *Phys.* II.1, 192b8–20.

they are the paradigmatic instances of natures, since they most of all have an intrinsic principle of motion. Not too many people doubt that animals move themselves, more doubt that plants do, and most (rightly) doubt that rocks and other inanimate objects do – they rather think that the latter only move when moved by some agent outside of themselves, like the gravity of the earth.

In another sense, though, we might say that nature is determined to one, as the scholastics used to say. Insofar as a thing acts naturally, it always acts in the same way; rocks always fall down, dogs always bark. This even seems to be how we recognize what is natural. Human beings from every culture have some language, so having a language is natural to men; but speaking this or that language, French or English, is not found always and everywhere, so it is not natural but conventional. Animate things do not always act the same way; even plants, to use Aristotle beautifully primitive example, grow both up and down.[35] In this sense, then, animate beings transcend mere nature. The more a thing acts from the determinate nature within it, the more it is determined to one and only one activity; but the animate can respond to its environment and so act in more than one way. This is especially true of animals and men, for, as Aristotle will argue, they take on new forms by way of knowledge, and these new forms can become for them new principles of activity. In this way, the animate things are rather the *least* natural of the natural things.[36]

The *De Anima* also assumes that nature acts for an end and, further, that the soul is the final cause of the organism.[37] The dependence on final cause will provoke loud protests from some. One might even cite Lucretius, the Roman atomist and poet:

Don't think that our bright eyes were made that we
Might look ahead...
Nothing is born in us that we might use it,
But what is born produces its own use.[38]

To paraphrase: "We have eyes not to see but we see because we have eyes." According to this interpretation of biology, in which temporally prior causes (matter and agent) are the only admissible causes, form and end either do not exist at all or are mere after-effects of other causes.

The modern theory of evolution might also give us pause, for it offers an explanation for the apparently purposeful behavior of organisms in terms of such prior causes. Jacques Monod, despite his commitment to "objectivity," by which he means a canon of scientific investigation which eschews final causality in all

---

35   II.2, 413a25–29.
36   See also Appendix 2, *The Definition of the Soul.*
37   II.4, 415b15–21.
38   Lucretius 1995 *De Rerum Naturae* IV, ll. 822–837.

its forms, admits that purpose, the "strangeness" of the living, needs to be explained, or more properly, if science is to be preserved, explained away.[39] In place of actual purposefulness, evolutionary theory offers us random mutations and natural selection. The genes which govern the structures and some of the fundamental behaviors of organisms are subject to random mutations, most of which will be harmful to the organism's reproductive success, but some of which may be beneficial. Those organisms with beneficial mutations will reproduce more often, and so eliminate their less well-equipped brethren from the scene. Here is, it seems, an account that needs no reference to actual purpose, but "explains" purpose as an illusory by-product of, in Monod's memorable formulation, chance and necessity.[40] Thus, the theory of random mutations of the genome gives some sort of explanation of the coming to be of the organs, which Lucretius simply has coming to be from the random confluence of atoms.[41] Both positions attempt to replace reason and purpose with random and mindless coincidences.

The position is in some ways attractive. One might wonder how, after all, what comes later in time can be a cause of what is prior in time, how the full-grown adult, say, can have caused the earlier development of himself as an embryo. Moreover, how can what is unintelligent, and even lacks sensation, act for any sort of end? The end only causes motion if it is desired, and nothing is desired if not known.

But evolution does not necessarily exclude final causality. The very mechanism of evolution belies this: The "struggle for life," if that is not a mere metaphor, implies some good struggled for. Do animals not really compete for food and mates? But if they do, are they not trying to get something good for themselves? If they are just machines programmed to fight over food, then there is no struggle for survival really, any more than there is a struggle to occupy the same spot when two billiard balls are on a collision course.

Besides, even if the organs come to be by random mutations, it does not follow that they do not have a purpose, and this for two reasons. First, there is no reason that random mutations cannot themselves be used as a tool. Why do clams and dandelions spread so many seeds abroad? They are using the random distribution of the seed to ensure that some of the seeds come to maturity. So too do we humans use the random distribution of shot-gun pellets to bring down a duck. We certainly do not want *all* the shot to hit the duck; that would make the duck inedible. The random distribution makes it more likely that some pellets will hit, but not many; hopefully, no more than one. Secondly, what comes to be

39 Monod 1971 pp.23–31.
40 Monod 1971, pp. 95–98. See also the epigraph to the work: "Everything existing in the universe is the fruit of chance and necessity." (Attributed incorrectly to Democritus).
41 Lucretius 1995 *De rerum Natura* II, ll. 217–25.

by chance need not continue to be by chance. If George meets Georgia by dent-
ing her car in a parking lot, there may be what the movie critics call a "meet-
cute," a merely chance encounter, but when our hero goes on to court that lovely
young lady, to marry her and start a family, that is not by chance but on purpose.
So even if we say that the random mutations of evolutionary theory produce
organs by chance, it does not follow that the things produced, the organs, etc.,
have no purpose.

Further, the claim is that nature produces what look like purposeful systems
and structures for no end, but the apparent good just happens to follow upon
these systems and structures. But what is so produced are all the parts and the
organization of the organism, both the unconsciously purposeful parts, like the
heart with its beating and the lungs with their breathing, etc., and *also* the con-
sciously purposeful parts, like the deliberative faculty. But these latter are certainly purposeful, as everyone knows by experience. It strains credulity to say
that when I buy a hamburger to eat, there is not really any purpose in such conscious acts. This is simply contradictory to our immediate knowledge and so
should be rejected out of hand. And the very same sorts of evolutionary processes which brought about the obviously purposeful conscious activities also brings
about the apparently purposeful unconscious activities of plants and animals. It
is only reasonable to attribute real purpose to these activities as well – the same
effect should be explained by the same cause.

Other experiences are not so irrefutable, but nearly so. When a lion chases
an antelope, is the lion not really trying to catch and eat it? Is the antelope not
really running to save its life? Aristotle points out that some animals, especially insects, so much seem to act for an end that some people think they are
intelligent: He mentions ants and spiders, but there are endless examples.[42] It
is not the statement that nature acts for an end that needs defense, really, it is
the strangely purblind claim that it does not.

Finally, we should note that the questions raised by Aristotle in this text are
in any case prior to the questions raised by evolutionary biology and even by
other branches of modern biological thought. For the question "what is it?" is
always more fundamental than the questions, "when did it arise" or "how did it
arise" – the questions of evolutionary theory. In fact, one cannot really even ask
the latter questions without at least some answer to the former. We could not
begin to ask "when" or "how" if we did not even know what we were asking
about. Nor could we ask about the behavior or structure of organisms if we had
no idea of what an organism is. As we saw earlier, everyone has some vague but
very certain knowledge of what life is. This may be enough for the modern biologists, both those who specialize in evolutionary theory and those who do not,
to get on with their project. It remains that there lies behind their inquiries an

---

42   *Phys.* II.8, 198b10–199b33. In this chapter, besides pointing out that some animals
      seem intelligent, Aristotle gives several other arguments.

assumed and usually unexamined notion of life. It is this notion that Aristotle, like them, takes for granted in his studies, but, unlike them, does not leave unexamined.

We have focused on this unique fact about biology, that we have inside information on the subjects of the science, and particularly that we know that those subjects are divided into two parts, a body and a soul. This fact is responsible for an anomaly in Aristotle's procedure. Given what he says elsewhere about how to proceed in science, namely, that we should proceed from the universal to the particular,[43] we might wonder why he begins here not with living being in general but with the first principle of such beings, the soul. The reason is that the very first experience proper to biology already includes the soul, not as to what it is but as to whether it is; we know there is a something, call it "soul," which is a principle of our motions and that it is other than what is moved by it. This experience tells us no more than that there is a principle of life within us, but it teaches this with certainty. With this initial grasp of the soul, we can begin our science of biology and without it we can do nothing. Thus, in a way, we do begin with "living thing" in general, for we start with the experience of living.[44]

The *De Anima* is the study of the soul in this generality and abstraction. We do not need detailed knowledge of biochemistry or anatomy to read this work, for the intimate knowledge of life which we have is not dependent on such determinations. Aristotle insists that every soul has its appropriate body, a plant soul needing a much less articulated body than a horse,[45] but he does not try to determine what belongs to the species of living thing in the *De Anima*, except, again, in the most general way. He distinguishes plants and animals and human beings, but goes no further in this work. Thus, what is determined in this work will be true of any species of being found under the universal natures treated.[46] Later works in biology delve more deeply into particular powers (e.g., *On Memory and Recollection*; *On Sense and the Sensible*) and finally into the concrete, material basis for life (e.g., *The History of Animals, The Parts of Animals, The Movement of Animals*, etc.). The working out of the doctrines taught here is left for later, not because it is of no interest or a mere footnote, but because the more concrete and particular understanding of organisms depends upon the more abstract and universal. For example, what is true of the

---

43 *Phys.* I.1, 184a16–24; *PA* I.1, 639a24–27.

44 The word "animate" is derived from the word "anima," Latin for "soul," and so shows us two facts: the inanimate is less known to us than is the living, and the living is recognized along with the perception of the soul.

45 I.3, 407b13–26; II.2, 414a21–27.

46 The possibility that there are non-material living things is hinted in *De Anima*, but not pursued. Some, though, think that III.5 is all about such a being. Cf. II.3, 430a22–23; Appendix 5, *The Intellectual Soul*.

sensing soul in general must be true of the particular kinds of sensing soul, though the reverse is not true. It is in these more concrete, particular, and so empirical inquiries that modern biology comes into its own.

The importance of the study is underlined by Aristotle when he says, "knowledge of the soul contributes great things in regard to every truth, but most of all in regard to nature."[47] The most interesting of natural things are the living ones, and in some way we even get the idea of nature, as a principle of operation, from the living. And all biological studies are subsequent to the considerations of this first work on biology. Further, even logic is illuminated by the study of life; at least we learn in the De Anima how it is that our minds can seize upon the first principles of the sciences, a question left unanswered in the Posterior Analytics.[48] The nature of universal predicates is also explained by the immateriality of the intellect, which later is shown in the third book of the De Anima.[49] The delineation of the powers of the soul is helpful, too, for ethics and politics.[50]

Finally, the study of the soul is of great help in metaphysics. In proving that the intellectual soul is not merely the form of a body but is separable from the body,[51] it provides a door into metaphysics. We do not know that immaterial things are even possible without an argument from material things, from the things we know naturally and without argument or effort. For it is not enough to say we do not see any contradiction in the notion of immaterial being; not seeing a contradiction is not the same as seeing there is no contradiction. We only know that there really is no contradiction if we see that the thing is real or is necessarily implied by what we know to be actually real; if not, we may simply be failing to note a contradiction, as we might think there can be a greatest prime number just because we don't see the contradiction latent in that idea. So without an argument like the one in the De Anima that the intellect is immaterial, or the one in the Physics that the first mover is immaterial, we have no reason to think there is another science, first philosophy, as Aristotle calls it, or metaphysics.

> If, therefore, there is not some other substance beside the ones constituted by nature, physics (i.e., natural philosophy) would be first science. But if there is some immobile substance, this (i.e., the science of this immobile substance) will be prior and will be first philosophy, and will be universal thus, because it is first. And its consideration would be about being as being, both what it is and the things which belong to it as being.[52]

47 I.1, 402a–7.
48 Po. An. II.19, 100a3–14; DA III.4–5, 430a5–17 and Appendix 5, The Intellectual Soul.
49 See III.4, 429b10–22 and Appendix 5, The Intellectual Soul.
50 Nic. Eth. I.13, 1102a22–26.
51 See Appendix 5, The Intellectual Soul.
52 Meta. VI.1, 1026a27–32.

In fact, insofar as the intellectual soul transcends matter, the study of it is not properly a part of natural science, but already is metaphysics.[53] Nevertheless, the proof that it is immaterial is one for natural science. Further, the discussion of the intellectual soul and, in particular, the argument that knowing is an "immaterial reception," is our basis for understanding what sorts of things these immaterial beings are, i.e., that they are intellects.

Order within the De Anima

The *De Anima* can be divided into the first chapter of Book I and all the rest. That first chapter forms a sort of proemium in which Aristotle tells us what he is up to, why it is important, what the difficulties are, and how he will approach the issues he is dealing with. In the rest of Book I, he considers the opinions of his predecessors and sifts them for insights which he can use himself, and for errors to be avoided.[54] In Book II, Chs. 1–2, he defines the soul.[55] After this, he divides the kinds of soul into three, the vegetative, the sensitive, and the intellectual,[56] and then goes on to treat each one.[57] Next, he considers the locomotive power of animals and their ability to desire,[58] and finally he considers the order of the powers of the soul.[59]

The order in the book as a whole can be understood in more than one way. Most obviously, and most in accord with Aristotle's explicit considerations about the order among the powers of the soul,[60] the movement from vegetative to sensitive to intellectual is a motion from what has fewer powers to what has more. The vegetative soul can feed, grow, and reproduce; the sensitive can, additionally, sense; the intellectual can also understand and think things though. Some of the sensitive and all, so far as we know, of the intellectual, can also move around in place.

There is also an order from outside to inside, as it were: the vegetative acts within itself by eating and growing. It takes food from outside, brings it into itself, and either uses that food for energy or to replace parts of its own substance. When it acts, it does so by one part doing something to another part.

---

53 Cf. *Meta*. VI.1, 1025b32–1026a6; *Phys*. II.2, 194b14–15.

54 Appendix 1, *Dialectic in Book I of the De Anima*, discusses briefly how Aristotle uses his predecessors' opinions to advance his inquiry.

55 See Appendix 2, *The Definition of the Soul*.

56 II.3, 414a29–b33.

57 The vegetative soul is treated in II.4, the sensitive in II.5–III.3, and the intellectual in III.4–8. See Appendices 3–5 for treatments of each of these sorts of soul.

58 III.9–11, 432a15–434a21.

59 III.12–13, 434a22–435b25.

60 II.3, 414a29–b33.

These parts are external to each other, though they are all within the organism.[61] When the senses act, they receive their objects from what is outside and cannot operate in the absence of those objects, but the activity that follows upon that reception, the sensing, remains within the sense organ – there is here no acting upon another part of the animal or upon an external object. The intellectual soul is even more self-contained, its activity more immanent and immaterial: Though it receives its object from experience, it considers them in itself and, unlike the senses, does not depend upon the presence of an external object to be in act. The abilities of the three sorts of souls to interact with their environments also increases dramatically as we move from the vegetative to the sensitive to the intellectual. Plants can take in food and to this extent interact with their surroundings; animals, at least those which can move in place, can respond to what they see and hear in their surroundings and either flee or pursue; human beings, because their intellects seize upon the universals, can affect their environments much more profoundly – they can change the courses of rivers, bore roads through mountains, and eventually build space stations in orbit and on the moon and other planets. Animals, but men much more so, can also simply know the world, take it in as a whole, as an object of knowledge. For animals, this knowledge is ordered to survival and reproduction, but for men, contemplation becomes a self-contained, self-justifying activity. Knowing the order and causes of the universe serves no useful purpose; it is simply good to know; in fact, if Aristotle is right, it is the end of human life.[62] The order is, then, from what is less perfectly to what is more perfectly a locus of operation and awareness, i.e., from what is less to what is more a "self."

After the general consideration of the three sorts of souls, more detailed studies are left to subsequent books. While those works, of course, shed light on Aristotle's meaning and purpose in the *De Anima*, and while there are important philosophical truths contained in those later works, especially the more general ones like *Sense and the Sensible* and *Memory and Recollection*, a great deal of what those works contain has been superseded by modern biology.

Notes on This Translation

This translation, like my translation of the *Physics*, is intended to permit those who do not know much or any Greek to carry out a careful study of the thought of Aristotle. I have tried to translate the same word by the same word as much as possible, but it is not always possible to do so and still be faithful to the

---

61 The case of reproduction will be considered in Appendix 3, *The Vegetative (or Reproductive) Soul*.

62 *Meta.* I.2, 982b11–28; *Nic. Eth.* X.7, 1177a12–18.

Greek. For in Greek, as in English and, I suppose, in all languages, there are many words which have many different meanings, and the extension of meanings in one language may not correspond to the extensions in another (though it is often surprising how alike these processes of extension are). I have provided a glossary to help track down the chief words and their translations. This glossary is essentially a simplified version of the one included in my *Physics* translation, with some alterations and amendments made because of the more particular use of certain words in this text. I have not aimed overly much at elegance, but tried to indicate in the English the difficulties of the Greek. I have tried not to "paper over" problematic texts, but I have often offered interpretations in the endnotes and appendices. The reader who desires a relatively unfiltered Aristotle has only to ignore my comments. I have tried to be sparing in expanding Aristotle's terse prose. The result is not easy to read, but, I hope, is accurate. Words which do not translate anything explicitly said in the Greek are included in square brackets, thus: [...]. When I provide an alternate translation or the original Greek, I include it in curved brackets, thus: {...}.[63]

This translation is based primarily on the text established by W.D. Ross in the Oxford Classical Texts Series.[64] I have also extensively consulted his slightly later edition,[65] as well as one other text and many translations.[66]

The notes and appendices of this edition are intended to help the reader see what Aristotle is saying "from the inside," i.e., not sitting in judgement over his work but trying to learn from it on its own terms. I am convinced that Aristotle has the basic points right and that we should not approach the text as an historical document or curiosity, but as the work of an extraordinarily intelligent person trying to explain some of the most significant aspects of our experience, in terms understandable without the sophisticated apparatus of modern science, terms, in fact, presupposed to that apparatus.

More particularly, the endnotes are intended to provide references, cross-references, and suggested explanations of some of the more difficult passages. The five appendices tackle issues demanding lengthier considerations: the use of dialectic, the definition of the soul, and the three main sorts of soul. These essays are not intended to engage modern scholarship or even ancient scholarship, but to tie back the considerations of Aristotle to our more basic experiences, to elucidate what Aristotle means, and to explain why he proceeds as he does.

The reader who wishes to think about the background of the *De Anima* has, of course, the first book of the *De Anima* itself to look to. The most important secondary source is Kirk, Raven, and Schofield's *The Pre-Socratic*

63 For more on the principles of translation, see Coughlin 2005, pp. xxiii–xxx.
64 Ross 1956.
65 Ross 1961.
66 See the bibliography for detailed information on these works.

Philosophers.[67] The commentary of David Ross in his critical edition,[68] is often helpful with regard to the positions Aristotle has in mind in his sometimes cryptic remarks. The imposing work of Ronald Polansky, *Aristotle's De Anima*, has much to commend it both with regard to interpretation and with regard to the historical background.[69] Also helpful in these ways are C.D.C. Reeve's notes on his translation,[70] and David Bolotin's on his.[71] I have, of course, compared many of my translations to those of others', including those already mentioned and also that of Joe Sachs.[72] I have consulted all these works in trying to unravel the text and its meaning. The commentary of Thomas Aquinas is most useful for a close analysis of pretty much every argument and for understanding the general sweep of the text.

67   G.S. Kirk, J.E. Raven, and M. Schofield 1983.
68   Ross 1961.
69   Polansky 2007.
70   Reeves 2017.
71   Bolotin 2018.
72   Sachs 2001.

Acknowledgements

This work was originally translated for use by the students of Thomas Aquinas College in Santa Paula, California, each of whom is required to spend a semester studying it. Innumerable teachers, students, and colleagues have contributed to it in both large and small ways and, while not all can be, some must be mentioned. First of all, Marcus Berquist (RIP), Duane Berquist (RIP), Warren Murray, and Thomas Dillon (RIP) were formative of my understanding of this and of Aristotle's other works. Ron Richard and Chris Decaen were tireless in bringing to my attention infelicities of expression and translation. A study group of Tony Andres, Blaise Blain, Peter Cross, Katherine Gardner, Joshua Lim, and Scott Strader was particularly helpful. Caleb Cohoe indicated to me several important texts and graciously allowed me to read his chapter from the forthcoming *Aristotle's On the Soul: A Critical Guide.*[73] Travis Cooper undertook to proofread and criticize the bulk of the work. Tony Andres, Ben Coughlin, and Steve Cain reviewed significant parts. Steve was also the one who pointed out to me how dialectic was being used in Book I, which led to my writing the first appendix. John Nieto, Mike Augros, and Tom Kaiser helped me clarify my thoughts on many points. Several of my children (Bridget, Tom, Jerry, Frank, and Charlie) read parts of the translation aloud to me while I read the Greek to be sure nothing was omitted. My wife, Maureen, was, as always, patient and supportive.

---

[73] Cohoe 2022.

Abbreviations Used in this Translation

Categories	*Cat.*
De Anima	*DA*
De Caelo	*De Cael.*
De Generatione et Corruptione	*De Gen.*
De Interpretatione	*De Int.*
De Memoria	*De Mem.*
De Sensu et Sensato	*De Sens.*
De Juventute	*De Juv.*
Generation of Animals	*Gen. An.*
History of Animals	*Hist. An.*
IA	*Progression of Animals*
MA	*Movement of Animals*
Metaphysics	*Meta.*
Nicomachean Ethics	*Nic. Eth.*
On Sleep	*Somn.*
Parts of Animals	*PA*
Physics	*Phys.*
Politics	*Pol.*
Posterior Analytics	*Po. An.*
Prior Analytics	*Pr. An.*
Rhetoric	*Rh.*

Book I

Chapter 1

Holding that knowledge is among things beautiful and honorable, while one sort is so more than another either according to its certitude[1] or by being of better and more wonderful things,[2] due to both of these [causes] we should reasonably put the inquiry about the soul among the first ones. It seems too / that knowledge of the soul contributes great things in regard to all truth, but most of all in regard to nature.[3] For it [, i.e., the soul] is in a way the principle of animals. We seek to look at {contemplate, consider, θεωρεῖν} and to know the nature and substance[4] of the soul and, next, whatever things are accidents of it.[5] Some of these accidents seem to be passions[6] proper to the soul, while some / seem to belong to animals because of that {the soul}.[7]

However, to attain any conviction about it is in every way among the most difficult of tasks.[8] For while this is a question common to many other things as well (I mean the question about the substance and the "what it is"[9]), perhaps it might seem to someone that there is some one method about everything of which we wish to know / the substance, as there is demonstration for properties which are accidental; whence this method ought to be sought. But if there is not some one and common method about the "what it is," the undertaking becomes still more difficult. For it will be necessary to grasp what the [proper] way [of approaching the question] is in each case. And if it should be clear whether [the right way] is demonstration / or division or even some other method,[10] still, {the question} whence the inquiry should begin presents many difficulties and [occasions for] errors. For the principles of different things are different, as, e.g., of numbers and of surfaces.

Perhaps it is first necessary to decide which one of the genera it falls into and what it is[11]; I mean whether [it falls] into "this something"[12] and substance or quality or quantity or / even some other one of the predicates {categories} we have distinguished[13]; again, [we must ask] whether it is among beings in potency or is instead some actuality.[14] For this makes no / small difference. And one must consider whether it is divisible into parts or is without parts,[15] and

402a1

5

10

15

20

25

402b1

1

whether every soul is of the same species or not; and if they are not
of the same species, whether they differ [only] in species or [even] in
genus. For until now, those who speak and inquire about the soul
seemed only to inquire into the soul of man.[16] / And one must be careful lest it escape one's notice whether the account of it is one, like that
of "animal," or is different for each, as are [the accounts] of "horse,"
"dog," "man," and "god." (The universal "animal" is either nothing
or is posterior [to the particulars], as would also be the case should
some other common thing be predicated.[17])

Moreover, if there are not many souls, but [rather] parts [of one
soul], [one must consider] / whether to ask first about the whole soul
or about its parts.[18] And it is difficult to determine how these [parts]
are by nature different from each other, and whether one needs to
inquire first about the parts or about the works of these, e.g., [should
we first ask about] understanding or [about] the mind,[19] [about] sensing or the sensitive, and likewise in the other cases. But if [one should
ask about] the works first, one will then / be at a loss about whether
he must first ask about the things corresponding to these, e.g., the sensible [object] before the sensitive [power] and the intelligible [object]
before the mind {intellect, understanding}.

Not only does knowing the "what it is" seem useful for considering the causes of the accidents in substances (as in mathematics
[knowing] what the straight and the curved are or what the line and
the plane / are [is useful] for grasping well that the angles of a triangle
are equal to so many right angles), but also, on the contrary, the accidents contribute greatly to looking at the "what it is." For when we
can give an account of the accidents, either all or most of them, in
accord with appearance, then we will also be able to speak / in the
best way about the substance. For the principle of all demonstration
is the "what it is."[20] Whence, with respect to any definitions according to which knowing / the accidents or even conjecturing about them
easily does not occur – it is clear that [such definitions] are said
dialectically and are all wholly empty.[21]

There is a difficulty also about the passions of the soul: whether
there is something of the soul proper to it or [whether] they are all
common as well to that which has [a soul].[22] / To grasp this is necessary but not easy. It seems that, in the cases of most [of the passions],
there is not a single suffering {πάσχειν} or doing {ποιεῖν} which is
without the body, e.g., to be angry, to take courage, to desire, to sense
in any way. To understand {νοεῖν} seems most of all to be proper [to
the soul]. But if even this is some imagination or is not without imagination, not even this could be / without body.[23] If, therefore, there is
something among the works or passions of the soul which is proper

to the soul, it can happen that the soul be separated. If, on the other hand, nothing is proper to it, it would not be separable, but [the case would be like that of the straight:] just as many things happen to what is straight, as straight, e.g., to touch the bronze sphere at a point, still, the straight, / being separated, will not touch [anything].[24] For if it [the soul] is always with a body, it is inseparable.[25]

    15

But it seems that all the passions of the soul do exist with the body: anger, gentleness, fear, pity, courage, joy, and both loving and hating. For the body suffers something with these. The following indicates this: sometimes when forceful and manifest / sufferings occur nothing is provoked or feared, yet sometimes (when the body is excited and is in a condition like that which it has when one is angered), one is moved by small and faint occurrences. Moreover, the following case is clearer: for [sometimes even when] nothing fearful is happening, the passions of one who fears come to be in the passions. If things / are so, it is clear that the passions have accounts which refer to material.[26] Whence their definitions are like this: "anger is some motion of this sort of body or of a part or of a power, under the influence of this, for the sake of that." And because of these things, the consideration of the soul (either of all or of one of this sort) falls immediately to the student of nature.[27]

    20

    25

The student of nature and the dialectician[28] would define / each of these [passions], e.g., what anger is, differently. For the one would define it as "an appetite for vexing in return," or something like that, while the other would define it as a seething of the blood and heat around the heart. / Of these, the one gives the material, the other the species and account. For this is the account of the thing; but if it is going to exist, it is necessary that it be in this sort of material, just as the account of a house is of this sort: that it is a shelter preventing destruction / by wind and rain and heat – while the one will say it is stones and bricks and lumber, the other will say it is the species in these [latter] for the sake of those [former]. Which of these is the student of nature? Is it the one concerned with the material but ignoring the account, or the one concerned with the account alone? Or is it rather the one concerned with [what is made] from both? But then who is each of the others? Is there not someone who treats of / the inseparable passions of material, and not as separable? But the student of nature treats all the works and passions which belong to such and such a body and such and such material. Whatever someone [else treats] are not such – about some such things, the artist,[29] the carpenter or doctor, maybe; about things which are not separable, but not insofar as they are the / passions of such a body and are [known] by abstraction, the mathematician; insofar as they are separated {separable}, the first philosopher.[30]

    30

    403b1

    5

    10

    15

But one must return whence the argument [began]. We said, then, that the passions of the soul are inseparable from the natural material of animals, at least such [passions] as belong in the way courage and fear do and not as line and surface do.[31]

Chapter 2

403b20 In looking into the soul, while we raise problems about what needs to be provided as we go forward,[32] it is necessary to take along with us the opinions of those who went before us, that we might grasp what has been well said, but if something was not well [said], that we might beware of it.[33]

25 The beginning of our inquiry is to set out the things / which most seem to belong to it [the soul] according to nature. The ensouled, then, seems to differ from the unsouled by two things: motion[34] and sensing. And these two things are just about what we have received about the soul from our predecessors. For some say that the soul is

30 both mostly and primarily the mover; but, believing that / what is not itself moving cannot move another, they supposed the soul to be something among moving things.[35]

404a1 Whence, Democritus says it is a certain [sort of] fire / and hot thing.[36] For there being infinite atoms and shapes,[37] he says the spherical ones are fire and soul (like the so-called "motes" in the air, which are seen in the sunbeams which come through windows); the totality

5 of seeds he (and likewise Leucippus) calls / the elements of the whole of nature; of these, [he calls] those which are spherical "soul," because such shapes are most able to slip through and to move the rest, being in motion themselves, supposing that the soul is what produces motion in animals. Whence also they say that the mark of life / is breathing.

10 For when the atmosphere constricts the bodies [of animals], and squeezes out the shapes (the ones which produce motion in animals because they themselves never rest), help comes from outside by other such shapes entering in by way of breathing. For these, repelling what

15 constricts and compresses, prevent the ones / within the animals from escaping. And they live so long as they can do this.[38]

It seems that what is said among the Pythagoreans contains the same reasoning, for some of them said the soul is the motes in the air, some,

20 what moves them. This was said about these [motes] because / they appear to be continuously moving, even when there is a complete calm.

Those who say that the soul is what moves itself are brought to the same [view]. For they all seem to assume that motion is most at home in the soul, and that all other things are moved by the soul, while the latter [is moved] by itself, because they see nothing moving [others] / which is not itself also moving.[39]

Likewise too, Anaxagoras says that the soul is what causes motion, as does anyone else who said that mind moved the whole.[40] But [these men speak] not altogether in the same way as Democritus. For [Democritus says that] soul and mind are simply the same. For [he says] the truth is what appears, so that Homer did well in saying / "Hector lay thinking other thoughts."[41] For he does not use "mind" for a power concerned with truth, but [says] the soul and mind are the same.[42] / Anaxagoras is less clear about these; for in many places he calls the mind the cause of what is beautiful and right, but elsewhere [he says] this [cause] is the soul. For it [mind] is in all the animals, the great and the small, the high and the low. / But mind (the one so called in reference to prudence) does not appear to belong to all animals alike; indeed, not even to all men.

All those, then, who looked to the fact that the ensouled thing is in motion assumed that the soul was the thing most able to cause motion, but all those who [looked to] the knowing and sensing of beings / said the soul was the principles, some making these many, some [making] this one.

So Empedocles made [it] from all the elements, and also [said] that each of these is soul, speaking as follows:

By earth we see earth, by water, water,
By ether, ether divine, but by fire destroying fire,
By love, love, and strife by mournful strife.[43] /

In the same way also Plato makes the soul out of the elements in the *Timaeus*; for like is known by like, while things are [made] out of the principles.[44] Likewise also, in the writings *On Philosophy*,[45] it is set out that animal itself is / from the idea of the one itself and of the first length, and breadth, and depth; and other things are [constituted] in the same way.[46] Moreover, [the position is presented] in another way as well: understanding is the one, science the two (for it is in a single way [from one and] to one), opinion, the number of the surface, sensation that of the solid. For the numbers were said to be the species and / the principles themselves, and they {numbers} are [also] from the elements; but some things are judged by mind, some by science, some by opinion, some by sense. But these numbers are the species of things.[47]

And since the soul seemed to be able both to cause motion and to know in this way, some have woven it out of both, stating that the soul is a / self-moving number.[48]

25

30

404b1

5

10

15

20

25

30

But they differ about the principles, what and how many they are, most of all those making them bodily from those making them unbodily / and from these those mixing [them] and stating that the principles are from both.[49] They differ also about how many [principles there are]. For some say one, some, more. They give an account of the soul in a way that follows these [opinions]. For they assume, not unreasonably, that what is able to cause motion according to its nature is / among the first things.[50] Whence it seemed to some to be fire, for this both has the smallest parts and is the most unbodily of the elements, and, moreover, it both itself moves and moves others primarily.

Democritus spoke in the most polished way, showing the "why" of each of these. For he said the soul is the same as mind, / while the latter is [made] from the first and indivisible bodies, being able to cause motion through [having] small parts and through its shape: he says the spherical are, among the shapes, the most mobile, and such are both mind and fire.

Anaxagoras seems to say the soul and the mind are different, as we said before,[51] but he uses / them as one nature, except that he rather posits the mind as the principle of all things. He says, at least, that among beings it alone is simple and unmixed and pure.[52] He gives an account of both knowing and moving by the same principle, saying that mind moved the whole.

Thales too, from what is remembered [about him], seems / to have supposed the soul to be something able to cause motion, if indeed he said the magnetic stone has a soul because it moves iron.

Diogenes, like some others, said it was air, believing this to have the smallest parts and to be a principle. And through this the soul both knows and moves,[53] insofar as it is first, and from this it knows the rest; insofar as it is smallest, / it is able to cause motion.

And Heraclitus said the soul is the principle, if it is the vapor from which the other things are constituted.[54] And it is the most unbodily [thing] and is always flowing. And he said a thing being moved is known by a thing being moved;[55] both he and the many believe [all] beings are in motion.

Alcmaeon seems to have supposed things about the soul / in a way very near to these. For he says it is undying through being like the undying things and that this belongs to it as always moving. For all the godlike things are / always continuously moving: the moon, the sun, the stars, and the entire heaven.

Of the cruder thinkers, some, like Hippo, have even said that it is water. They seem to have been persuaded from seeds, because [the seeds] of all things are watery. For he also refutes those who say the soul is blood, [saying] that the seed is / not blood and that this is the

405a1

5

10

15

20

25

30

405b1

5

first soul. Others, like Critias, said it is blood, supposing that what is most proper to the soul is sensing and that this belongs through the nature of blood.

In fact, all the elements have received a judge [in their favor] except earth.[56] No one has pronounced for this, except those who said the soul is / from or is all the elements.[57]   10

So all men define, so to speak, the soul by three things: by motion, by sensation, and by being unbodily;[58] each of these is led back to the principles. Whence also, except for one thinker,[59] those who define it by knowing make it either an element or from the elements, saying nearly the same thing as each other. / For they say like   15
is known by like.[60] For since the soul knows all things, they constitute it from all the principles.[61] Whoever, therefore, says there is some one cause and one element also sets out the soul as one, like fire or air. Those who say the principles are many make the soul more too. / But   20
Anaxagoras alone says the mind is impassible and has nothing in common with any of the other things.[62] Being such a thing, how it will know and through what cause, he neither has said nor is it clear from what he has said.[63] Whoever makes contrarieties in the principles also constitutes the soul from contraries; those who make one of the contraries / [the principle], like hot or cold or some other such thing, also   25
likewise posit the soul as some one of these. For which reason they also follow up the names, some calling [the soul] the hot because through this also living is named, some calling it the cold, through this that it is called the soul through breathing and cooling down.[64]

These are, therefore, the things handed down / about the soul and   30
the causes due to which they spoke in this way.

Chapter 3

One should first look into [the questions] about motion.[65] For perhaps   405b31
it is not only false that its [the soul's] substance is such as some say, / that it is a self-mover or a thing able to move [another], but it is even   406a1
an impossibility that motion should belong to it.[66] It has already been said, then, that it is not necessary that a mover also itself be in motion.[67] But there are two ways in which anything is in motion: / for   5
it is so either according to another or according to itself. We call "[in motion] according to another" whatever is in motion by being in a moving thing, like sailors; for they are not in motion in the same way as the ship. For the one is in motion in virtue of itself, but the others [are in motion] by being in something which is in motion, as is clear in the case of the parts [of a mobile]. For walking is the proper motion

of the feet, and this [act of walking] also belongs to the men; but it does not belong / to the sailors [as sailors].[68] Since being in motion is said in two ways, we should now look into what concerns the soul, whether it is in motion in virtue of itself and shares in motion.[69]

As there are four motions, locomotion, alteration, diminution and growth, it would move with one of these, or with some, or with all.[70] But if it is not in motion / accidentally, motion would belong to it by nature. If so, place too [would belong to it by nature]. For all the motions mentioned [occur] in place.[71] But if the substance of the soul is to move itself, being in motion will not belong to it accidentally, as [it does] to white or to "three feet [long]." For these too are in motion, / though accidentally; for what they are in, body, is in motion. Because of which also they have no place [as such]. But there will be [a place as such] of soul, if it shares in motion by nature.[72]

Moreover, if it is in motion by nature, it might also be in motion by force, and if by force, by nature. And things are the same way in regard to rest. For whatever it moves into by nature, in that it rests / by nature; likewise also, whatever it moves into by force, in that it rests by force.[73] Even for those who are willing to make things up, it will not be easy to give an account about what sorts of forced motions and rests would belong to the soul.

Moreover, if it will move up, it will be fire, if down, earth; for these are the motions of these bodies. But the same account also / concerns the things [elements] in between.[74]

Moreover, since it is apparent that it moves the body, it is reasonable that it move it according to those motions by which it itself is in motion. If so, it is also true to say, conversely, that that according to which the body is in / motion is also that motion according to which it {the soul} is in motion. But the body moves by locomotion. Whence also the soul would change either as a whole or by its parts shifting around. But if this is possible, it would be possible that it enter [the body] again after having left it. From this / the resurrection of dead animals would follow.

And it would also be moved by another according to accidental motion, for an animal may be pushed by force. But what is moved by itself in its substance must not be moved by another, except accidentally, just as what is good according to or through itself is not so through another or / for the sake of another. But one should say that the soul is moved most of all by the sensibles, if indeed it is moved.

But if it itself also moves itself, it would move; whence, if every motion is a removal of what is moving insofar as it is moving, the soul too would be removed from its own substance, if it does not

move itself accidentally / but the motion belongs to its substance   15
according to itself.

And some, like Democritus, say that the soul moves the body in
which it exists in the same way as it itself moves, speaking perhaps like
the comic poet Philippus. For he says that Daedalus[75] made the wooden
Aphrodite[76] move by pouring in molten silver. / And Democritus   20
speaks in the same way, for, because they are naturally apt never to rest,
he says that the indivisible spheres drag around and move the whole
body. But we will ask whether this same thing causes resting. But how
it would do so is difficult or impossible to say. Generally, the soul does
not seem to move / the animal in this way, but [rather] through some   25
choice and thought.

In the same way, Timaeus too argues, in the manner of a student
of nature, that the soul moves the body. For, being entwined with it,
by moving itself it also moves the body.[77] For when it had been composed out of the elements and apportioned according to the harmonic
numbers / so that it might have sensation and connatural harmony and   30
the whole might be carried by a harmonious locomotion, [the demi-
urge] having bent the straight into a circle, dividing, from one [of
them] he made two circles, joining them again in two places, / [and]   407a1
he divided one [of them] into seven circles, as though the locomotions of the heavens were the motions of the soul.[78]

First, then, saying that the soul is a magnitude is not said well,
for it is clear that he wishes that the [soul] of the whole [cosmos] / be   5
such as is whatever the so-called mind is. For it is neither like the sensitive nor like the spirited [parts of the soul]. For the motion of these
is not revolution. But the mind is one and continuous the way understanding {νόησις} is; but understanding is the things being understood, while these are one by succession, like number, and not in the
way magnitudes [are one].[79] Because of which the mind is not continuous in this way but is either without parts / or is something not   10
continuous in the way a magnitude is.

For, if it is a magnitude, how will it understand? Will it be by any
one of its parts whatsoever? [And will it be by one] of its parts
according to magnitude or according to a point, if one must call this
a part too? If, then, according to a point, and these are infinite, it is
clear that it will never go through them; but if according to magnitude, it will understand the same thing often / or infinitely many   15
times. But it is apparent that it may happen [to understand a certain
thing only] once. But if it is sufficient that it have touched [the intel-
ligible] with any one of its parts, why must it move in a circle or even,
generally, have magnitude? But if it is necessary to understand by the
whole circle touching, what is [the activity corresponding to] the

touching by the parts? Moreover, how will it understand what has parts by what is without parts or what is without parts by what has parts?

20 But it is necessary that / the mind be this circle. For the motion of the mind is understanding, but [the motion] of the circle is revolution. If, therefore, thinking is revolution, the mind would also be the circle, the revolution of which is understanding. What, then, will it always be understanding? For it must [always be understanding something] if the revolution is eternal. For there are limits of practical understanding, for all such [understanding] is for the sake of some-

25 thing, / while contemplative {speculative} [understanding] is similarly determined by accounts. But every account is a definition or a demonstration. Demonstration, then, is both from a principle and also somehow has an end, the syllogism or the conclusion. But if they do not conclude, still, they do not return again to the principle, but, always taking a [new] middle and extreme they go on in a straight

30 line, / while revolution returns again to the beginning. And all definitions are limited.

Moreover, if the same revolution often [occurs], it will be necessary to understand the same thing many times.

Moreover, understanding seems to be a certain [sort of] resting and standing rather than motion, and syllogism [seems to be] the same way.

407b1 But indeed, what is not easy / but forced is not blessed; but if its {the soul's} motion is not its substance, it would be moved against nature.[80] And for it {the soul} to be mixed with the body and unable to be freed would be painful, even something to be fled from, if

5 indeed it is better for the mind not to be with the body, / as is said customarily and believed by many.[81]

Also, it is unclear what the cause of the heaven's being carried around in a circle is; for the cause is not the substance of the soul being carried around in a circle, but it {the substance of the soul} moves like this accidentally; nor is the body the cause, but the soul is [a cause] more so than it. But indeed, it is not said that it is better,

10 though it is due to this / that the god should have made the soul be carried in a circle – because it is better for it to be moved than to remain still, and to move this way rather than otherwise. Since, however, such an inquiry is more at home among other arguments, let us leave this for now.

15 But this strange thing happens also / in this account and in many of the [other] ones about the soul. For they join and place the soul into the body, not at all determining why [this happens] and how the body is disposed. And yet this would seem to be necessary, for, through

their partnership, the one does something and the other suffers something and the one is moved and the other moves [it], but none of these
belongs to just any chance things in regard to each other. / Some take   20
it in hand only to say what sort of thing the soul is but they determine
nothing further about the receptive body, as though, as in the
Pythagorean myths, any chance soul could be put into any chance
body. For it seems that each [body] has its proper species and form.
They talk as if one were to say / that carpentry is put into flutes. For   25
an art must use its [own] tools[82] and the soul its [own] body.[83]

Chapter 4

And a certain other opinion has been handed down about the soul,   407b27
one not less convincing to many than those that have been mentioned,
a position which has had to give accounts as before a tribunal even in
popular writings. / For they say it [the soul] is a certain [sort of] har-   30
mony.[84] For harmony is a mixing and composition of contraries and
the body is composed from contraries.[85]

    And yet harmony is a certain [sort of] ratio or composition of
things mixed, while the soul can be neither of these. Moreover, moving [another] does not belong to harmony, / but all, so to speak, assign   408a1
this most of all to the soul. It harmonizes more to say harmony about
health and generally of the bodily excellences than about the soul.
This is most apparent if one should try to give an account of the passions and the works of the soul by some harmony, / for it is difficult   5
to make it fit.

    Moreover, when we say "harmony," we are looking to two
[meanings]: the chief one being the composition of magnitudes in
things having motion and position, when they are so joined that nothing of the same kind can be introduced, and, next, the ratio of things
mixed. In neither way is it [the position] / reasonable. The composi-   10
tion of the parts of bodies is very easy to test. For the compositions
of the parts are many and various; of what, then, or how must one
assume the mind to be a composition, or even the sensitive or the
desiring [part]?[86] Likewise, it is strange that the soul is the ratio of the
mixture, / for the ratios of the mixtures of the elements according to   15
which a thing is flesh and that according to which a thing is bone are
not the same. It will happen, then, that a thing has many souls also
according to the whole body, if indeed, all have been mixed from the
elements, while the ratio of a mix is a harmony and a soul.

    One might also ask Empedocles (for he says each of them / [i.e.,   20
bone, flesh, etc.] is in some ratio) whether, then, the ratio *is* the soul

or is it rather that, being some other thing, it comes to be in the parts? Moreover, is friendship the cause of any chance mixture or [only] of one according to a ratio {reason}?[87] And is it [friendship] the ratio or some other thing beside the ratio? These [positions], then, involve these sorts of difficulties.

25   However, if the soul is other / than the mixture, why in the world is it destroyed at the same time as 'to be flesh' and ['to be] the other parts' of the animal? Besides, if indeed each of the parts does not have a soul, if the soul is not the ratio of the mixture, what is it which is destroyed when the soul is removed? It is clear from the things said,
30   then, that the soul cannot be either a harmony / nor can it be carried about in a circle. But it can be in motion accidentally, just as we said, and can move itself insofar as that in which it is can be in motion and this latter can be moved by the soul. But otherwise, it is not able to be in motion according to place.[88]

408b1   One might more reasonably raise the difficulty about its being / a thing in motion by looking into such concerns as the following. For we say that the soul is pained and rejoices, takes heart and fears, again, is angry and senses and thinks things through; but all these seem to be
5   motions. Whence one might believe that it is in motion. / But this is not necessary. For even if being pained or rejoicing or thinking things through are most of all motions and each of these is being in motion (e.g., being angry or fearing is for the heart to move in a certain way, while thinking things through is perhaps some such thing or some-
10   thing else), and of these, it / happens that some are motions according to locomotion, some according to alteration (but of what sort they are and how [this happens] belongs to a different discussion), the being in motion is due to the soul. Saying, then, that the soul is angered is as if one should say the soul weaves or builds a house. For perhaps it would be better not to say that the soul pities or learns or thinks things
15   through, but / that the man [does so] in virtue of the soul, and this, not as though the motion is in it, but in some cases [the motion] goes towards it, in others away from it, as sensation is [to it] from [exter-nal] things, while recollection is from it towards motions or rests in the sense organs.

But the mind seems to come to be within, being some substance,
20   and not to be destroyed.[89] For mostly it would be destroyed / by the weakening of old age, but [it is rather] as now happens in the case of the sense organs. For if an old man should receive a certain kind of eye, he would see just like a young man. So that old age does not occur by the soul having suffered something [directly], but [rather by] that in
25   which it is [having suffered], just as in bouts of drinking or / in sick-nesses. Understanding and contemplating are quenched by something

else inside being destroyed, then, but are themselves impassible. And thinking things through and loving and hating are not passions of that [mind], but rather of the thing that has that [, i.e., has mind], insofar as it has that. Because of which also, if this latter thing [which has a mind] is destroyed, it {the soul} neither remembers nor loves. For they did not belong to that {the soul}, but to what is common, which [latter] is destroyed. (But perhaps the mind is something more divine and impassible.)[90] /

From these things, then, it is clear that the soul is not able to be moved. But if it is not moved in general, it is clear that neither [is it moved] by itself.[91]   30

Of the things which have been said, the most unreasonable one by far is that which says that the soul is a self-moving number. For those who hold this, the first impossible things are the ones which result from [the soul's] being in motion, and proper ones / from saying it is   409a1 a number. For how must one think the units move, and by what, and how, being without parts and indivisible? For insofar as it both is able to cause motion and is a mobile, one must [be able to] divide it.[92]

Moreover, since they say that when a line moves it makes a surface, a point / a line, the motions of units will also be lines. For the point   5 is a unit having position, while the number of the soul is somewhere and has position to start with. Moreover, if someone subtracts a number or a unit from a number, there remains another number. But plants and many of the animals, being divided, live and [the parts] / seem to have   10 the same species of soul [as the whole did].

It would seem to make no difference to speak of units or very small bodies. For even if Democritus' spheres should become points, as long as some amount remains, something in them will be the mover and something the moved, just as in what is continuous. For what was mentioned [, i.e., that the body must be divided into a mover and a moved,] does not happen through a difference in greatness / or smallness but because [it is] an amount. Because of which,   15 it is necessary for there to be something that moves the units.

But if the soul is the mover in the animal, then also in the number, so that the soul is not both the mover and the moved, but the mover only. How, then, can this be a unit? For there must be present in it / some difference from others. But what would be the difference   20 of a monadic unit except position?

If, then, the units in the body and the points are different, the units will be in the same [position]. For it will occupy the space of a point. And indeed, if two [can occupy the same space], what prevents an infinity being in the same [space]? For those things of which the place is undivided / [are] themselves [undivided]. But if the points in   25 the body are the number of the soul or if the soul is the number of the points in the body, why do not all bodies have souls? For points (even an infinity of them) seem to be in all.

30   Moreover, how is it possible for the points to be separated and removed from the bodies if / indeed lines are not divided into points?

Chapter 5

409a31 In one way, as was said,[93] this opinion comes to the same thing as that of those who posit it {the soul} to be some body divided into small parts; but in another way, as Democritus says it {the body} is moved
409b1   by the soul, it has a strangeness all its own. / For if the soul is in every sensitive body, it is necessary that two bodies be in the same [place], if the soul is a certain [sort of] body.[94] For those who say it {the soul}
5   is a number, many points / are in one point, or else every body has a soul, unless [the view is that] some different [sort of] number, and something other than the points [already] existing in bodies, comes to be within [the body]. It happens, too, that the animal is moved by the number just as we said Democritus moves it.[95] For what difference
10   does it make whether we say little spheres or big units, or / generally units which move in place? For in both ways it is necessary that the animal move by these things being moved.

These and many similar things, then, happen for those who weave motion and number into one thing. For not only is it impossible that the definition of the soul be like this, but even that an accident [of the
15   soul be such]. This is clear if / someone should try to explain from this account the passions and the works of the soul (e.g., reasonings, sensations, pleasures, pains and any other such things). For as we said before, it is not even easy to make a guess from these things.[96]

20   There being three ways handed down according to which the / soul is defined (some having said it is what is most able to cause motion by itself being in motion, some, the body with the smallest parts, or the one more unbodily than the others – and these [positions] have certain difficulties and contrarieties, which we have pretty much gone through), it remains to be seen how it is said to be from the elements.

25   For they say this so that it might both sense / and know each of the beings, but many impossible things must also happen on this account.[97] For they posit that like knows like, as if positing the soul to be the things [known]. But these [i.e., the elements or principles] are not the only things, but there are also many others, [i.e.,] the things [made] from these [elements], perhaps infinite in number. Let
30   it be, / then, that the soul knows and senses from each of these

[elements]. But by what will it know and sense the composite, e.g., what a god is, or a man, or flesh, or bone? So too, / any other composite thing: for each of these does not have elements in just any way, but in a certain ratio and composition, as even Empedocles says about bone:

410a1

> The earth, well-favored, in its broad melting pots /
> Took two of the eight parts of the shimmering water,
> Four of Hephaistos: and white bones were born.[98]

5

[Saying] that the elements are in the soul, then, does no good, if the ratios and the compositions are not also within it. For it knows each thing like itself, but not bone or man, if these / are not within it. But that this latter is impossible does not need saying. For who would question whether a stone or a man is inside the soul? So too the good and the not-good and likewise also in each of the other cases.[99]

10

Moreover, being is said in many ways (for it signifies this something, or amount, or quality, or even / some one of the other predicates {categories} which we have distinguished[100]): so will the soul be [made] from all of these or not? But there do not seem to be elements common to all. Is it, then, only from those which are substances? Then how will it know each of the others? Or will they say there are proper elements and principles for each of the genera, from which [proper elements and principles] the soul / is composed? It will therefore be amount and quality and substance. But it is impossible that from the elements of an amount a substance and not an amount will exist. To those who say [the soul] is from all [sorts of things], then, these and other such things happen.

15

20

And it is also strange to say both that like is impassible to like, and that like is sensed by like and / like is known by like.[101] For they posit that sensing is a certain [sort of] suffering and being moved. So too understanding and recognizing.[102]

25

The things just now said witness that many strange and difficult things follow upon saying, as does Empedocles,[103] that each thing is known by way of bodily elements and in relation to the like. / For whatever is simply earth in the bodies of the animals, like / bones, tendons, and hair, does not seem to sense anything, so that they are not [sensible] of the like.[104] And yet this should follow. Moreover, in each of the principles there would be more ignorance than comprehension. For each will know one, but will be ignorant of many, for [it will not know] all the others.

30

410b1

For Empedocles / it happens that the god is most unwise, for it

5

does not know one of the elements, namely strife, but mortals [know] all, for each [mortal] is [made] from all.[105]

Generally, why would not every being have soul, since every being is either an element or from one or more or all of the elements? For it is necessary / to know some one or ones or all.[106]

Someone might doubt also about what in the world makes them be one. For the elements seem like material. For the chief thing is that which composes, whatever it might be. But it is impossible that something be stronger and more of a principle than the soul; and still more impossible [that there be a thing stronger and a ruler] more so than the mind. For it is reasonable that this be first-born and lord according to nature.[107] But they say the elements are the first of the beings.[108] /

All, however, both those saying the soul is from the elements due to its knowing and sensing beings, and those saying it is most able to cause motion, do not speak of all souls, for not even all things which sense are capable of motion. For there appear to be some animals / which stay still according to place. And yet it seems that the soul moves the animal only according to this one of the motions. And the case is similar for those who make mind and what is sensitive out of the elements. For it seems that plants live, though they do not share in locomotion or sensation, and many of the animals do not think things through. But if one were to put / these aside and posit the mind to be a part of the soul, and the sensitive part likewise, one would still neither be speaking generally about all souls nor about the whole of any one of them. The account in the so-called Orphic [poems] also has done this. For they say that the soul, being carried on / the winds, enters [the living thing] when things breathe. But this is not possible for plants / and some of the animals, if, in fact, not all breathe. But this escaped the notice of those who make this supposition.

And if one must make the soul from the elements, one need not make it from all of them. For either part of the contrariety is sufficient to judge both itself and its opposite. / For by the straight we know both itself and the curved. For the rule is the judge of both (though the curved [is the rule] neither of itself nor of the straight).[109]

And some say it {the soul} is mixed in the whole, which is perhaps why Thales believed that all things are full of gods.[110] But there are some difficulties with this. For, if the soul is / in the air or in fire, why does it not make an animal, though in the mixed [bodies it does do so], (even though it seemed [to him] better that it be in these [simple bodies])? One might also ask due to what cause the soul in the air is better and more deathless than in the animals. But something strange and irrational happens in either way. For saying that / air or fire is an animal is irrational and not saying a thing with a soul within it is an animal is strange.

They seem to suppose the soul is in these because [they assume that] the whole is of the same species as the parts; whence, if it is by taking something away from the surroundings into the animals that animals become ensouled, / it is necessary for them to say also that 20 the soul is of the same species as these parts. But if, when air is divided, [the parts are] of the same species, but the soul is made of dissimilar parts, it is clear that some [part] of it {the soul} will be present [by coming in from the surrounding air], though some [other part] will not be. It is necessary, then, that the soul either be made of similar parts or that it not be present in every part of the whole.

From what has been said, then, it is apparent that neither does knowing / belong to the soul due to its being from the elements nor 25 is it well or truly said that it moves itself.

But since knowing belongs to the soul, and also sensing and forming an opinion, and, again, desiring and willing and, generally, appetites, and motion according to place comes to be in animals due to / the soul, and, again, growth, maturity, and decay, does each of 30 these belong / to the whole soul and do we understand and sense and 411b1 move and do and suffer each of the others by means of all of it, or different ones by different parts? And is living, then, in a certain one of these parts, or in many, or all, or is there some other / cause [of life]? 5

Some, then, say that it is able to be divided into parts and that it understands by one [part] but desires by another.[111] What in the world, then, holds the soul together, if it is naturally apt to be divided into parts? For certainly it is not the body. For it rather seems, on the contrary, that the soul holds the body together. At least, when it has left, [the body] gives off vapors and rots. If, then, some other thing makes it one, / that would most of all be the soul. But one will have 10 to ask again whether *that* is one or has many parts. For if it is one, why not [say] right away [that] the soul is one? But if it is divisible into parts, the argument will again ask: "what holds that together?" And so one will go on to infinity.

One might doubt about its parts too, / what power each one has 15 in the body. For if the whole soul holds together the whole body, it is also fitting that each of the parts holds together some part of the body. But this seems impossible. For it is difficult even to concoct something about what sort of part the mind would hold together or how.[112]

It appears also that plants live when divided and, / among ani- 20 mals, some of the insects [do too], as if the parts have the same soul in species, if not in number. For both of the parts have sensation and move according to place for some time. But if they do not continue doing so, that is nothing strange. For they do not have the organs {tools} to preserve the nature. But nonetheless all the parts of the

25   soul / are present in each of the parts and they are of the same species
both with each other and with the whole, with each other insofar as
they are not separable, with the whole soul insofar as they are not
divided [from it].[113]

It seems also that the principle in plants is a certain [sort of] soul.
For animals and plants share only this, and though this [sort of soul]
30   is separable from / the principle of sensation, nothing has sensation
without this.[114]

Book II

Chapter 1

Let what was handed down about the soul by our predecessors, then, have been said. Let us begin again as if from the beginning, trying / to determine what the soul is and what would be the most common account of it.[1]

We call, then, some one genus of beings substance[2]; of this {substance}, one is as material, which in virtue of itself is not a "this something," while another is form and species, in virtue of which [form], right away, a thing is called "this something," and a third is what is from these.[3] But the material is potency, / the species actuality; and this latter is two-fold, one like science, another like contemplation [of the object of science].[4]

Bodies seem to be substances most of all, and of these, the natural ones, for these latter are the principles of the others.[5] Of natural bodies, some have life, while some do not;[6] by life we mean self-nutrition and growth and / diminution.[7]

Whence every natural body which shares in life will be a substance – substance, however, in this way, as composite.[8] But since it is also a body of certain sort (for it is one which has life), the soul could not be the body. For the body is not among things which belong to an underlying, but rather is itself something which underlies and is material [for another]. Therefore, it is necessary that the soul be substance / as the species of a natural body having life potentially. Substance, however, is actuality. Therefore, it is the actuality of such a body.

But this [actuality] is said in two ways, one as science, the other as contemplation [of the object of science]. It is clear, therefore, that [the soul is actuality] as science. For both sleep and waking exist in the presence of the soul. But waking is / analogous to contemplation [of the object of science], while sleep is analogous to having science and not [actually] using it. But in the same [individual], science is prior in generation.[9] Whence, the soul is the first actuality of a natural body having life potentially.[10]

But such [a body] would be composed / of tools {would be

412a3

5

10

15

20

25

412b1

organic}. The parts of plants are tools {organs}, too, though they are very simple, e.g., the leaf is the covering of the pod, while the pod is of the fruit. And the roots are analogous to the mouth, for both take in food. If, then, one must say something common about all souls, / it would be the first actuality of an natural body composed of tools {organic}.[11]

Whence also one need not ask whether the soul and the body are one, just as neither does one ask this about wax and its shape, nor, generally, about the material of each thing and that of which it is the material. For, while "one" and "being" are said in many ways, the main one is actuality.[12] /

Universally, therefore, it has been said what the soul is. For according to its account, it is substance. But this is the "what it was to be"[13] for this sort of body, just as if some tool, e.g., an ax, were a natural body. For being an ax would be its substance, and the soul is this. But if the latter were separated, it would no longer be an ax, except equivocally; / but as it is, it is an ax. For the soul is not the "what it was to be" and the account of this sort of body, but of a natural body such as has in itself a principle of motion and of standing.

One must also consider what was said in the case of the parts. For if the eye were an animal, its sight would be its soul. For this is the substance / according to account of the eye. But the eye is the material of sight, and if sight departs, the eye is no longer an eye (except equivocally, like a sculpted or a painted eye). So one must grasp what is said in the case of the part about the whole living body. For there is a proportion: as the part is to the part, so the entirety of sensation is to the whole / sensitive body, as such.

It is not what has lost its soul which exists in potency so as to live, but what has [a soul].[14] The seed and fruit are potentially such bodies.[15] As, therefore, cutting and seeing are actualities, and so too / is being awake, the soul is like the sight and the power of the organ. The body is what is in potency. But just as the eye is the pupil and sight, so also the living thing is the soul and the body.

On the one hand, then, it is not unclear that the soul (or some / parts of it, if it is naturally divisible into parts) is not separable from the body. For in some cases, the actuality is of these parts [of the body]. Yet nothing prevents some parts [being separated], because they are the actualities of no [part of the] body.[16] On the other hand, it is unclear whether the soul is [also] the actuality of the body in the way that the sailor is of the ship.[17] Generally, therefore, let this be determined and / drawn in outline about the soul.

Chapter 2

But since what is clear and more known according to account comes
to be from what is unclear but more apparent, one must try to
approach the soul once more in this way.[18] For it is not only necessary
for the definitive account to show the "that," as most terms {defini-
tions} / do, but also to include and show the cause. But now the
accounts of terms are like conclusions. For example, "What is squaring?" "Making an equilateral rectangle equal to an oblong rectangle."
Such a term has the account of a conclusion. But he who says that
squaring is the finding of a mean proportional says / the cause of the
thing.[19]

Taking the beginning of the inquiry, therefore, we say that the
ensouled is to be divided from the unsouled by living. But living
being spoken of in many ways (e.g., understanding, sensation, motion
and standing according to place, moreover, motion according to
nutrition, / and both diminution and growth), even if only one of these
be present, we call the thing living.[20]

Because of which, too, all plants seem to live. For they are apparently such things as have in them this sort of power and principle,
[i.e., one] through which they receive growth and diminution according to opposite places. For they – whatever things / feed continuously
and live until the end, so long as they are able to take in food – do not
grow up but not down, but in both [directions] alike and in all ways.[21]

This power is able to be separated from the others, but in mortal
things it is impossible that the others be separated from this.[22] This is
apparent in plants. For no other power of the soul is present in these.
/ Living, therefore, belongs in living things through this principle.[23]

But an animal lives primarily through sensation. For we call
"animals" (and not merely "living") even the things which do not
move or switch place, but do have sensation. Of sense, touch / is present in all first. Just as the nutritive power is able to be separated from
touch and from all sensation, so touch [can be separated] from the
other senses. We call the "nutritive" power that part of the soul in
which even plants share. But all animals appear to have the sense of
touch.

We will say later through / what cause each of these [facts]
occurs.[24] Now, however, let this much alone be said, that the soul is
the principle of the things named, and is defined by these: by the
power of nutrition, of sensation, of thinking things through, and of
motion.

413a11

15

20

25

30

413b1

5

10

But whether each of these is a soul or a part of a soul, and if a
15   part, whether such as to be separable / only in account or even in
place, is not a difficult thing to see in some cases, though some present a difficulty.[25] For just as among plants some, when divided,
appear to live, even when [the parts] are separated from each other, as
if the soul in these were one in actuality in each plant, but many in
20   potency, so we see this happening in other, / different [sorts of] soul:
in the case of insects which are divided. For each of the parts has sensation and motion according to place – but if sensation, then imagination and appetite too. For where there is sensation, there is also pain
and pleasure, and wherever these are, there is necessarily also
desire.[26]

25   About mind and / the power of contemplation, nothing is yet
clear, but it seems to be a different kind {genus} of soul, and this
alone can be separated, as the eternal from the corruptible. It is manifest from these [considerations], however, that the remaining parts of
the soul are not separable, as some say [they are].[27]

But it is manifest that these [parts] are different in account. For if
30   sensing / and forming an opinion are different, then to be able to sense
and to be able to form an opinion are different (and likewise for each
of the other parts mentioned). Moreover, in some living things all
these [parts] are present, in some, some of these, in others, however,
414a1   only one. This [fact] will make / the difference among living things.[28]
(Afterwards we must look into the cause.[29]) Something akin happens
in the case of the senses. For some have all, some have some, and
some have [only] the most necessary one, touch.

Since, however, that by which we live and sense is said in two
5   ways, / just as that by which we know – we say that one is science
and the other is the soul, for we speak of knowing by each of these –
and likewise too that by which we are healthy – the one is, health and,
the other, some part of the body, or even the whole – while of these
science and health are form and a certain species and account and are
10   as the act / of the receptive, the one of the scientific power, the other
of what can be healed (for it seems the act of doers is present in what
suffers and is disposed[30]), but the soul is this, i.e., that by which we
primarily live and sense and think, it [the soul] would thus be some
account and species, and not material and underlying. For substance
15   / is said in three ways, as we said,[31] one of which ways is species, one
material, and one what is from both, and of these, the material is
potency, while the species is actuality; since what is from both is the
ensouled, the body is not the actuality of the soul, but the latter is [the
actuality] of a certain body.[32]

And because of this fact, those to whom it seems that the soul

neither / is without body nor is a certain body are making a good   20
assumption. For it is not a body, but something of a body.[33]

And because of this it {the soul} is present in a body, and in a
certain sort of body, and [things are] not as our predecessors said, fitting it {the soul} into a body without defining in any way in which
one and in what sort of body, even though it does not appear that any
chance thing receives any chance thing. / And this happens according   25
to reason: for the actuality of each thing is in that which is in potency
and [the actuality] is naturally apt to come to be in its proper matter.[34]
From these considerations, therefore, it is clear that the soul is some
actuality and account of what has a potency to be such.

Chapter 3

Of the aforesaid powers of the soul, all are present in some, / as was   414a29
said,[35] some of them are in some, and in some only one. We call
"powers" the nutritive, sensitive, appetitive, what is able to cause
motion according to place, and what is capable of thought. Only the
nutritive power is present in plants, but in other things / both this   414b1
power and the sensitive power. But if the sensitive power [is present],
the appetitive is as well. For appetite is desire and anger and will, and
all animals have one of the senses, [namely,] touch: but in anything
in which sensation is present, in this pleasure and pain and / the pleas-   5
ant and the painful [are also present], and in whatever these things are
[present], desire is too. For this is appetite for the pleasant.[36]
Moreover, they have the sense of food, for touch is the sense of food.
For all living things are fed by the dry and the moist and the hot and
the cold, while touch is the sense of these, but they are fed by the
other sensibles accidentally. / For sound and color and odor con-   10
tribute nothing to food, while flavor is one of the tangibles.[37] Both
hunger and thirst are desires, hunger for what is dry and hot, thirst for
what is moist and cold. Flavor is like some seasoning of these. One
must be more certain about these things later;[38] but now let so much
/ be said about them: that in living things which have touch, appetite   15
too is present. The case of imagination is unclear; one must look into
it later.[39] But in addition to these [powers], the power of local motion
also is present in some, and in others also both the power to think
things through and the mind, e.g., in men and, should it be the case,
in some other such thing, or something more honorable.[40] /

So it is clear that the account of the soul and that of shape would   20
be one in the same way. For in the one case there is no shape beyond
the triangle and the consequent shapes, nor in the other case is there

soul beyond the sorts mentioned. There can be a common account
with regard to shapes, an account which will befit all shapes but will
25   be proper to no shape. Likewise in the case / of the souls mentioned.
Whence it is laughable, in these cases and in others, to seek a common account, [one] which will be the proper account of no beings and
will not be about the proper and indivisible species, while omitting
such [a proper account]. In this, [considerations] about shapes and
30   about the soul are similar. For among shapes and the ensouled, / the
prior always is in the subsequent in potency, as the triangle in the
square, the nutritive in the sensitive.[41]

Whence one must ask about each, what is the soul of each, e.g.,
what is the soul of the plant and what of man or of beast.[42]

415a1   One must inquire due to what cause / they are in sequence in this
way. For the sensitive power is not without the nutritive, while the
nutritive is separated from the sensitive power in plants.[43] Again, not
5   one of the other senses is present without touch, but touch / is present
without the others. For many of the animals have neither sight nor
hearing nor the sense of smell. And of sensitive things, some have the
power of local motion, while some do not. Lastly, the fewest things
have calculation and the power to think things through. Among mor-
10   tal things, in whatever calculation is present, in these all the rest / [of
the powers are present] too, while calculation is not in all those in
which each of these [other powers] is, but in some there is not even
imagination, while some live by this alone. But [there is] a different
account in the case of speculative {contemplative} mind.[44]

It is clear, therefore, that the most proper account of the soul is
the account which is about each of these [particular sorts of soul].

Chapter 4

415a14   For one intending to make an inquiry about these [powers], however,
15   it is necessary / to grasp what each of these is, and then to seek out in
this way the things following [upon them] and the other things [con-
nected with them]. Yet if one needs to say what each of these is, i.e.,
what the intellectual power or the sensitive power or the nutritive
power is, one must first say, further, what understanding is and what
20   sensing is. For the works and the deeds are prior to the powers / in
account. If so, however, one must further have considered first the
things corresponding to these [works and deeds]; due to the same
cause, one ought to determine first about these, e.g., about food and
the sensible and the intelligible.[45]

Whence, one must speak first about food and generation. For the nutritive soul is also in the others {living things}, and is / the first and most common power of the soul, that according to which living is in all living things – the works of which soul are generating and using food. For the most natural of works for living things which are complete and not disabled or spontaneously generated[46] is the making of another like themselves (an animal an animal, a plant a plant), so that they might always share, insofar as they are able, in what always exists and in the divine. / For all things have an appetite for this and do whatever they do according to nature for the sake of this. However, that for the sake of which is two-fold: that which or that for whom.[47] Since, then, it is impossible to take part in what is always and in the divine in a continuous way, because not one of the destructible things can persist the same and one / in number, insofar as each thing is able to share, it takes part in this [way], this one more and that one less, and the same thing does not persist, but what is like the same [persists], not one in number, but one in species.[48]

　　The soul, however, is the cause and principle of the living body. These [i.e., cause and principle] are said in many ways[49]; likewise, the soul is a cause according to / three of the determined ways. For the soul is a cause as whence is the motion, and as that for the sake of which, and as the substance of ensouled bodies. It is clear, then, that it is a cause as substance.[50] For, in all things, substance is the cause of being, while for living beings, to live is to be – but the soul is the cause and principle of this. Moreover, the actuality / of a being in potency is the account {λόγος}.[51] But it is clear that the soul is also a cause as that for the sake of which. For just as the mind acts for the sake of something, nature acts the same way, and this is its end. In living things, the soul is such according to nature. For all natural bodies are tools {organs} of the soul, and just as some are [the tools] of animals, so too some are / of plants, as being for the sake of the soul. That for the sake of which, however, is two-fold, that which and that for whom. But indeed, the soul is also that whence first is motion according to place. This same power, however, is not in all living things. Yet alteration and growth are also according to the soul. For sense seems to be a certain [sort of] alteration,[52] / but nothing which does not share in soul senses. So too in the case of growth and diminution. For nothing which does not feed decays or grows naturally, while nothing feeds which does not take part in life.

　　Empedocles did not speak well, when he added this, that / growth happens in plants by sending roots down because earth is carried in this way naturally, up because fire is [carried upwards] likewise. For he does not grasp up and down well. For up and down are not the same for each thing and for the universe as a whole. But as are the heads of

animals, so are the roots of plants, if one needs to call the organs different or same by their works.[53] / In addition to these [considerations,
one might ask him] what is it that keeps together the things which are
carried to contrary places, the fire and the earth? For they will be torn
asunder, if there be not something preventing this. But if there is, this
is the soul and the cause of growth and of feeding.

It seems to some, however, that the nature of fire / is the cause of
feeding and growth simply. For this alone of the bodies or the elements seems to feed and grow, due to which someone might assume
that this is what is at work in both plants and animals. It is somehow
a joint cause, but is not simply the cause; / rather the soul [is the
cause]. For the growth of fire is unlimited, as long as there is fuel,
while of all the things constituted by nature there is a limit and ratio
both of magnitude and of growth. These are from the soul, but not
from the fire, and from the account more than from the material.[54]

However, since the same power of the soul is nutritive and generative,[55] / it is necessary to determine about food first, for by this
work it is separated from the other powers of the soul.

It seems that contrary is food for contrary, though not all for all,
but whichever of the contraries have not only generation from each
other, but also growth. For many things come to be from each other,
but not all / are amounts, as health [comes] from illness. But it
appears that not even [all of] these are food for each other in the same
way, but a liquid [, e.g., oil,] is food for fire, while fire does not feed
water. Among the simple bodies, then, these seem most to be, the one,
food, and the other, what is fed.

But there is a difficulty. For some say / that like is fed, just as it
grows, by like. But to others, as we said,[56] the reverse seems [to be
the case], that contrary is fed by the contrary, like being impassible to
like, while food changes and is digested. But for all things, change is
to an opposite or middle. Moreover, food suffers / something due to
what is eating, but not the latter due to food, just as / the artist does
not suffer due to the material, but the latter due to the former. The
artist changes only from rest to act.[57]

Whether the food is what is finally added or what exists at first
makes a difference. If both (the one / undigested, the other digested),
in both ways it might be called food. For as undigested, contrary is
fed by contrary, but, as digested, like by like. Whence it appears that
in some way both [parties] speak rightly and not rightly.[58]

Since nothing that does not share in life feeds, the ensouled /
body, as ensouled, would be what is fed. Whence also food is relative
to the ensouled, and not accidentally.[59]

But to be food and to be able to cause growth are different. For insofar as the ensouled is an amount, [what the living feeds on is] able to cause growth, but insofar as [the ensouled is] a "this something" and substance, [what the living feeds on is] food. For it conserves the substance, and [the substance] exists so long as / it can feed. And it [food] is productive of generation, not of the generation of the one fed, but of one like the one fed; for the substance of this already exists, while nothing generates itself, but [a thing] conserves [itself].[60] Whence such a principle of the soul is a power such as to conserve the one having it, as such, while food helps it to be at work. Whence, deprived / of food, it is not able to exist.

Since there are three things – what is fed, that by which it is fed, and the one feeding – the one feeding is the first[61] soul, what is fed is the body having this soul, [and] that by which it is fed is the food.

Since, however, it is just to name each thing from its end, while the end [here] is to generate one like itself, / the first soul would be "reproductive" {"generative of one like itself"}.

However, that by which a thing feeds is two-fold, like that by which a thing is steered, both hand and rudder, the one moving and being moved, the other only being moved. Yet it is necessary that all food be able to be digested, while warmth works for digestion. Whence, every ensouled thing has heat. /

In outline, therefore, what food is has been said. Later, it must be more clearly treated in the appropriate works.[62]

Chapter 5

These things having been determined, let us speak about every sense in common.[63] Sensing occurs in being moved and suffering, as was said. For it seems to be a sort of alteration.[64] / Some, however, say that like suffers from like. / How this is possible and how impossible, we have said in our general works on acting and suffering.[65]

There is a difficulty as to why a sensation even of the senses themselves does not occur; and why they do not bring about sensation without what is outside [them, though] fire and earth / and the other elements (of which there is sensation in virtue of themselves or in virtue of their accidents[66]) are within [the sense organs]. It is clear, then, that what is sensitive is not in act, but only in potency; whence it does not sense, just as what can be ignited does not ignite itself through itself without what can ignite it. For it would ignite itself, and nothing would need fire in actuality.[67]

But since / we say "sensing" in two ways (for we say that what potentially hears or sees hears or sees, even if it should happen to be sleeping, and also what is already at work), "sensation" too might be spoken of in two ways, the one as in potency, the other as in act, and likewise sensing: one is being in potency, the other being in act.[68]

15   First, then, let us speak as if / suffering and being moved and being in act are the same. For motion too is a certain [sort of] act, though imperfect, as was said in another work.[69]

All things, however, suffer and are moved by what is productive and is a being in act. Whence it is that a thing suffers in one way by 20   what is like [itself] and in another way by what is unlike, / as we said. For the unlike suffers, while what has suffered is like.[70]

One must also distinguish, however, in regard to potency and actuality; for just now we were speaking about them simply. For there is something which knows in the way in which we say a man knows, because man is among the things which are knowers and which have 25   knowledge, while / [there is something which knows] in another way, as we call the one who already has the science of grammar a knower. These two are not potential in the same way, but the one is potential because the kind and the material are such, while the other is so because he is able to contemplate [the object of science] whenever he wishes, should nothing outside prevent him. But the one already contemplating [the object of science] is being in actuality and is chiefly 30   the one who knows this "A." / Both of the first ones are knowers in potency [and come to be knowers in act], then, but the one [does so] having been altered through learning and often changing from the contrary state {habit, disposition, condition}, while the other, from having grammar or arithmetic though not being at work {in act}, 417b1   [changes] in / another way to being at work {in act}.[71]

But "suffering" is not simple either: one sort is a destruction due to the contrary, while another sort is more the preservation of a being in potency by a being in actuality and by something similar in the way that 5   potency / is related to actuality.[72] For the one who has knowledge comes to be contemplating [the object of science], a change which is either not altering (for the progress is into itself and into actuality) or is a different kind of alteration. Whence, it is not good to say that the one thinking, when he thinks, is being altered, as neither is the housebuilder [being altered] when he builds. It is right, then, that the process 10   by which one who [already] understands and judges goes / into actuality from being in potency not have [the name] "teaching" but a different name.[73] One must say either that one who, from being in potency, learns and grasps knowledge by means of one who is in actuality and capable of teaching does not suffer, as was said, or that there are two 15   modes / of alteration, the one a change to the privative dispositions and the other to the states {habits, dispositions, conditions} and nature.[74]

The first change of what is sensitive, however, comes to be due to what generates; when a thing has been generated, it already has sensing, as [a thing] also has knowledge. But sensing according to act is said in the same way as contemplating [the object of science]. They differ, / however, because the things productive of the act of the one, the visible and the audible, are outside (and likewise the rest of the sensibles). The cause is that sense according to act is of particulars, while science is of universals: but these are somehow in the soul itself. Whence understanding is in a man whenever he wishes, / but sensing is not in him [whenever he wishes]. For it is necessary for a sensible to be present. This is so too in the sciences concerned with the sensibles, and due to the same cause, because the sensibles are among particulars and things outside. But the opportunity to clarify these things will come later.[75] /

For now, however, let this much be determined: that being in potency is not spoken of simply, but in one case it is said as we might say a boy is able to command an army, in another, as one who is in his prime; / so too the sensitive. Let it be determined about these that they are other and how they are other; but since the difference of these is unnamed, it is necessary to use "suffering" and "altering" as the chief names.[76] The sensitive in potency, however, is like the sensible already in actuality, as was said.[77] / Therefore, not being like, it suffers, while, having suffered, it has been made like and is such as is that [sensible].[78]

Chapter 6

First, however, one must speak about the sensibles with regard to each sense.[79] But "the sensible" is said in three ways, two of which we say are sensed in virtue of themselves {*per se*}, while one is sensed accidentally {*per accidens*}. / Of the two, one is proper to each sense, the other common to all.

I call "proper" what cannot be sensed by another sense, and about which it cannot err, as sight is of color, hearing of sound, taste of flavor, while touch has [reference to] many differences.[80] But each sense discerns / these things, and does not err that this is color or that it is sound, but [it does err about] what or where the colored thing is, or what or where that which sounds is.[81] Such things, therefore, are called the proper sensibles of each [sense].

The common [sensibles] are motion, rest, number, shape, magnitude. For such things are not sensibles proper to any one [sense] but are common to all.[82] For a certain motion is / a sensible both for touch and for sight.

A sensible is called accidental if, e.g., a white thing is the son of Diares. For one senses this thing accidentally, because it happens to the white, which is sensed. Whence also the sense suffers nothing from this sensible as such.[83]

25   Of those which are sensibles in virtue of themselves, the proper sensibles are chiefly / sensibles, and are those [objects] for which the substance of each sense is naturally apt.[84]

Chapter 7

418a26   That of which there is sight is the visible, but the visible is color, and also something which can be said in speech, but happens to be unnamed.[85] What we mean will be clear by going on.[86]

For the visible is color; this, however, is what is upon / what is visible in virtue of itself: in virtue of itself and not in account, but because it has in itself the cause of being visible.[87] However, all color

418b1   / is able to move the transparent according to act, and this is its nature.[88] Whence, the visible is not without light, but every color of each thing is seen in light. Whence, one must say first, about light, what it is.

5   There is, then, something transparent. I call the transparent / what is visible, not visible in virtue of itself, as if speaking simply, but through an extraneous color. Such are air and water and many of the solids. For these are transparent not as air or water, but because there is some nature present, which is the same in both of these and in the eternal body above.[89]

10   Light, however, is the act of this, / of the transparent as transparent. In that in which this is, there is darkness also, in potency.[90] Light, however, is like the color of the transparent, whenever the transparent is in actuality due to fire or something of this sort, like the body above. For even in this something one and the same is present.

What the transparent is, then, and what light is, has been said,
15   that it is neither fire, nor any / body, nor a stream from some body (for in this way it would be a certain [sort of] body)[91], but it is rather the presence of fire or some such thing in the transparent. For two bodies are not able to be together in the same [place]. And it seems that light is contrary to darkness. Darkness, however, is the privation of such a
20   state in the transparent. Whence, it is clear that / light is the presence of this.

And Empedocles [did] not [speak] correctly, nor anyone else who spoke in this way, speaking as if light were carried along for some time and comes to be between the earth and the containing

body, though escaping our notice. For this is opposed to what argument makes clear and to the appearances. / For it might escape our   25
notice over a small distance, but not noticing this [when the motion
is] from the extreme east to the extreme west is a very great require-
ment.[92]

What is without color is receptive of color, what is without sound
of sound. The transparent is the uncolored and the invisible or what
is barely seen, as, it seems, the dark. Such is the transparent, / but not   30
when it is transparent in actuality, but when in potency. For the same
nature is sometimes dark and sometimes light. /

However, not all visible things are in light, but only the proper   419a1
color of each thing. For some things are not seen in the light, while
they bring about sensation in darkness, like things that appear fiery
and shining, like fungi, horns, heads, scales, and eyes of fishes / (but   5
these things are unnamed by one name). But of none of these is the
proper color seen.[93] Due to what cause these are seen, then, is another
story, but for now so much is apparent, that what is seen in light is
color. Whence, [color] is not seen without light: for this was being /   10
color for it, being able to move the transparent in act. However, the
actuality of the transparent is light. A sign of this is apparent: for
should someone place upon his eye a thing that has color, it will not
be seen. But the color moves the transparent, such as the air, while the
sense organ is moved by this / [air] when the latter is continuous.   15

For Democritus does not speak about this well, believing that if
what is between [the eye and the color] should become void, even if
an ant should be in the heaven, one would see [it] distinctly. For this
is impossible. For seeing comes to be by the sensitive suffering something; it is impossible, therefore, that it be [directly acted upon] by the
color which is seen. It remains, then, that it be / by what is between;   20
whence it is necessary that there be something between. But were
there a void, [it would follow] not that it would be seen distinctly, but
that nothing at all would be seen. It has been said, therefore, due to
what cause it is necessary to see color in light.

Fire, however, is seen in both, in darkness and in light, and this
by necessity. For the transparent comes to be / transparent due to   25
this.[94]

The same account, however, is [found] in sound and odor. For
neither of these brings about sensation when touching the sense
organ, but what is between is moved by the odor or sound, while each
of the sense organs is moved by this [middle thing]. Should someone
place what sounds or what has odor upon the sense organ itself, it will
bring about no sensation. The case is akin in touch and taste, / though   30
it does not appear to be – the reason for this will be clear later.[95]

The medium for sound is air, while that for odor is unnamed. For there is some common passion in the case of air and of water; as the transparent is for color, so for what has odor there is / what is present in both of these. For it appears that even the water animals / have the sense of smell. But man and whichever land animals breathe are unable to smell when not breathing. The cause of these things too will be discussed later.[96]

Chapter 8

And now let us first determine about sound and hearing. Sound is / two-fold. For one is a certain act, the other a potency. For we say that some things do not have sound, such as sponge and wool, but others do have sound, like bronze and whatever things are solid and smooth, because they are able to sound. But this {to sound} is to make sound in act in between itself and what hears [it]. Sound according to act is always of something, / against something, and in something. For what makes it is a blow. Because of which, it is impossible that sound come to be if there is [only] one thing [present]. For what hits is different from what is hit. Whence, the sounding sounds against something. But a blow does not occur without locomotion. And, just as we said, sound is not the striking of any chance thing. For should one strike against wool, / no sound is made. But bronze and things which are smooth and hollow [do make sounds], the bronze because it is smooth, the hollow by making many reverberations after the first, [the air] which is moved being unable to get away.

Moreover, one hears in air and, though less so, in water. The chief thing in the case of sound is not the air or the water; rather, there must be / a striking of solids against each other and against the air. But this happens when the air, when struck, remains and is not dispersed. Because of which, if it be struck quickly and strongly, it sounds. For the motion of what strikes must outstrip the breaking up of the air, as if someone should strike at a heap or swirling cloud of sand which is being / quickly carried along.

An echo occurs when, [a portion of] air being made one due to a container which encloses it and prevents its dispersal, the air rebounds like a ball. It seems an echo always occurs, but not clearly, since in the case of sound things happen as in the case of light. For light too is always reflected / (for [otherwise] light would not be in every place, but there would be darkness outside of the [direct] sunshine), though it does not [always] reflect as it does from water or

35
419b1

419b4
5

10

15

20

25

30

bronze or certain other smooth things, [i.e.,] so as to make a shadow
by which we can mark off the light. But the void is rightly said to be
the chief thing in hearing. For air seems to be void, and this is what
produces / hearing, when, being continuous and one, it is moved.[97]   35
But if what strikes be not smooth, / it {sound} does not come to be,   420a1
because it {the air} is easily dispersed. But [when what strikes is
smooth], then it {the air} all at once becomes one due to the surface,
for the surface of the smooth is one.

What can make sound, therefore, is what is able to move air
which is one by continuity right up to the organ of hearing. But air is
of one nature with the organ of hearing. Through being in air, / what   5
is inside is moved when what is outside is moved. Because of which,
the animal does not hear throughout [its body], nor is there air everywhere in it. For [even] the part which will be moved and have sound
in it does not have air everywhere.

Air itself, then, is without sound because it is easily dispersed,
but when the dispersal is prevented, its motion is sound. But the air
in the ears is enclosed so as / to be unmoving, that it might sense more 10
precisely all the differences of the motion.

Due to these things we also hear in water, because it does not
enter into the air which is naturally present, nor even into the ear,
because of its spiral shape. When this does happen, one does not hear,
nor if the eardrum is damaged, just as in the case of the eye, if its skin
/ is damaged.   15

But it is not a sign of whether the ear is hearing or not that the
ear murmurs like a horn. For the air in the ears is always moved with
a certain motion of its own, but sound belongs to another and is not
one's own. And because of this they say hearing is by means of the
void and echoing, because we hear by having some air which has
been bounded. /

Is it what is struck or the striker that makes a sound? Or is it not   20
both, in different ways? For the sound is a motion of what is able to
be moved in the way in which things which bounce back from a
smooth thing do when one hits them. So, as was said,[98] not everything struck and everything which strikes make a sound (for example,
a pin might hit a pin), / but what is struck must be regular, so that the 25
air might bounce back and vibrate all at once.

The differences of things which sound are manifest in sound
according to act. For just as without light colors are not seen, so too
the sharp and the flat [are not heard] without sound. But these are said
according to a metaphor / from things which are touched. For the   30
sharp moves the sense much in a short time while the flat moves little
in a long time.[99] The sharp is not fast, then, nor the flat slow, but such

a motion comes to be, of the one through quickness, of the other
420b1 through slowness. / And this even seems to have a proportion to the
sharp and the dull in the case of touch. For the sharp is like something
which stabs, while the flat is like a thing that presses, because the one
moves in a little [time], the other in much; whence the one happens
5 to be fast, the other slow. / So about sound, let things have been determined in this way.

Voice is a certain sound of the ensouled. For none of the unsouled
[things] vocalize, though they are said to vocalize according to a likeness, e.g., the flute and the lyre and other unsouled things have an
arrangement of sound and melody and articulation, for it seems that
voice too has these [attributes].

10 Many of the animals do not have / voice, e.g., the ones without
blood and, of ones with blood, the fishes. And this happens reasonably, if indeed sound is a certain [sort of] motion of the air. But the
fish which are said to vocalize, like the ones in the river Achelous,
make sound with their gills or by some other such part.

Voice, however, is a sound of an animal, and not [one made] by
15 any chance part. But since all things make sound by something / striking, and [striking] something, and in something, and this latter is air,
it is reasonable that only those things would vocalize which take in
air. For nature uses what has been inhaled for two works: just as [it
uses] the tongue both for tasting and for discourse, of which the one,
taste, is necessary (because of which also it belongs to more [ani-
20 mals]), while the other, giving an explanation, / is for the sake of well-
being, so too [it uses] breath for both heating the interior, as a necessary thing (the cause will be said in other writings[100]), and for voice,
so that well-being may be present.

The throat is the organ for breathing, while that for the sake of
which this part exists is the lung, for by this part animals which have
25 feet / have more heat than the others. There must be breathing, and
the first place [it is needed is] around the heart. Because of which it
is necessary that the air be brought in by breathing. So that voice is
the striking of the air breathed in upon the so-called wind-pipe by [the
action of] the soul in these parts. For not every sound of an animal is
30 voice, / as was said (one can also make noise with the tongue or by
coughing), but the part which strikes must be ensouled and [the sound
must be made] with some imagination. For voice is indeed a certain
sound which signifies, and is not, like a cough, [a mere striking] by
421a1 the inbreathed air, / but by means of this [inbreathed air] it {the ani-
mal} strikes the air in the wind-pipe against it [i.e., the wind-pipe].

A sign [of this] is that one cannot vocalize while breathing in or
breathing out, but [only] while holding one's breath. For the one who

holds [his breath] moves [the wind-pipe] with this [held air]. It is apparent also why fish are voiceless; for they have no throats {wind-pipes}. / But they do not have this part because they do not receive air nor do they breathe. Through what cause [this is so], then, is another story.[101]

5

Chapter 9

It is less easily determined about smell and odor than about the fore-going. For it is not clear, as it is about sound and color, what sort of thing odor is. The cause is that / we do not have this sense with pre-cision, but [in a way] inferior to many of the animals. For man senses odors poorly and does not smell any odors which are without pain or pleasure, as though the sense were without precision. It is reasonable that the hard-eyed animals[102] sense colors in this way, and that / the differences of colors are for them not distinguished, except as fright-ful or not frightful. So too in the case of odors for the race of men.

For there seems to be a proportion to taste, and the species of fla-vors are similar to those of odor. But we have more precise taste because it is a certain [sort of] touch, while / this latter sense is the most precise [sense] man has. For in the other senses, he is left behind by many of the animals, but according to touch he is precise in a way differing greatly from the others. Because of which, also, he is the most intelligent of the animals. A sign of this is that even in the race of men one is naturally well disposed or not naturally disposed [to understanding] in dependence on this sense organ and / not any other. For the hard-skinned are not naturally disposed to thought, while the soft-skinned are well disposed. Just as one flavor is sweet and one bitter, so too are odors. But some things have a proportion according to odor and flavor, I mean, e.g., [they have] a sweet odor and a sweet flavor, but some are opposite. Similarly too, / odor is pungent and harsh and acidic and oily. But, as we said, because odors are not strongly distinguished, as flavors are, the names have been taken from these[103] / according to the likenesses of the things. For the sweet is from saffron and honey, while the pungent from thyme or such things, and it the same way for the others.

Just as in hearing and each of the other senses, one [sense] is of the hearable and the unhearable, one of the visible / and the invisible, so too the sense of smell is of what has an odor and of what is odor-less. (What has no odor is either what is entirely unable to have odor or what has little and weak [odor].) The untastable is spoken of in the same way.

421a7
10
15
20
25
30
421b1
5

The sense of smell is also through a medium, like air or water. /
For even the water animals seem to sense odor, the ones with blood
and the ones without blood alike, just as do the animals [which live]
in the air. For some of these too approach food from afar, having
smelled the odor. Due to which it seems strange, if all animals smell
in the same way, that man does so [only] while breathing in and does
not sense while not breathing in / but breathing out or holding his
breath, whether [the object] be far away or close by or even placed
within the nostril. And being unable to sense when placing [the
object] on the very sense organ is common to all [animals]. But not to
sense without breathing is proper to men. This is clear to those who
try it. Whence, / since they do not breathe, the bloodless [animals]
would have another sense besides the ones spoken of.[104]

But this is impossible, if they are indeed smelling an odor. For
smelling is the sensing of an odor, both of what smells bad and of
what smells good. Moreover, it is apparent that they {animals which
seem to smell without breathing in} are destroyed by the strong odors
by which man is destroyed, like those of tar / and sulfur and things of
that sort. It is necessary, then, that they smell, though not while
breathing.

It seems that this sense organ in men differs from the other animals, just as the eyes from those of the hard-eyed [animals]. For the
ones have eyelids as a screen, like a case, and do not see when their
eyelids are not moved / or raised. But the hard-eyed have no such
thing, but see right away what comes to be in the transparent. In this
way too the organ of smell is uncovered / for some [animals] as is the
eye, but for those which take in air there is a covering which is uncovered in breathing, the passages and pores being widened. And because
of this the animals which breathe do not smell in the water. For it is
necessary / to breathe while smelling, but it is impossible to do this in
water.

As flavor is of the wet, so odor is of the dry, while the organ
which is able to smell is such [, i.e., dry,] in potency.[105]

Chapter 10

What can be tasted is a certain [sort of] tangible thing, and this is the
cause of its not being sensed through an extraneous body as a medium, / for neither in touch is it so.[106] And the body in which the flavor
is, what can be tasted, is in water as in material, and this is something
tangible.[107] Because of which, even if we were in water, we would
sense it if something sweet were thrown in; our sense of it would not

be through a medium, but by its being mixed with water, like a drink. But color / is not seen in this way, i.e., by being mixed, nor by things streaming off [of the thing seen].[108] So there is no medium [for taste]. But as color is the visible, so is flavor the tastable.[109]

Nothing, though, produces the sense of flavor without moistness, rather, [everything with flavor] has moistness in act or in potency, like salt. For it is both easily dissolved itself and is also able, when on the tongue, to dissolve [other things]. /

Just as sight is of the visible and of the invisible (for darkness is invisible but the eye judges even this) and also of the exceedingly bright (for this too is invisible, though in a different way from darkness), so hearing is of both sound and silence, one of which is audible, the other inaudible, and also of very loud sound, / as sight is of the bright. For just as a small sound is inaudible, so too, in a way, is a great and violent one. And the "invisible" is, in some cases, what is completely so (the impossible too [is spoken of] in this way in some cases), but in other cases, while [a thing may be] naturally apt [to be seen], it is not or is barely [visible] (compare "footless" or "seedless." So too, then, taste is of the testable / and the tasteless, while this is what has little flavor or a bad flavor or is destructive of taste. The principle seems to be the drinkable and the undrinkable. For there is a certain taste of both, but the one is of what is bad and destructive of taste, the other of something which is according to nature. The drinkable is common to touch and to taste. /

Since, however, the moist is the tastable, it is necessary also that the sense organ [of taste] neither be moist in actuality nor unable to be moistened. For the taste suffers something from what can be tasted, insofar as it can be tasted. It is necessary, then, that the organ capable of taste be able to be moistened but not moist, and yet still be preserved when it is moistened.[110] /

A sign [of this] is that the tongue does not sense when dried out or excessively moist. For in the latter case, [sensation] occurs at the touch of the moist which was present at first, as when someone who has first tasted a strong flavor tastes another, or as to those who are sick all things seem bitter because they are sensed by a tongue full of such moisture. /

The species of flavors, as in the case of colors, are simple contraries, the sweet and the bitter, while the oily is next to the one and the salty to the other. Between these are the pungent, the harsh, the sour, and the acidic. For these seem, perhaps, to be the differences of flavors. / Whence, what can taste is what is such in potency, while the tastable is what can make it be in actuality.

15

20

25

30

422b1

5

10

15

Chapter 11

422b17   The account is the same about the tangible and touch. For, if touch is
not one sense but many, it is necessary that the tangible be many as
20   well. There is a difficulty / about whether they {the objects of touch}
are many or one and about what the sense organ of that which can
touch is, whether it is the flesh (and in the other [animals] what is
analogous [to flesh]) or not, but this [i.e., flesh] is rather the medium,
while the first sense organ is something else within [the animal's
body].[111] For every sense seems to be of one contrariety, as sight of
25   white and black and hearing of high / and low and taste of bitter and
sweet. But in touch there are many contrarieties: hot and cold, dry and
moist, hard and soft, and whatever other such things there are.
     It is some resolution of this difficulty that even in the other sens-
30   es there are many contrarieties, e.g., in sound there is / not only high
and low, but also loudness and quietness and smoothness and rough-
ness of sound, and other such things. And in the case of colors there
are other such differences. But it is not clear what that one thing is
that underlies touch as sound does hearing.
     It does not seem to be a sign of whether the sense organ is within
423a1   or not, / but is immediately flesh, that sensation occurs at once when
it is touched. For even now, if someone should stretch something
around the flesh, making it like a membrane, sensation would be inti-
mated in the same way as when directly touched, and yet it is clear
5   that the sense organ is not / in this [membrane]. And if it should come
to be naturally united, the sensation would go through even faster.[112]
Because of which, this part of the body seems to be disposed as if the
air were naturally around us in a circle. For we would then think that
we sensed both sound and color and odor by some one thing, and that
10   sight, hearing, and smell were / some one sense. But now, because
that through which the motions come to be is distinguished, it is
apparent that the senses mentioned are different. Yet in the case of
touch this is at present unclear.[113] For it is impossible that an ensouled
body be constituted from air or water [alone]. For it must be something solid. It remains, then, that it is a mix from earth and of these
15   [other elements], as flesh / and what is analogous to it look to be.
Whence it is necessary also that the body which is a medium of what
is able to touch be naturally joined to it, through which the sensations,
being many, come to be.[114]
     But touch on the tongue makes clear that they are many. For it
senses all the tangibles with the same part that senses flavor. If, therefore, the rest of the flesh also sensed flavor, taste and touch would

seem / to be one and the same sense. But now [they seem to be] two   20
because they do not correspond.

But someone might doubt: if every body has depth (this is the
third magnitude) and, when there is a body between two bodies, these
are not able to touch each other, while water is not / without body (nor   25
is liquid, but it must be water or have water in it), and things touching
each other in the water, since their ends are not dry, must have water
between them, with which their extremes are full – if this is true, it is
impossible for things to touch each other in the water, and so too in
the air. / For air is to the things in it in the same way as water is to the   30
things in water, but this escapes our notice more, just as also [it
escapes] the animals in the water / if, being wet, they touch some-   423b1
thing wet.[115]

Is sensation of all things similar, then, or is it different for different things, just as now it seems taste and touch occur by touching
while the others happen from afar? But this is not so; rather, we sense
even the hard and the soft / through other things, just like what can   5
sound and the visible and what has an odor.[116] But the ones are from
far off, the others from nearby (because of which it escapes notice),
since we sense all things though a medium, but in these cases it
escapes notice. And yet (as we said before[117]), even if we should
sense all tangible things through a membrane, without noticing / that   10
it lies between, we would be in the same position as we are now in
water or in air. For we seem now to touch them {the objects} and
nothing [seems] to be between.

But the tangible differs from the visible and the hearable because
we sense the latter by the medium doing something to us, but [we
sense] the tangibles not by / the medium but together with the medi-   15
um, like one struck through a shield. For he is not struck by the shield
which has been struck but both are struck at the same time.

Generally, it seems that just as air and water are related to sight
and hearing and smell, so too, just like each of those, flesh and the
tongue are to the sense organ. / Neither here nor there would sensa-   20
tion occur, if the sense organ itself were touched, just as if someone
should put a white body on the surface of the eye. It should be clear
too that the sense organ of touch is within. For in this way things
would happen just as in the other cases. For it would not sense were
something placed upon / the sense organ, but when placed upon the   25
flesh it is sensed. Whence, flesh is the medium of touch.[118]

The tangibles, therefore, are the differences of body as body; I
mean the differences which determine the elements – hot, cold, dry,
moist – about which we have spoken earlier in the [writings] on the
elements.[119] / The sense organ for these is the tactile, that in which the   30

sense called touch first is present, the part which is such in potency. /
424a1 For sensing is a certain [sort of] suffering. Whence, the maker makes
that other, what is in potency, such, like itself. Whence, we do not
sense what is equally hot and cold or hard and soft, but we sense
5 things that are excessive, the sense being / like a certain mean of the
contrarieties in the sensibles. And because of this it discerns the sensibles. For the middle is able to discern. For it is, in relation to each
of these, the other one of the extremes. And, just as what is going to
sense white and black must be neither of these in act, but in potency
10 both (and so too in the other [senses]), / in touch also [it must be] neither hot nor cold.

Moreover, just as sight was somehow of the visible and invisible,
and likewise the rest [of the senses are] of opposites, so touch is of
the tangible and intangible. The intangible is what has an altogether
small difference of the tangibles, as air which has suffered [some
15 affection], and the excesses of the tangibles, like things / which are
destructive.[120]

In outline, then, each of the senses has been discussed.

Chapter 12

424a17 We must grasp generally, about all sense, that sense is what is receptive of the sensible species without the material, as wax receives the
20 sign of the signet ring / without the iron and the gold. However, it
takes on the golden or the brazen sign, but not as gold or bronze.
Likewise, too, the sense of each thing suffers by what has color or flavor or sound, but not insofar as each of those things is called [a certain substance], but insofar as it is of such a [sensible] sort, and
according to its account.[121]

25 The first sensitive thing is that in / which there is such a power.
They {the sensitive thing and its power} are therefore the same, but
their being is different. For what senses would be a certain [sort of]
magnitude; yet surely to be sensitive or the sense [itself] is a not a
magnitude, but is a certain ratio {account} and power of that magnitude.[122]

From these [considerations], however, it is apparent why the
30 excesses of the sensibles sometimes destroy / the sense organs. For if
the motion [caused by the sensible thing] be more powerful than the
sense organ, the ratio is dissolved – but this was the sense – just as, if
one strikes the chords strongly the concord and tone [are
destroyed].[123] And [it is apparent] why plants do not sense, though
they have some part of soul and suffer something due to the tangible.

For they too are cooled / and heated. For the cause is that they do not have a mean, nor such a principle as to receive the species of the sensibles, but they suffer with the material.[124]

However, one might be at a loss as to whether what is unable to smell could suffer something by an odor, or / what is not able to see by color, and likewise in the other cases.[125] If an odor is what can be smelt, if it brings about anything, an odor brings about the sensation of smell. Whence, none of the things which cannot smell can suffer anything due to an odor. The same argument also [applies] in the other cases. Nor in the case of what is able [to sense can anything be affected by the sensible] except insofar as each one is sensitive. At the same time this is clear in this way too: / for neither light and darkness nor sound nor odor brings about anything in bodies, but that in which these exist brings something about, as the air in which thunder is present splits the wood.

But tangible things and flavors do bring something about.[126] For if they do not, by what would the unsouled suffer and be altered?[127] Will others also, therefore, bring something about? Or is it that not all bodies can suffer by odor / and sound, and those that do suffer are indeterminate and do not remain, such as air, for it has a smell, as if it suffers something.

What, then, is smelling except suffering something? Or is not smelling also sensing, while the air, suffering quickly, becomes sensible?[128]

Book III

Chapter 1

One might believe from the following [considerations] that there is no sense other than the five (I mean these: sight, hearing, smell, taste, and touch). For if we already have sense of all things of which touch
/ is the sense (for all the passions of the tangibles as tangible are sensible to us through touch), it is necessary, if indeed some sense is missing, that some sense organ is also missing in us, and whichever ones of these [sensibles] we sense when touching, are sensible by touch, which we happen to have, but whatever things [we sense]
through a medium / and not by touching them, [we sense] by means of the simple [elements] (I mean such as by air or by water), and they are such that, if through one [element we sense] many sensibles different from each other in kind, it is necessary that what has such a sense organ be able to sense both (e.g., if the sense organ is made from air, and air is [the medium] of both sound and color); if, however,
[we sense through] / more than this (as, e.g., both air and water [are media] of color, for both are transparent), what has either of these alone will sense through both; but sense organs are [made] from only two of the simple elements, from air and from water (for the pupil is
of water, the organ of hearing / of air, the organ of smell from one or the other of these, while fire is either of none or is common to all – for nothing without heat is sensitive – and earth is either of none or most properly mixed in touch; whence, it would remain that no sense organ is without water and air): but some animals have these [sorts of
sense organs] already, therefore all the senses are had / by those which are not imperfect or mutilated (for it appears that even a mole has eyes under its skin), so that if there is no other body, and no passion which is not of the bodies here [around us], no sense would be missing.[1]

But neither can there be some proper organ of the common sensibles / which [common sensibles] we [then] sense by each sense
accidentally,[2] like motion, standing still, shape, magnitude, number, one. For we sense all these by motion[3] (e.g., we sense magnitude by motion, whence also shape, for shape is a certain magnitude; while

[we sense] resting by its not being moved; and number by the denial
of the continuous) and by the proper sensibles, / for each sense sens-   20
es one [proper object]. Whence it is clear that it is impossible for
there to be a proper sense for any of these, e.g., for motion.[4] For [oth-
erwise] it would be just as we now sense the sweet by sight. This is
because we happen to have the sense for both; whenever they come
together, we know [them]. But if [we did] not [have both], we would
not have sensed [at least one of them] at all, / except accidentally, as,   25
e.g., [we sense] the son of Cleon not because he is the son of Cleon
but because he is white, while it happens to the white to be the son
of Cleon. But we already have common sensation, not accidentally,
of the common sensibles. There is not, therefore, a proper sense [for
them]. For in no way would we have sensed [the common sensibles]
except in the way that it was said that we sense / the son of Cleon.[5]   30
Whenever sensation occurs at the same time about the same [object],
e.g., [in the case of] bile, that it is bitter and yellow, the senses sense
each other's proper sensibles accidentally, / not insofar as [they are]   425b1
these senses, but insofar as [they are] one. For to say that the two
[sensibles] are one is certainly not [a job] for either one [of the sens-
es] – due to which, also, one is deceived, and, should a thing be yellow, one believes it is bile.[6]

One might ask, "For the sake of what do we have many senses /
instead of only one?" Or is it that the accompanying and common   5
sensibles might less escape us, e.g., motion and magnitude and number? For if there were only sight, and this of the white, they would
escape notice more, and all these would seem the same, because color
and magnitude would [always] accompany each other. But as it is
now, since the common ones / also belong to a different sensible   10
thing, this makes it clear that each of these is something other.[7]

Chapter 2

Since, however, we sense that we see and hear, it is necessary to sense   425b12
that one sees either by sight or by a different [sense].[8] But the same
sense will be of sight and of the underlying color. Whence either there
will be two senses / of the same [sensible] or the same [sense will have   15
sensation] of itself.[9] Moreover, if a different sense were the sense of
the seeing, either these will go on infinitely or some same thing will
be [the sense] of itself. Whence, one ought to do this in the first case.

Yet there is a difficulty. For if sensing by sight is seeing, while
color or what has color is what is seen, if something will see the seeing, the first seeing thing will also have color.[10] /

20   It is apparent, therefore, that sensing by sight is not one. For even when we are not seeing, we discern both darkness and light by sight, but not in the same way.[11] Moreover, the thing which sees is also, as it were, colored. For each sense organ is receptive of the sensible without the material. (Whence, even in the absence of the sensibles /

25 there are sensations and imaginings in the sense organs.) The act of the sensible and of the sense are one and the same, but to be these is not the same; I mean, e.g., sound according to act and hearing according to act.[12] For what has hearing may not be hearing, and what has

30 sound does not always sound. Yet whenever / what is able to hear is at work {in act} and what is able to sound sounds, then the hearing according to act and the sound according to act come to be together;

426a1 / which things one would call, the one, hearing, the other, sounding.[13]

        If, then, the motion and the activity and the passion are in the one which is acted on, it is necessary also that the sound according to act and the hearing according to act be in what is according to potency.

5 For the act of what is active and of what can move something / comes to be in the thing which suffers.[14] (Whence, it is not necessary for the mover to be moved.[15]) Therefore, the act of what can sound is the sound or sounding, that of what can hear, hearing or listening. For hearing is two-fold, and sound is two-fold. And the same account [is found] in the other senses and sensibles. For just as the activity and /

10 the passivity are in what suffers but not in what acts, so also the act of the sensible and that of the sensitive are in the sensitive. But in some cases they are named, e.g., sounding and listening, while in some one of the two is unnamed. For the act of sight is called vision but the act of color is unnamed, and the act of what can taste is tast-

15 ing, / but the act of flavor is unnamed.[16]

        Since, however, the act of the sensible and of the sensitive are one, while to be [these] is different,[17] it is necessary that what are in this way called hearing and sounding are destroyed and conserved together, and flavor and tasting also, and the others likewise. But this is not necessary in the case of things said according to potency.[18] /

20   But the earlier students of nature[19] did not speak well about this, forming the opinion that the white and the black are nothing without sight, nor flavor without taste. In saying this they spoke rightly and not rightly. For sense and sensible are said in two ways, in some cases according to potency and in other cases according to act, and in the latter cases what is said occurs, but in the others it does not occur. /

25 But those [thinkers] spoke simply about what is not spoken of simply.

        If, however, sound is a certain concord, while the sound and the hearing are as one, and concord is a ratio, it is necessary that hearing

30 be a certain ratio. / And because of this also each excessive thing, both

the shrill and the strong, destroys hearing. So too in flavors, [the excessive destroys] / taste, and in color, the very bright or dark [destroys] sight, in odor, strong odors, both the sweet and the bitter, as sense is certain ratio.[20] Because of which also, things are pleasant whenever, being pure and unmixed, they are brought into ratio, as the acidic or / sweet or salty, for then they are pleasant. Generally, the mixed, the concord [is pleasant] rather than the sharp or flat, and what can be warmed or what can be chilled [is pleasant] to touch. Sense is a ratio but excessive sensibles loosen or destroy [the senses]. Each sense, therefore, is of its underlying sensible and is present in the sense organ as sense organ, and / discerns the differences of its under- lying sensible, as sight [discerns] white and black, taste, sweet and bitter. This is so in the other cases as well.

However, since we also discern white and sweet and each of the sensibles in relation to each [other sensible], we also sense that they differ by something – necessarily, then, / by a sense, for they are sen- sibles. By which it is also clear that the flesh is not the ultimate sense organ. For [if so] it would be necessary for what discerns to discern by touching.[21] Nor can one discern that the sweet is different from the white by separate things, but both must be made clear to some one thing.[22] For otherwise, even if I should sense this and you should sense that, / it would be clear that they are different from each other. Rather, something one must say that they are different. For sweet is different from white. The same thing, therefore, says this. Whence, as it says, so does it understand and sense. It is clear, therefore, that it is not possible to discern separate things by separate [powers]. Nor in a separate time, as is seen from the following. For just as the same thing / says that the good is different from the bad, so also when it says the one to be different from the other, the "when" is not accidental: I mean, e.g., [when] I now say that it is different, but not that it is dif- ferent now. But it speaks in this way, both now and that [they are dif- ferent] now; therefore, at the same time. Whence it is an unseparated [power] and [acts] in an unseparated time.

But indeed, it is impossible that the same thing, / insofar as it is undivided, be moved at the same time according to contrary motions, and in an undivided time. For if [a thing is] sweet, it moves the sense / or the understanding in one way, and the bitter [moves them] in a contrary way, and the white differently. Is it the case, then, that the thing which discerns is together and undivided in number and unsep- arated, while it is separate in being? In a way, then, it is as divided that it senses divided things, but in a way, as undivided. / For in being it is divided, while in place and number it is undivided. Or is this not possible? For what is the same and undivided is the contraries in

potency, but not in being, yet it is divided by being worked on
{brought into act}. And it is not possible to be white and black at the
same time; whence, neither [is it possible] to suffer the species of
these, if sense and understanding are such. But, / like what some say
about a point, insofar as [it is both] one and two, in this way [it is]
divisible. Therefore, as undivided, what discerns is one and [it dis-
cerns] at one time, while, as divided, it uses the same point twice at
the same time. Therefore, it discerns two [things] insofar as it uses the
limit twice, and it discerns the separate things as if separately; as one,
[it discerns something] one and at one time.[23]

About / the principle by which we say an animal is sensitive,
then, let it be determined in this way.[24]

Chapter 3

427a17   Since, however, [men] mostly define the soul by two differences, on
the one hand, by motion according to place and, on the other hand, by
understanding {τὸ νοεῖν} and judging {τὸ φρονεῖν} and sensing
{τὸ αἰσθάνεσθαι},[25] while understanding and judging seem to be
like / a certain [sort of] sensing (for in both of these the soul discerns
{κρίνει} and knows {γνωρίζει} beings, and the ancients even say
judging and sensing are the same, as Empedocles said, "For in men,
skill is increased with what is present,"[26] and elsewhere, "whence for
them judging always / presents something different,"[27] and Homer
intends the same thing as these thinkers: "[f]or the mind {νόος} is
such...."[28]), for all these thinkers assume understanding {τὸ νοεῖν}
to be bodily, like sensing, and that like is sensed and judged by like,
as we determined in the first arguments.[29] And yet it was necessary
427b1   for them also to speak at the same time / of erring, for this is more
proper to animals, and the soul remains in this [condition of error] for
a longer time. Whence it is necessary[30] either, as some[31] say, that all
appearances are true,[32] or else that touching the unlike is error, for this
is the opposite of / knowing like by like, though it seems that the error
and the science of opposites is the same;[33] it is apparent, therefore,
that sensing and judging are not the same. For the one is present in
all, but the other in few of the animals.[34]

But neither is understanding – within which one finds [under-
standing] correctly and not correctly (correctly: / prudence {judg-
ment, φρόνησις} and science {ἐπιστήμη} and true opinion {δόξα
ἀληθής}; not correctly: the opposites of these) – neither is this the
same as sensing. For sensation of what is proper is always true,[35] and
exists in all the animals, while thinking things through {διάνοια}

can also occur falsely, and is present in nothing in which reason {speech, λόγος} is not also present.

For imagination {φαντασία} is different from both / sense and the power to think things through {διάνοια}, and does not come to be without sense, and without this, there is not belief {ὑπόληψις}.

That imagination and understanding {νόησις} are not the same is apparent. For this passion {πάθος} is in us whenever we wish, for something is made before the eyes, as those do who make up images in the mnemonic arts and place them [before the mind's eye], / while to form an opinion {δοξάζειν} is not in our power. For it is necessary that it be either true or false.[36] Moreover, whenever we form the opinion that something is terrible or fearful, we are affected right away; and likewise in the case of the hopeful. But with regard to imagination we are disposed as if we are seeing something terrible or hopeful in a picture.

There are also differences / of this belief: science and opinion and prudence and the opposites of these; let the account of the differences of these be left for a different occasion.[37]

But concerning understanding {τὸ νοεῖν}, since it is different from sensing, and, of the former, one sort seems to be imagination, the other, belief, [after] determining about imagination, one must speak too of the other {belief}.[38] /

If, therefore, imagination {φαντασία} is that according to which we say some image {φάντασμα} comes to be in us (and if we do not mean something metaphorical), is it a power or habit among those according to which we discern and speak truly and speak falsely? These are sense {αἴσθησις}, opinion {δόξα}, / science {ἐπιστήμη}, and understanding {mind, νοῦς}.

It is clear from the following, then, that it is not sense. For sense is either a power or an act, like sight or seeing, but something (e.g., the things in sleep) appears even though neither of these two is present. Again, sense is always present, but not imagination.[39] But if it is the same [as the sense] in act, it would happen / that imagination is in all beasts. But it seems not to be, as it is in ants and bees but not in worms.[40] Again, the senses are always true, while imaginings are more often false.[41] And we do not say, in fact, when we are working with certitude in regard to the sensible, that this *appears* {φαίνεται[42]} to us to be a man, but rather when we do / not sense clearly whether that is either true or false. And what we said earlier then: something appears even when the eyes are closed.

But indeed, neither will imagination be one of the [powers which are] always true, like science or understanding {νοῦς}.[43] For imagination is also false.

15

20

25

428a1

5

10

15

It remains, then, to see if it is opinion.[44] For opinion comes to be
both true and false.[45] But / conviction follows opinion. For one cannot
form opinion about things concerning which one does not seem to be
convinced. Yet conviction is present in none of the beasts, while
imagination is in many. Moreover, conviction goes with every opinion, while having been persuaded [goes with] conviction and reason
{speech} [with] persuasion. Imagination, however, is in some of the
beasts, but not reason.

It is, therefore, apparent / for these reasons that imagination
would be neither opinion with sense, nor [opinion] through sense, nor
a twisting together of opinion and sense,[46] and also because it is clear
that the opinion would not be of another thing, but, if it {such an opin-
ion} exists, [it would be] of that of which there is sensation. I mean
that imagination would be what is twisted together from the opinion
of white and the sensation of white. For it surely is not / from the
opinion of the good and the sensation of / the white. Imagining, then,
would be forming an opinion about just what is sensed, not accidentally.

But, in fact, false appearances arise about that concerning which
one has at the same time a true belief, e.g., the sun appears to be a foot
in diameter, but one is convinced that it is greater than the inhabited
world. If the thing stays the same, / then, it happens either that the true
opinion which he had is abandoned by him, though he neither forgets
it nor is persuaded [otherwise], or else, if he still has it, it is necessary
that the same thing be both true and false. (But [the true opinion]
would become false when it escapes notice that the thing is changing.) Imagination, therefore, is not some one of these, nor is it from
these.[47] /

But[48] since, when a thing has been moved, another is moved by
this,[49] and imagination seems to be a certain [sort of] motion,[50] and
does not come to be without sense, but is in what has sensation and is
of that of which there is sensation, while motion can come to be from
the act of sense, and it is necessary that this same [motion] is similar
to the sensation, this {imagination} / would be a motion, one occurring neither without sense nor present in what does not have sense.
But the one having it {imagination} does and suffers many things due
to it and it is both true and false.

This happens because of the following things. The sensation of
the proper sensibles is true or is what has least falsity, but second is /
sensing those things which are accidents of the sensibles. And here one
can already be deceived. For one is not deceived that white is, but one
is deceived [as to] whether the white is this or something else. Third
[is sensation] of the common [sensibles] and the things following upon

the accidental [sensibles] in which the proper [sensibles] are present (I mean, e.g., motion and magnitude), concerning which, / right away, erring according to sense is greatest. But the motion (the motion which comes from these three sensings) which occurs due to the act of sense will differ.[51] And the first, when sensation is present, is true; but the others may be false both in the presence and in the absence of sensation, and most of all when / the sensible is far away. If, therefore, nothing else has the above mentioned [characteristics][52] except imagination / (and this is what was said), imagination would be a motion coming to be due to sense according to act.

25

30

429a1

However, since sight is most of all a sense, even the name of imagination {φαντασία} was taken from light {φῶς}, because one cannot see without light.

And because what remains / is also similar to the sensations, animals do many things according to these [images], some because they do not have understanding, like the beasts, some, like men, because the understanding is at times eclipsed by passion or disease or sleep.

5

About imagination, therefore, what it is and why it is, let so much be said.

Chapter 4

Concerning that part of the soul by which the soul both knows {γινώσκει} and judges {φρονεῖ} (whether that part be separable, or not separable according to magnitude but [only] according to account), one must look into what difference it has, and how understanding {τὸ νοεῖν} can ever come to be.[53]

429a10

If, then, understanding is like sensing,[54] either it would be suffering something from the intelligible, or [it would be] / some other such thing. It must be impassible, then, but receptive of the species, and be such {the species} in potency though it is not this [, i.e., the species]. And it must be related in the same way: as the sensitive [is related] to the sensibles, so is the mind to the intelligibles.[55]

15

It is necessary, therefore, since it understands all things, that the intellect {mind} be unmixed, as Anaxagoras says, that it might command; but this is [necessary] that it might know.[56] / For what is outside, appearing within, hinders and screens.[57] Whence there is no one nature of this [part] but this, that it is a possible {potential} thing.[58] Therefore, what is called the intellect of the soul (I call the intellect that by which the soul thinks things through and takes things up[59]) is none of the beings in act before it understands.[60]

20

Whence it is reasonable / that it not be mixed with the body. For

25

[then] it would come to be qualified somehow, either cold or hot, and there would be some organ [for it], as [there is] for the sensitive. But as it is, there is none.[61]

And therefore those who say the soul is the place of species speak well,[62] except that it is not the whole [soul which is such] but the intellectual [power], nor is it the species in actuality but in potency.

30   But it is clear from the sense organs and sensations / that the impassibility of the sensitive and the intellectual parts is not alike. For
429b1   the sense is not able to sense / after sensing what is very sensible, e.g., sound after a great sound, nor is it able to see or smell after strong colors or odors. But whenever the intellect understands something very intelligible, it does not understand less [intelligible] things less, but
5   even more so. / For the sensitive is not without body, but this {intellect} is separate [from body].

When it [i.e., the intellect] comes to be each thing as the knower according to act is said [to do] (this happens when it is able to work through itself), even then it is in potency in some way,[63] but not in the same way as before learning or discovering: and then it is able to understand itself.[64] /

10   But[65] since a magnitude is other than to be magnitude, and water than to be water (and so it is also in many other things, but not in all, for in some they are the same[66]), [the soul] discerns to be flesh and flesh either by different [powers] or by one disposed differently. For the flesh is not without material, but, like the snub, [it is a] this in a
15   that. / Therefore, although [the soul] discerns the hot and the cold by the sensitive power, and the flesh is some ratio of these, it discerns to be flesh by [something] different, either by a separate power or by one which is as the bent is related to itself when extended.[67]

Again, among beings in abstraction,[68] the straight is like the snub, for the straight exists with the continuous.[69] But the "what it
20   was to be"[70] is other, if to be / straight and the straight are different. Let it be "duality."[71] Therefore, the soul discerns it by something different or by what is related differently.[72] Generally, therefore, as things are separable from material, so too are they things which concern the intellect.[73]

But if the intellect is simple and impassible and has nothing in common with anything, as Anaxagoras says, one will be at a loss about how it will understand, if understanding is suffering something.
25   For one thing seems to act and another to suffer / insofar as there is something common that belongs to both;[74] moreover, is it {the intellect} itself intelligible too? For either intellect will belong to the other [intelligibles], if it is not itself intelligible due to something else

(while the intelligible is something one in species), or else it will have something mixed with it, which something makes it intelligible just like the other intelligibles.[75]

Indeed, suffering in virtue of / something common was distin-   30
guished earlier, [so we hold] that the intellect is somehow the intelligibles in potency, but, before it understands, it is nothing in actuality.
It is in potency in this way: / as in a writing tablet in which no writing   430a1
is present in actuality. This is just what happens in the case of the
intellect.[76]

And it is itself intelligible just as are the intelligibles. For in the
case of what is without material what understands and what is being
understood are the same, for speculative knowledge and / what is   5
known in this way are the same.[77]

However, one must look into the cause of not always understanding. Among things having material, each one is among the intelligibles in potency. Whence the mind will not belong in these, for the
mind is a potency for such things without [their] material. But what
is intelligible will belong to that [thing that has material].[78]

Chapter 5

But since in the whole of nature there is one thing [which is] the mate-   430a10
rial in each genus (this is what is in potency all those [in the genus]),
and another, the cause and what brings [them] about by making them
all, in the way an art does in relation to its material, it is necessary
also that these differences exist in the soul.[79] And there is, on the one
hand, the sort of intellect in which all things / come to be[·80] and, on   15
the other hand, the sort by which all things are made, like some state
{habit, disposition, condition, ἕξις} like light. For, in a way, light too
makes what are potentially colored to be colored in act.[81]

This intellect is also separable and impassible and unmixed,
being in substance act. For what makes is always more honorable
than what suffers, and the principle than the material.[82] /

But science according to act is the same as the thing [known].[83]   20
However, according to potency science is prior in time in one [mind],
yet universally it is not prior in time.[84] But it {the intellect according
to act} does not sometimes understand and sometimes not understand.[85]

When separated, this alone is that which truly is, and this alone
is immortal and eternal.[86] But we do not remember because, while
this is impassible, / mind which is able to suffer {παθετικός} is   25
destructible[·87] And without this it understands nothing.[88]

Chapter 6[89]

430a26 So the understanding of undivided things is among those about which
there is no falsehood, but in those {acts of understanding} in which
there is truth and falsehood, there is right away some putting together
of things understood, as if they were one – just as Empedocles says,
"In which way the heads of many without necks were germinated,"[90]

30   / later being put together by friendship[91] – so too these separated
[things understood] are put together, like incommensurable and diam-

430b1 eter.[92] But with respect / to things in the past or in the future, the time
is [also] thought about and put together. For the false is always in
what is put together. For even if [one says] "white is not white," "not
white" is put together [with "white"]. (One can say all these accord-

5   ing to division as well.[93]) It is not only true or false / that Cleon is
white, then, but also that he was or will be.[94] And that which makes
each thing one is an intellect.[95]

Since, however, the undivided[96] is two-fold, being either in
potency or in act, nothing prevents one from understanding the undivided when one understands a length (for it is undivided in act), and
doing so in an undivided time. For the time is divided and is undivid-

10   ed in the same way as / the length. So one cannot say what one was
understanding in each half [of the time], for, unless it {the line} be
divided, it {the part of the line} does not exist, except in potency.
However, by understanding each of the halves separately, one also
simultaneously divides the time, and then it {the time} is just like the
lengths. Yet if [one is thinking of the undivided] as [composed] from
both [parts], [one is] also [thinking of this] in the time of both.[97]

But what is undivided not according to quantity, but in species, /

15   it understands in an undivided time and by an undivided [part] of the
soul.[98] But [it understands the parts of the species] accidentally, and
not insofar as the things which it understands and the time in which
[it understands] are divided, but insofar as [they are] undivided. For
even in these there is something undivided (though perhaps not separable), which makes the time and the length one. And this happens

20   alike in time and in length and / in everything continuous.[99]

However, the point, and every division, and what is indivisible in
this way, are made manifest in the way privation is. And the account
is similar for other things, e.g., how one knows evil or black. For one
somehow knows [it] by its contrary. But what knows must be in
potency, and one [of the contraries] must be in it. If, however, in some

25   one of the causes there is no / contrary [when it knows a contrary],
this knows itself and is in act and separate.[100]

There is a speech [which says] something about something, just

as there is also denial, and all such are true or false; still, not all under-standing {νοῦς} [is such]. Rather, [the understanding] of what a thing is according to the "what it was to be" and [which] does not [say] something about something is true; like the seeing of the proper [sensible], it is always true. Yet [saying] whether / the white thing is a man / or not is not always true.[101] Whatever things are without material are disposed in this way.[102]

430b30

Chapter 7

Science according to act is the same as the thing.[103] But science according to potency is prior in time in one thing, yet generally [it is] not even [prior] in time. For all things coming to be are from being in actuality.

431a1

The sensible appears to make / the sensitive in act from being in potency. For [the sensitive] does not suffer nor is it altered.[104] Whence this [, i.e., sensation,] is another species of motion. For motion is the act of the imperfect, while what is simply act is differ-ent, the [act] of the perfected.[105]

5

Sensing, therefore, is similar to merely speaking [a name] or understanding [what a thing is], but when there is pleasure or pain, the soul pursues / or avoids as if affirming or denying. And to be pleased and to be pained is for the sensitive mean to be at work in regard to what is good or evil as such.[106] Both aversion and appetite according to act are the same [with this], and the faculties of appetite and aversion are not different either from each other or from the sen-sitive, but their being is other.[107]

10

The phantasms, however, / are like the sensibles to the soul which is able to think things through.[108] When it says or denies the good or the bad, it avoids or pursues. Therefore the soul never under-stands without a phantasm.[109]

15

As the air made the pupil of a certain sort, while the pupil [made] another [of a certain sort], so too in hearing. But the extreme [of the senses] is one and it is one mean, though its being / is many.[110] What that by which the soul discerns sweet and hot has been spoken of before, but must be spoken of again as follows.[111] For there is some-thing which is one, in this way, as a terminus; and these being one by proportion and in number, it relates to each of the two as the former to each other. For how does it differ to ask how it discerns the things not in one genus / or the contraries, like white and black? Let then, A, the white, be to B, the black, as C to D, as those are to each other. Whence also alternately. If, then, C and D should be present to one {thing in

20

25

the soul}, they will be disposed in this way, just as are A and B, being the same and one though their being is not the same; and that other likewise. The same / account [applies] if A is sweet and B white.[112] /

431b1 The intellectual [part], then, understands the species in the phantasms. And as in those there is defined for it what is to be pursued and avoided, so, even apart from sensation, when it is concerned with the

5 phantasms, / it is moved. For example, in sensing that the beacon is aflame, it knows that the enemy [is present], seeing by what is common[113] that there is motion; but sometimes, as if it were seeing, it reasons and deliberates about future things in relation to present things by what is imagined or understood in the soul.[114] And as in the other case, when it says the pleasant or the painful is there, it avoids or pur-

10 sues, / and so it is generally in action.[115] And what is without action, the true and the false, are in the same genus with the good and the bad. But they differ in this, [by considering things] simply or in relation to someone.[116]

But [the mind] thinks the so-called abstract things just as if someone should understand the snub not as snub but separately as curved

15 in act, he would understand it without / the flesh in which the curved is. Whenever it understands these things, it understands the mathematicals, as separated [though] they are not separable.[117] Generally, the intellect according to act is the things.[118]

One must inquire later whether it can understand something among the separated things or not, [when] it is itself not separated from magnitude.[119] /

Chapter 8

431b20 Now, however, summing up the things said about soul, let us say again that the soul is somehow all beings.[120] For beings are either sensible or intelligible things, while science is somehow the knowables and sense the sensibles. But one must ask how this is so. Science and

25 sense, therefore, are divided to correspond / to things: what is in potency to things in potency, what is in actuality to things in actuality. The sensitive [part] and the scientific [part] of the soul are these things in potency, the one what is knowable, the other what is sensible.[121]

It is necessary [for the soul] to be either the things themselves or else the species. But it is certainly not the things themselves. For the

432a1 stone is not in the soul, but its species.[122] / Whence the soul is like the hand. For the hand is the tool of tools,[123] and the intellect is the species of species, and the sense the species of sensibles.

But since there is nothing beyond the magnitudes, [i.e.,] the separate sensibles (so it seems), the intelligibles are / in the sensible   5
species, both those said in abstraction and whatever are states and passions of the sensibles. And because of this no one not sensing can learn or understand, and whenever one contemplates [the object of science], it is necessary to contemplate {look at} some phantasm at the same time. For the phantasms are like the sensibles, except [they are] / without material.[124]   10

However, the imagination is different from affirmation and negation. For the true or the false is a twisting together of thoughts.[125] But by what will the first thoughts differ so as not to be phantasms? Yet not even these are phantasms, though they are not without phantasms.[126]

Chapter 9

Since, however, the soul of animals is defined according to two   432a15
powers – by being able to discern, which is the work of the power to think things through and of sense, and, moreover, by moving according to local motion – let so much be determined about sense and intellect;[127] but now we must inquire about the moving [power]: what it is of the soul, whether a certain part of it / (separable either in magnitude or in account[128]) or is it the entire soul, and, if it is a certain part,   20
is it something proper beyond those usually named and mentioned, or is it a certain one of these?

There is a difficulty right away:[129] how one should name the parts of the soul and how many [there are]. For in some way they appear to be unlimited, and [to be] not only those which / some   25
who determine [this question] say, [namely] the rational and the spirited and the desiring [parts],[130] while others [say the parts are] what has reason and what is irrational.[131] For, according to the differences through which they separate those [parts], other parts also appear, parts which stand further apart than those about which something has already been said: the nutritive, which is both in plants and / in all animals, and the sensitive, which one may not   30
easily put down as irrational or as having reason. Moreover, if one will put down separate parts of the soul, the imaginative, / which is   432b1
different in being from all [the others], presents a great difficulty: with which of these is it the same or different?[132] Besides these, there is the appetitive, which both in account and in power would seem to be different from all.[133] Yet it is strange / to tear this apart.   5
For will comes to be in the rational part, and desire and spirit in the

irrational. But if the soul is three-fold, appetite will be in each.[134] And, indeed, about that with which the present argument is concerned, what is the mover according to place for an animal? For in regard to motion according to growth and diminution, being in all, / that which is in all would seem to cause motion, [namely] the generative and the nutritive [power]. (But we must look into breathing in and out and sleeping and waking later. For these also pose a great difficulty.[135])

But concerning motion according to place one must inquire what moves the animal in regard to progressive motion.[136] It is clear, then, that / this power is not the nutritive one. For this motion is always for the sake of something and is with imagination or appetite. For nothing which does not have appetite or aversion is moved, except by violence.[137] Moreover, even the plants would be able to cause motion, and would also have some organic part for this motion.[138] Likewise, neither is it the sensitive power. For there are many / animals which have sense, and yet are stable and unmoved till the end [of their lives].[139] If, therefore, nature makes nothing in vain and does not lack anything necessary,[140] (except in mutilated and incomplete things), while these sorts of animals are complete and not mutilated (a sign [of which] is that they are generative and / have full growth and diminution), then they would have the organic parts for progression.

But in fact neither the rational power nor what is called the intellect is what moves [the animal]. For the speculative power does not consider a thing to be done, nor does it speak about what is to be fled from and what is to be pursued, while motion always belongs to something which is fleeing or pursuing. But neither does / it immediately urge fleeing or pursuing whenever it looks at some such thing; e.g., often something fearful or pleasant is thought on, but it does not urge being frightened, though the heart / is moved, or, should it be pleasant, some other part. Moreover, even when the intellect urges on and the power of thinking things through says to flee or to pursue something, one is [sometimes] not moved, but acts according to desire, like a man who lacks self-control. And, generally, we see that he who has the doctor's art does not [necessarily] doctor, as if / something else were the ruler in acting according to the science, not the science [itself].

But, indeed, neither is appetite the ruler of this motion. For men who have self-control, when they have an appetite and [actually] are desiring, do not do those things for which they have appetite, but instead they follow the intellect.

Chapter 10

It appears, however, that these two, either appetite or mind, / are movers,   433a10
should one put down imagination as a certain [sort of] understanding.[141]
For many men follow imaginations contrary to science, and in the other
animals there is neither understanding nor reasoning, but [there is] imagination. Therefore, both of these, mind and appetite, are able to cause
motion according to place. [I mean that sort of] mind which reasons for
the sake of something and is practical: it differs / from the speculative   15
[mind] by its end.[142] And all appetite is for the sake of something. For
that for which there is an appetite is the principle {beginning, ἀρχή} of
the practical mind. The last thing, however, is the principle of the
action.[143] Whence, these two things reasonably appear to be the movers:
appetite and practical thought. For the appetible moves [us], and through
this, thought moves [us], because its principle is / the appetible.[144] And   20
whenever the imagination moves [us], it does not move [us] without the
appetite. There is some one mover, therefore: the appetible object.[145] For
if two things, mind and appetite, were moving, they would move
according to some common species.[146] But now the mind does not
appear to be a mover without appetite. For will[147] is an appetite; howev-
er, when one is moved according to reason, one is also / moved accord-   25
ing to will. Appetite, however, moves even against reason. For desire is
a certain [sort of] appetite.[148]

And while every understanding is right, appetite and imagination
are both right and not right.[149] Whence, the appetible always causes
motion, and this is either the good or the apparent good; not every
[one], but the practical good.[150] (The practical / is what can also be   30
otherwise.[151]) It is apparent, therefore, that this sort of power of the
soul, that called / appetite, causes motion.   433b1

For those who divide the parts of the soul, very many [parts]
come to be, if they divide and separate them according to powers: the
nutritive, the sensitive, the intellectual, the deliberative, and, further,
the appetitive. For these differ from each other more than do the desiring and the spirited [parts].[152] /

Since, however, appetites come to be contrary to one another, and   5
this happens when reason and the desires are contraries, [this situa-
tion] comes to be in things having a sense of time. For the mind com-
mands restraint because of what is to come, while desire [commands
pursuit] because of what is immediate. For the immediately pleasant
thing appears to be both simply pleasant and simply good / because   10
of our not seeing what is to come.[153]

The mover would be one in species, the appetitive as appetitive – but the appetible first of all: for this, though not being in motion, moves by being understood or imagined. In number, however, the movers are many.[154]

Since, however, there are three things – one, the mover, second, that by which it moves, and further, third, the thing moved, while the mover is two-fold, / one immobile, the other mover and moved – the immobile is the practical good, but what is [both] mover and moved is the appetitive power (for the thing desiring is moved insofar as it desires, and the appetite in act is a certain motion), while the thing being moved is the animal. However, the organ by which the appetite moves is already bodily, whence / one must consider this among the works {acts} common to the body and the soul.[155] But to speak now in summary, what moves organically is where the beginning and the end are the same, like a joint. For there the curved and the hollow are the end and the beginning (whence the one rests while the other is moved), being in account different / but unseparated in magnitude. For all things are moved by pushing and pulling.[156] Whence something must rest, just as in a circle, and the motion must begin from there.[157]

Generally, therefore, as was said, insofar as the animal is appetitive, it is able to cause its own motion.[158] But it is not appetitive without imagination, while all imagination is rational or sensitive.[159] / The other animals, then, also share in the latter.

Chapter 11

433b31 Even in the case of those imperfect animals[160] in which the sense of
434a1 touch alone exists, however, / one must inquire what the moving power is, [and] whether imagination and desire occur in them or not. For it appears that pain and pleasure are present, while if these [are present], desire is necessarily also present. But how could imagination be in them? Or is it that, just as it {such an animal} is moved indeterminately, / so too this [imagination] is in it, but in an indeterminate way?[161]

The sensitive imagination, therefore, is also present in all the other animals, as was said, while the deliberative [one] is in the rational ones. For whether one will do this or that is already a work of reason. And it is necessary to measure by one thing. For it pursues the greater. Whence, it is able to make something one from / many phantasms.[162] And the cause of [the other animals] not seeming to have opinion is that they do not have that [imagination] which is from a gathering together {syllogism}[163]; but this [deliberative imagination] does have that [opinion].[164] Whence, the appetite does not have the deliberative power,[165] but sometimes it conquers and moves the will, sometimes that [conquers and moves] it: like a ball, appetite moves appetite, whenever a lack of self-control occurs.[166] By nature, however, the higher always is more a principle and moves, so that it is already moved according to three local motions.[167] /

Yet the scientific power is not moved, but remains.[168] Since, however, one belief and account is universal while another is of the particular (for one says that this sort of person must do such and such a thing, while the other that this here is indeed such a thing, and I am this sort), either then, this latter opinion moves, / not the universal one, or both do, but the one is more resting, the other not.[169]

Chapter 12[170]

It is necessary, therefore, for everything that lives and has a soul to have the nutritive soul, from generation to destruction. For it is necessary that what comes to be has growth, maturity, / and diminution, but these are impossible without food. It is necessary, therefore, that the nutritive power be in all things which are born and decay.

But it is not necessary that sense be in all living things. For that whose body is simple cannot have touch, nor can anything be an animal without this, nor can whatever is not receptive of the species / without the material [be an animal].[171] But it is necessary that an animal have sense, if nature does nothing in vain.[172] For all things which are by nature are for the sake of something, or will be the concomitants of things which are for the sake of something. If, therefore, any body which can move forward did not have sense, it would be destroyed and / not arrive at the end, which is the work of nature. For how would it feed? For [food] is present to the stationary [living things] there where they are naturally apt to be, but it is not possible that a body which is not stationary, though generable, have a soul and a discerning intellect without sensation (though neither, in fact, can / the ungenerable). For why would it not have it? For it is better either for the soul or for the body, but then it would be [better for] neither. For the soul would not understand more, while the body would not be more through that. Therefore, no non-stationary body has soul without sense.

But if in fact it does have sense, the body would have to be simple / or mixed. But it cannot be simple. For it would not have touch, but it must have this.[173] This is clear from the following. For since an animal is an ensouled body, and every body is tangible, while the

15

20

434a22

25

30

434b1

5

10

tangible is what is sensible by touch, it is also necessary for the body of the animal to be tactile, if the animal is to be preserved. For the

15   other senses sense / through a different [medium], e.g., smell, sight, and hearing. But if it did not have sense, when it is touched, it would not be able to flee some things and grasp others; if this [were so], it would be impossible that the animal be preserved.[174]

Whence also taste is like a certain [sort of] touch. For it is [a

20   sense] of food, and food is a tangible body. But sound / and color and odor do not nourish [an animal] nor do they bring about growth or diminution. Whence, it is also necessary for taste to be a certain [sort of] touch, because it is a sense of the tangible and nutritive. These are, therefore, necessary things for the animal, and it is apparent that an animal without touch is not possible.[175] The other senses, however,

25   are for the sake of well-being and / are not right away in any kind of animal at all, but in certain ones, as, for example, they must be in the ones that can move forward. For if the animal is to be preserved, it must sense not only when touched, but also from afar. But this would happen if it is able to sense through a medium, in virtue of that [medium] suffering and being moved by the sensible, while the animal itself [is moved] by that [medium].[176]

30   For just as / what moves according to place brings about a change up to a certain point, and what impels [something] makes that other thing able to impel, and the motion comes about through a medium, so too the first mover impels without being impelled, while the extreme is only impelled and does not impel, and the middle does

435a1   both / (and there may be many middles).[177] So in alteration too, except that [that which alters] alters while remaining in the same place, just as if one were to dip something into wax, the wax will be moved so far as the thing was dipped. But a stone [would] not [be moved] at all, while water [would be moved] even further. The air is

5   moved / and brings something about and suffers over the greatest distance, supposing it remains and is one. (Whence also, in the case of reflections, it is better [to say that] so long as it is one, the air suffers from the shape and color rather than [to say] that the sight issuing out [of the eye] is reflected.[178]) In the case of something smooth, [the air] is one. So this moves the sight again, as if the sign [pressed] into the

10   wax passed through / to the other side.

Chapter 13

435a11   It is apparent, however, that it is not possible for the body of an animal to be simple, I mean, to be [merely] fiery or airy. For without touch it can have no other sense. For every ensouled thing is a tactile body, as was said.[179] The other [elements] / besides earth can become sense organs, but they all bring about sensation by sensing through something other [than themselves] and through a medium. Touch, however, occurs by touching the things themselves; whence also it has this name. And indeed, the other sense organs sense by touching, but through something different, and this sense alone seems [to sense] through itself.[180] Whence, / no body of an animal would be [composed] from such elements, nor, then, of something earthy. For touch is like the mean of all the tangibles, and the sense organ is receptive not only of whatever differences there are of earth, but also of hot and cold and all the other tangibles. And because of this too, we do not sense / in the bones and in hair and in other such parts, because they are of earth.[181] / And because they are of earth, no plants have sense. No other sense can be present without touch, and this sense organ is neither of earth nor of any one of the other elements alone.

It is therefore apparent that animals necessarily die when they are deprived / of this sense alone. For it is not possible [for something] to have this one {sense} if it is not an animal, nor, if it is an animal, is it necessary that it have any [sense] other than this one.[182] And because of this the other sensibles (like color and sound and odor) do not thoroughly destroy the animal when they are excessive, but only the sense organs [are destroyed by them] – except / accidentally, as when there is an impulse and blow together with the sound, or when different things are moved by what is seen or smelled, which things destroy by touch. And a flavor, insofar as it happens at one and the same time to be tangible, destroys in virtue of this. But the excess of the tangibles, e.g., of hot or cold or hard, kills the animal. / For any excess of the sensible kills the sense organ; whence also, the tangible [destroys] touch. But it is by this that the animal is defined. For it was shown that there cannot be an animal without touch.[183] Whence, the excess of the tangibles destroys not only the sense organ / but even the animal, because it is necessary to have this alone.

An animal, however, has the other senses, as was said, not for the sake of being but for the sake of well-being.[184] For example, since it {the animal} is in air or water (or generally, in the transparent), it has sight that it might see; taste, due to the pleasant and painful,[185] that it might sense this in food, and desire it and be moved; hearing, that something might be signified to it; a tongue, / that it might signify something to another.[186]

15

20

30

435b1

5

10

15

20

25

Endnotes to Book I

1 The contrast here is between the quality of the object of knowledge and the strength of our grasp of it. "Certitude" (ἀκρίβεια) might also have been translated "precision" or "exactness." The study of the soul would seem to be certain because we all have a very definite and certain knowledge that we are alive, that we move and sense and think. If we mean by "soul," then, as Aristotle does, simply the "principle of life," the starting points of this science will be very certain. He does not seem to mean that everything in the science is very certain or exact, because he goes on to say that it is very hard to know. See I.1, 402a10–11. (References to the *De Anima* will be by Book, Chapter, and Bekker number only; the initials, *DA*, will be provided when confusion may result from their absence. See the *Introduction* for a list of abbreviations used in this translation.)

2 Cf. *PA* I.5, 644b31–33.

3 It is clear that knowing what the soul is, if that word be understood to refer to the principle, whatever it might be, which makes things alive, would greatly advance the study of nature, since many natural things, and those which especially engage our attention, like dogs and horses and men themselves, are living. In some sense, too, animate things are among the most evidently natural things in that they clearly have a principle within them of moving and resting (See *Phys.* II.1, 192b8–10). (As we will see later, though, living things are in a sense beyond nature. See II.2, 413a25–31; II.4, 415b28–416a18.) Besides, even the inanimate is, as the name indicates, understood at least initially through the animate, rather than the reverse (as is often presupposed). In Aristotle's view, knowledge of the soul would also advance the understanding of ethics and politics (see *Nic. Eth.* I.13, 1102a5–32), of metaphysics (compare III. 4–5 with *Meta.* XII, 7–10), and even of logic, insofar as logic deals with things as they are conceived in the soul Cf., e.g., *Po. An.* II.19, 99b26–100b5. See the *Introduction*.

4 "Substance" translates "οὐσία" which can mean (among other things) an individual existing thing, like a horse or a man, or the essence of a thing. See *Meta.* V.8, 1017b23–26. This word will be consistently translated, "substance."

5 By "accidents of it," Aristotle here means aspects of the soul which do not belong to its "what it is" (its essence or nature), but aspects which follow from that, i.e., he means what might be called properties or *per se* attributes. He does not mean merely adventitious attributes. The word can also mean the merely accidental or coincidental. This translation will not presume to distinguish these by translating the one Greek word with two different English words, but will leave it to the reader to determine which meaning is intended in each case.

6 "Passions" translates "πάθη" and does not necessarily refer to something emotional or even to something which one "experiences" or has done to one (though that would be a more proper meaning), but can merely refer to an attribute. One might translate the word, "affections" or "undergoings" or "things one undergoes."

7   This is to say that some attributes belong to the soul alone and others belong to the body in virtue of its having a soul.

8   If, as Aristotle has just said, the study of the soul is particularly certain (or, perhaps, "precise" or "exact"), how can it also be so difficult to know? See the *Introduction*.

9   The "what it is" is that which answers the question, "what is it?," in other words, the essence of the thing or what corresponds to the definition of the thing.

10   For demonstration, cf. *Po. An.* I.1–6; for division, *Meta.* VII.12, 1037b27–1038a30, *Pr. An.* I.31, 46a31–b37 and Plato's *Sophist* 218d–221b. In II.1, 412a3–b9 Aristotle uses division, while in II.2, 413a11–414a19 he presents the definition as one differing from a demonstration by position. In *Po. An.* II.8–10, 93a1–94a19, Aristotle explains how a definition and a demonstration can both be about the nature.

11   Generally, it seems we know the genus first. We are, according to *Phys.* I.1, 184a21–26, more certain of the more universal than of the less universal. For example, we are more sure that the thing chasing us through the woods is an animal than that it is a wolf or a dog. So it seems reasonable to try to determine the genus first. See Coughlin 2005, pp. 207–208.

12   "This something" is a literal translation of τόδε τι (in Latin, *hoc aliquid*). It signifies an individual, concrete thing like "this man" or "Socrates" as opposed either to universals like "man," on the one hand, or, on the one hand, accidents like black or white.

13   The ten "categories" or predicates are the ten highest univocal predicates, i.e., the ten most universal or embracing names of things, leaving aside those which embrace many things but in doing so must be defined in many different ways. (*Cat.* 4, 1b25–2a4) Aristotle argues that, e.g., "being" does not mean the same thing when said of a horse and of the horse's size, as seems obvious enough. (*Meta.* IV.2, 1003a33–b10) But "substance" or "thing" do mean the same thing when said of horse and of dog, and "size" does mean the same thing when said of sixteen hands tall and two feet tall. The categories are the ten most universal genera, and so would seem, according to the teaching of *Phys.* I.1, to be the first things to look into when trying to give a definition.

14   The Greek words translated by "potency" and "actuality" are, respectively, δύναμις and ἐντελεχέια. For the sense and translation of the latter, see Coughlin 2005, pp. xxv–xxvii and the *Glossary*.

15   Aristotle will divide the soul into "parts," but not in the normal sense of "parts," that is, not ones which form the whole of which they are parts by composition, but rather parts which are really powers, e.g., the nutritive "part" and the sensitive "part." (See, e.g., II.2, 413b7–8; II.2, 413b13–15; III.4, 429a10–11; III.9, 432a15–23) Such powers need not exhaust that of which they are the powers, as neither the sensitive nor the vegetative power alone can express all that an animal can do; for this reason, that of which they are powers can be called a "whole" and they can be called "parts."

16   This complaint will form the basis of certain objections leveled at his predecessors. Aristotle's view is evidently that there are different sorts of soul in different sorts of living things and that a complete treatment must take this into account. See II.3, 414b32–33.

17   The thought seems to be that there is no animal which is merely an animal; each one is a particular sort of animal. There may be a generic definition of soul, but that would not be a sufficient account of any real soul since genera do not have independent existence. See II.3, 414a29–b33.

18 Here the question is whether the soul is one thing with many powers or many things each of which has a power all its own. Does a horse, e.g., digest by one power and see by another power of one soul, or are these several activities rooted in several souls?

19 See the *Glossary*, "mind."

20 *Po. An.* I.4, 90a14–15.

21 That is, a definition which does not help us toward scientific demonstration, in which we see properties of the subject as due to the essence of the subject, is empty and cannot be anything but dialectical.

22 Does the soul have properties of its own, properties which are independent of body, or do all its attributes belong to the body, even if because of the soul, as feeding, we might say, belongs to the body because of the soul?

23 Aristotle will return several times to the question of the mind as a possibly separate part of the soul. He will discuss the imagination in: III.3, 427b29–429a9; III.7, 431a14–17, b2–10; III.8, 432a3–14 and intellect at length in III.4–5.

24 As the straight can be considered just insofar as it is straight, or insofar as it is in a body, so can the soul, and as the abstract line cannot touch a bronze sphere at a point, so neither, if it has no operation outside the body, could the soul considered in abstraction do anything.

25 This important paragraph indicates that if a thing has an operation proper to it, it must exist on its own, but if it does not, it cannot exist on its own. The operation of seeing, e.g., is the operation of a bodily organ, the eye; if the operation of the mind is like this, then it is not separable from the body any more than sight is. But if the operation of thinking is separate from the body, then the power to think (and what has that power, if it is distinct from the power itself) can be separated from the body. Plato had often expressed the view that the soul is an entity separate from the body in which it dwells (see, e.g., *Phaedo*, 106d–e); Aristotle is indicating an interest in settling that question and will come back to this question primarily in the third book (III.4–5). There he will use this claim about independent operation as a premise to show that the intellect is able to exist on its own.

26 More literally, "enmattered accounts" (λόγοι ἔνυλοι) but see Ross 1961, *ad loc.* Ross points out that the expression seems to mean that the definition of the thing includes a material element, as the definition of a house might include brick or wood.

27 The student of nature (φυσικός) deals with material things. Since Aristotle has just shown that many affections of the soul are involved with material, the study of the soul belongs to natural philosophy. This is qualified at *Meta.* VI.1, 1026a4–6.

28 The dialectician is one who would approach the truths of things by way of the opinions of men, either common opinions or the developed opinions of noteworthy thinkers. The method of dialectic is taught in the *Topics*. The doctrine is intended to allow us to make initial forays into whatever subjects we are interested in. From these, we can sift the opinions and test them against each other to try to determine the truth, or at least the direction in which the truth lies. See Appendix 1, *Dialectic in Book I of the De Anima*.

29 The artist does not consider "every work and passion of such a body and of this sort of matter," but only those aspects of his material which will bear on his work; he considers things which have his art as a principle, not things that have nature as a principle. See *Meta.* VI.1, 1025b18–24.

30 Cf. *Meta.* VI.1, 1025b3–1026a32.

31 Ibid. Lines and surfaces do not exist apart from physical bodies, but their definitions do not include the sensible qualities characteristic of such bodies; the passions of animals, on the other hand, both exist in material and have definitions containing reference to matter as subject to sensible qualities.

32 Cf. *Meta.* III.1, 995a27–b4.

33 In Chapter 2, Aristotle will present the views of his predecessors. For information about some of the thinkers mentioned in Book I, cf. Ross, 1961, *passim*; and also G.S. Kirk, J.E. Raven, and M. Schofield 1983. References to the "fragments" of the pre-Socratic philosophers are usually made according to the format standardized by H. Diels, *Die Fragmente der Vorsokratiker* (often cited as Diels, Diels-Kranz, or simply DK). The fragments in Kirk, Raven, and Schofield are designated using the numbering of Diels and all those referenced in this translation can be found, with English translations, in the text of Kirk, Raven, and Schofield. I will refer to such fragments by the name of the author and the DK number, e.g., "Democritus, Frs. 67–68." See Appendix 1, *Dialectic in Book I of the De Anima*, for a discussion of the use of dialectic in I.2–5.

34 Motion may be taken here broadly to include nutrition, growth, and locomotion, but it seems most obvious to name locomotion. In any case, most of the opinions which Aristotle will discuss look to locomotion.

35 Aristotle will later show that the soul is the actuality or form of the body. (II.1, 412a27–28; II.2, 414a12–14) His predecessors, trying to explain how the soul could move the body, assumed it must itself be in motion. It seems that Aristotle is implicitly holding that actuality is sufficient as a principle of motion (*Meta.* XII.6, 1071b12–20), whereas his predecessors thought only another imperfect actuality, i.e., another motion (*Phys.* III.2, 201b27–202a3) could explain it.

36 Democritus, Frs. 67–68.

37 Cf. *De Cael.* III.4, 303a3–8; *Phys.* I.5, 188a23–26.

38 Democritus' theory of breathing is more fully described in *De Juv.* 10, 471b30–472a25.

39 Cf. Plato's *Phaedrus*, 245c5–246a2.

40 Anaxagoras, Frs. 12–13.

41 The reference would seem to be rather to Eurylaus. See *Iliad* XXIII, l. 698.

42 Cf. *Meta.* IV.5, 1009b26–33.

43 Empedocles, Fr. 109.

44 On Plato's construction of the soul, see *Timaeus*, 35a1–37b3.

45 Likely a work written by Aristotle himself. See Ross, 1961, *ad loc.*

46 Cf. Plato, *Timaeus*, *loc. cit.*

47 Cf. *Meta.* I.6, 987b14–988a1.

48 Plutarch attributes this view to Aristotle's contemporary, Xenocrates. Ross, 1961, *ad loc.*; cf. also I.4, 408b32–409a30.

49 Those making them unbodily may be those who use less palpable material, as will be clear from the ensuing discussion, and perhaps also those whose principles are mathematical.

50 Perhaps they look to the fact that all beings in our experience move and so think that what moves of itself is most of all a principle, since there are no immobile things to be principles and things that do not move of themselves must be moving in virtue

of those that do. Aristotle himself argues, in the *Physics*, that there is an immobile mover and will argue later in this book that the intellectual power is immaterial. See *Phys.* VIII.10, 267b17–26; *DA* III.4, 429a18–27; *DA* III.5, 430a17–19.

51　I.2, 404b1–6.

52　Anaxagoras, Fr. 12.

53　Diogenes, Frs. 4–5.

54　Heraclitus, Fr. 36.

55　Perhaps Aristotle is saying that Heraclitus makes an advance by choosing an element which is in motion not only to explain motion, but also to explain our knowledge of motion.

56　Cf. *Meta.* I.8, 989a5–8.

57　E.g., Empedocles.

58　Earlier, Aristotle said they all use motion and sensation. Here he adds, "being unbodily." The thinkers discussed seem to have moved toward the unbodily in their efforts to explain motion and sensation, so here, at the end of the summary of the opinions of others, we find this interesting additional "defining" aspect. Aristotle will himself define the soul in a way that makes it, in a sense, immaterial, insofar as it is not material but formal.

59　Anaxagoras. Cf. I.2, 405b19–21.

60　This premise of the earlier philosophers may be held because we seem to have what we know in our minds or in our senses, for it is our eyes that see and our minds that know, but the things we see or know must be present to the knowing powers in order to be known.

61　Perhaps they limit the soul to the principles of all things (rather than saying the soul is all things *tout court*) because they think knowing the principles of things is a sufficient for knowing all things.

62　One might wonder if Anaxagoras is implicitly saying Mind (his first mover) is not bodily, and if so, how he would understand that term. It seems that some of those to whom Aristotle attributes the notion of an unbodily principle only mean something with small parts or something very rarified.

63　Whereas Empedocles said that the soul is in a way everything, insofar as it is composed of the elements of everything, Anaxagoras took the opposite position, that the Mind or soul is completely different from everything else. Aristotle's position will take both positions into account. See III.4, 429a18–24; III.8, 431b21.

64　Aristotle is apparently thinking of the following words: ζεῖν (to boil), ζῆν (to live), ψῦχος (cold), and ψυχή (soul).

65　Aristotle begins in Chapter 3 to evaluate his predecessors' views. This will continue to the end of Book I. He will first consider the possibility that the soul moves in place *per se*; later he will ask whether we could say it moves *per se* when it experiences emotions or thought, at I.4, 408a34 ff.

66　This is a position with which Aristotle ultimately agrees, though in a qualified way. See I.4, 408a29–34.

67　*Phys.* VIII.5, 257a35–258b9. In Chapter 2, Aristotle had attributed to his predecessors the view that what is a mover must be in motion at I.2, 403b29–30.

68　Cf. *Phys.* IV.4, 211a16–23; *Phys.* V.1, 224a21–30.

69　The dialectic developed out of this concern concludes at I.4, 408a29–31 with the claim that the soul cannot be in motion in virtue of itself or *per se*, but must be in motion in virtue of the motion of another or *per accidens* (in particular, in virtue of the body it animates).

70   That there are four sorts of motion is argued at *Phys.* V.1–2, 225b5–226b1. In the *Physics*, Aristotle puts growth and diminution together. Note, however, that he divides "change" (μεταβολή) into three kinds, generation, corruption, and motion (κίνεσις), and then subdivides the latter into three. (*Phys.* V.1, 224b35–225b5)

71   That locomotion, growth, and diminution occur in place is obvious; Aristotle provides an argument concerning alteration at *Phys.* VIII.7, 260b1–5.

72   Cf. I.5, 409b2–4. For an understanding of this and the following arguments, see Appendix 1, *Dialectic in Book I of the De Anima*.

73   Cf. *De Cael.* IV.5, 312b2–19.

74   The elements in between are water and air.

75   A mythical craftsman.

76   The goddess of love, equivalent to the Roman goddess Venus.

77   Plato, *Timaeus*, 36e.

78   *Timaeus*, 35a–37c. The discussion of these views may seem peculiar, given how very unlikely they are. Moreover, in presenting these views, Plato presumably did not mean them to be taken at face value. Even though he must be aware that Plato did not intend these positions literally, Aristotle may respond to the text of Plato as written either because he is concerned that some people will take them to be literally true or because of some value found in their consideration. For example, thought does seem to come about by way of contact with the intelligible (since we think about things by having them in mind), and contact is first of all said of magnitudes. The comparison of the "contact" of thought with the "contact" of lines or surfaces (coming up in the next few lines) may help point us toward important likenesses and differences.

79   That is, thought is like number in that one thought succeeds another with nothing of the same kind (i.e., another thought) coming between. Magnitudes are one by continuity, i.e., because the end of one part of the magnitude is the beginning of the next. Cf. *Phys.* V.3, 226b18–227a17.

80   *Timaeus*, 34b.

81   Timaeus holds that the soul is made apart from and before the body, but body, as soon as formed, is joined to the soul and the soul is not able to free itself from this alien element. *Timaeus*, 34c–37d. Elsewhere, Plato expresses the view that the soul is better off if it is separated from the body. Cf. e.g., *Phaedo*, 66b–67b.

82   Note that the Greek word for tool, ὄργανον, is the root of the English word "organ."

83   Aristotle's predecessors seem to have treated all souls as if they are of one kind. Cf. II.2, 414a21–27. The fact that the soul is a principle of life and that life is found in such diverse bodies, all of which are animated by souls which use their bodies for their own peculiar sorts of functions, points to a proportion between body and soul. Aristotle will immediately go on, at the beginning of I.4, to take up a view that emphasizes this proportion to such a degree that it identifies the soul with the articulation of the living body.

84   The Greek word here need not be restricted to the musical sense, though it can mean that; it may also simply mean a "fitting together." The view that the soul is a harmony is ascribed to the Pythagoreans and is discussed in Plato's *Phaedo*, 86b–d and

92a–95a. In some way, this view seems to approach Aristotle's own, because saying the soul is a harmony looks at it as a sort of form; the difficulty is that it is an accidental form. Combining the plausible position with the objections against it, it becomes probable that the soul might be form in the genus substance. Cf. II.1, 412a3–b6 and Appendix 2, *The Definition of the Soul.*

85   The distinction is explained further immediately below; see I.4, 408a5–18.

86   If the soul or its powers are compositions of the elements, one should be able to deduce or at least make a good guess about what arrangement of elements might give rise to the properties of the soul or of its powers. For the characteristics of compounds are derived from those of their elements. See *De Gen.* I.10, 327b22–31.

87   Empedocles posited four elements (earth, air, fire, and water) as well as two movers, friendship and strife. Cf. Empedocles, Fr. 17. In Fr. 109, quoted above at I.2, 404b13–15, he said all these were in the soul.

88   We seem here to have a definite conclusion being drawn from the dialectical inquiry: The soul can move, but only in virtue of something else, the body, being in motion, i.e., the soul moves only *per accidens.* This dialectical conclusion points in the direction of saying that the soul is something of a living body, not an independent entity.

89   Aristotle continually makes room in this dialectical inquiry for a possibly immaterial intellect, as one might expect a disciple of Plato to do.

90   Aristotle seems to claim that the soul is another substance from man, enters into him in some way, and is what thinks, loves, and hates. And it is indestructible, a claim he argues to by analogy to sight and a belief that old age dims sight only because the organ wears away, not because the power itself is destructible. Some commentators take this text to support the view that the intellect, according to Aristotle, is a separate substance, perhaps even a divine one. But there are several problems with this reading. For one thing, the text stands amidst a plethora of dialectical arguments; why would Aristotle suddenly start stating his own views? It is at least premature for him to make these remarkable claims here, without the hint of an argument. Moreover, when he does get to his own views, in III.4–5, they differ significantly from what is presented here. Most importantly, he does not think the intellect works through an organ (III.4, 429a18, 24–25; 429b4–5), so the argument in this text, based on an analogy to sight and its organ, simply misfires. Moreover, his final statement in this passage seems rather to call into doubt the view of intellect presented here. For a detailed study of this text, see Cohoe 2018.

91   Aristotle concludes that the soul is not in any sort of motion *per se*, though it is the cause or principle of motion. See I.4, 408a29–30.

92   Cf. *Phys.* VIII.5, 258a20–25.

93   I.4, 409a10–11.

94   This may be taken as another indication that soul must be something of a body, though not itself a body. Cf. I.3, 406a12–22.

95   I.4, 408a3–5.

96   The reference may be to I.4, 408a3–5, though there he was speaking of the view that the soul is a harmony. Cf. also I.1, 402b25–403a2.

97   But see III.8, 431b28–432a3.

98   Empedocles, Fr. 96. The god Hephaistos was often associated with fire because he was a smith.

99 Aristotle's argument grants his predecessors' claim that like is known by like and adds that not only are elements known, but so are composites. Whence the arrangements or forms of the elements must also be present in the soul, and the soul must have in it even rocks and men, since these too are objects of knowledge. The argument points to the need to find a way of being in the soul which is not merely as in a place (like the elements) or as in a material subject (like the form or arrangement of the elements), but which can nevertheless explain how the soul knows things. The determination of this way will begin in II.5 and culminate in III.4–8.

100 Cf. *Cat.* 4, 1b25–27; *Meta.* V.7, 1017a22–27.

101 Cf. I.2, 405b19–21.

102 How is the known present to the knower? The sensible object seems to act on the senses, and what acts on another is other, as the cool is heated not by what is equally cool, but by something hotter than itself. And yet what is known is supposed to be like the knower. Cf. II.4, 416a29–b3; II.5, 416b32–417b16.

103 Cf. Empedocles, Fr. 109, quoted above at I.2, 404b13–15.

104 Cf. *Timaeus*, 64b–c.

105 The text implies that Aristotle thinks it at least strange that God should not know more than other minds do. This contrasts with the view of those who say, based on *Meta.* XII.7, 1072b19–26 and XII.9, 1074b15–1075a5, that Aristotle's God knows only himself. Cf. also *Meta.* III.4, 1000a24–32.

106 The argument points to there being a unique way of existing for the thing known; if it were simply the sort of presence we see in all physical things, everything would be a knower.

107 Cf. I.5, 411b6–14.

108 This argument brings up something Aristotle's predecessors did not seem too concerned with, namely, the soul as the unifying principle of a living thing. The living being is one being, and the principle of this unity would seem to be the soul. What could it be that it would cause such unity of disparate organs as eyes and livers and such disparate materials as earth and fire (or carbon and hydrogen)? Cf. II.1, 412b6–9.

109 Another indication of the oddity of knowledge: Knowing powers know opposites, as the curved and the straight by the straight, and the knowing power in some way has to be like the thing it knows. But no material thing could be both curved and straight.

110 Cf. Ross, 1961, *ad loc.*

111 The reference may be to Plato's *Republic*, 435d–441c, or, as Ross suggests, to a popular opinion presented in *Nic. Eth.* I.13, 1102a26–1103a10.

112 Why is this so hard? Perhaps Aristotle is reflecting on those arguments which dispose us to think the knowing powers are not merely material.

113 There is not only the question of how the soul holds together the body, but also of how the parts or powers of the soul, though distinct, remain together.

114 This fact will be used to lend unity to the study of the soul. Cf. II.3, 414b20–32.

Endnotes to Book II

1   Cf. Appendix 1, *Dialectic in Book I of the De Anima*, for an account of how this new beginning has profited from the first beginning, the recapitulation and refutation of Aristotle's predecessors in I.2–5.

Whether there is a common account of all souls was in question in I.1, 402b5–9 and the manner in which the account is common will be discussed in II.3. The ground for assuming here that there is a single definition is found at I.5, 411b27–30, where it was noted that all living things have the powers which even plants share, i.e., nutrition, growth, and reproduction; at II.3, 414a29–b32, he will argue that it is just the presence of this power in all living things which permits a unified definition of the soul. For the presence of this sort of power in all living things shows that they all have a certain sort of life in common, even if some, the animals and human beings, have additional and more perfect modes of life as well.

2   *Cat.* 4, 1b25–7; *Meta.* V.7, 1017a30.

3   This is not a division of the genus substance into species of substance, but of the name "substance" into three related meanings, meanings founded upon the analysis of natural substance in *Phys.* I.7, 189b30–191a22.

4   "Contemplation" here translates a word which originally means "looking" and might also be translated "consideration" or "speculation" (which is itself from a Latin word which means "looking"). The connotation of indecision or uncertainty in these English words ("I am contemplating buying a new car," "that's just speculation," etc.) is not reflective of the Greek. The word is intended to name the operation of actually knowing or exercising knowledge as opposed to having merely habitual knowledge.

5   That is, artificial bodies and the accidental conglomerations that come about by nature have natural bodies as their components.

6   A second division of substance. This one is a division of a genus into species, namely, into corporeal and incorporeal (presumably), then into natural and non-natural (probably the artificial or naturally occurring conglomerations of natural bodies, like stones of mixed elements), while natural is further divided into living and non-living. The point of making the division into artificial and natural bodies might be to indicate that, being different sorts of bodies, they would have different principles, and, since we know that the principles of artificial bodies are accidental arrangements, it is reasonable to think that the principles of natural bodies are not accidental arrangements. In fact, the natural are principles of the artificial because the former really are substances while the latter are just combinations of substances.

7   Note that Aristotle distinguishes life by way of certain vital operations. Though he does not here mention sensation, locomotion, reasoning, or even reproduction, he does not mean to exclude these from the definition. At any rate, he claims that his definition is general at 412b4–6, and he seems to include sensation and perhaps the thinking at 412b17–413a10.

8   Aristotle does not see a need to prove there are living things, nor even that the living and the non-living are distinct in kind. Rather, he relies on our experience that we know ourselves and others as things that have the operations through which we distinguish the living and the non-living – in fact, as the expressions "non-living" and "inanimate" imply, we know we are alive even better than we know that other things are not. See the *Introduction* for a discussion of the roots of Aristotle's arguments in our common experience of living.

9   One might think the activities precede the science because, like other habits, science is generated by the repetition of the acts which are appropriate to that habit: We learn to play piano by playing piano, we learn geometry by going over proofs, and we become courageous by acting courageously in the face of painful situations. Still, these acts are not acts of the habit, but acts leading to the habit, even if they are in a way the sorts of acts that the habit gives rise to. So the habit is prior in generation to the acts which proceed from it, even if the ones that lead to it are akin to the ones that arise from it. They are only akin and not identical because they do not have as their principle the habit but, perhaps, some desire to form the habit or whatever else might motivate the acts.

10   This is common to all souls because all mortal living things have the operations of life mentioned above. See 412a14–15; 413a25–32.

11   The Greek word for "tool" (ὄργανον) is the root of our English word, "organ." The thing that has the operations of life must have organs appropriate to those operations. See Appendix 2, *The Definition of the Soul* for further discussion of the shift from "natural body having life potentially" to "organic natural body."

12   Cf. *Meta.* VIII.6, 1045a7–b23.

13   The "what it was to be" is the essence or whatness of a thing. Cf. *Meta.* V.8, 1017b21–23.

14   What is "potentially alive" here is not what is able to become a living thing, but what is a living thing able to perform (or "potentially" performing) the operations of life. See Appendix 2, *The Definition of the Soul.*

15   That is, they are potentially the sorts of bodies (namely, living ones) which potentially perform (i.e., are able to perform) the operations of life.

16   Once again, Aristotle implies that some part of the soul may be able to exist separately. For earlier texts, see I.1, 403a5–10; I.4, 408b18–32; I.5, 411b14–19; for later texts, see II.2, 413b13–29; II.3, 415a7–12; III.3, 427a17–b14; III.4, 429a10–b5, 429b22–26, 429b29–430a2; III.5, 430a10–25; III.7, 431a14–b2, 431b17–19; III.8, 432a3–14.

17   This seems an odd claim: Hasn't Aristotle just argued (at 412b6–9) that the soul is the form or species and so is one with the body? This would seem to imply that it is not in the body as a sailor in a ship. Perhaps he means that it is not clear whether the soul is *also* in the body as a sailor in a ship, that is, as a sort of pilot. One might think this because the intellect (which he implicitly mentioned in saying that some part of the soul may not be the actuality of any body) is in the body in another sense than the soul, not as a form of a body, but as a sort of pilot or sailor.

18   This chapter approaches the definition in a different way than did Chapter 1. For a discussion of this fact, cf. Appendix 2, *The Definition of the Soul.* On what is more known (or "knowable") according to account, see *Phys.* I.1, 184a16–23 and *Meta.* VII.3, 1029b3–12.

19 Cf. *Po. An.* II.2, 89b36–90a34; *Po. An.* II.8–10, 93a1–94a19; Euclid, *Elements* VI, 17.

20 "The beginning of the inquiry" seems to be the observation that some things have peculiar activities, ones which are found only in the living. They all involve a sort of self-motion, which implies immanent operations, that is, operations that do not pass over into exterior objects. When we burn wood, the fire we apply to the wood burns something outside of itself, namely, the wood. But when we walk, we walk ourselves, and when we grow, we digest food and transform it into our own bodies, and when we sense, the seeing is a sort of alteration which takes place inside our eyes (and brains). For a more complete discussion of the vital operations and their role in coming to know the soul, see the *Introduction* and Appendix 2, *The Definition of the Soul.*

21 Because plants grow in all directions, they seem to transcend the elemental bodies, which, according to Aristotle, have each a single motion: earth down, fire up, the middle elements of water and air moving in either direction depending on where they are to begin with. I.3, 406a27–30; *De Cael.* I.3, 269b18–29.

22 The immortal things which have thought but not nutrition are the separated intelligences and the souls of the celestial spheres, if souls they have. Cf. *Meta.* XII.6, 1071b3–22; *De Cael.* II.2, 285a29.

23 That is, in mortal things life is present first of all through the vegetative functions. Other living powers seem to be possible only in the presence of these powers. Even in the cases of animals and men, we believe they live so long as they perform these vegetative operations, sometimes with artificial help (such as a respirator). The presence of these powers in all mortal living things allows us to have a universal definition said univocally of all mortal living things. See II.3, 414b20–32 and the note on that passage.

24 Cf. III.12, 434a22–b18.

25 In Book I, Aristotle raised the question whether the soul has parts and if so how they were distinguished. I.1, 402b9–16. Cf. also II.3, 414a32–b6.

26 Cf. II.3, 425a7–11; III.11, 433b31–434a10.

27 This is the most overt statement yet that the intellect may be separable from the body; Aristotle's earlier remarks seemed more tentative. I.1, 403a8–11; I.2, 405a13–17, 405b19–23; I.4, 408b18–29. He will be more explicit below: III.4, 429a18–27, 429b22–26; III.5, 430a17–19, 430a22–23. Those who assert that the other parts of the soul are separable are probably the Platonists (Cf. *Timaeus*, 69d–72d). It is noteworthy that Aristotle speaks of the "remaining parts of the soul," thus affirming (counter to some commentators), that the intellect is among the parts of soul and is not a separate being. Cf. Appendix 5, *The Intellectual Soul* and the notes on III.4–5. Aristotle is asking whether the parts of the soul are separable only in account or definition, or are they also separable in place? Some cases, he says, are easily judged: If we cut certain plants in two, both parts grow and nourish themselves. These two parts of the soul, therefore, have not been divided from each other in place. Some insects, too, are like this. These parts or powers of the soul are therefore also present together in place, however easily we can distinguish some of them in definition. But the mind "seems to be a different kind of soul, and this alone can be separated, as the eternal from the corruptible." Now, this is not just a separation in definition but in place, so that it can exist without being joined to the others. This could be by

being a separate substance, an "intelligence," divine or semi-divine, but it cannot simply be referring to a difference in definition. In any case, the passage is more easily read as suggesting that the power of the soul called the intellect can be separated from the other powers of the soul, all of which are powers *of the soul* and none of which is a separately existing thing. For he says the intellect and the power of consideration "seem to be a different kind of soul," and he speaks immediately of the "remaining parts of the soul," implying by both these manners of speech that the intellect, like the other powers, is something of the soul and not a separate being.

28   Since living things as such have vital operations, we should divide their species by the different vital operations they have.

29   Cf. III.12–13.

30   *Phys.* III.3, 202b19–22.

31   II.1, 412a6–11.

32   See Appendix 2, *The Definition of the Soul* for a discussion of this argument.

33   At this point, Aristotle has avoided two extreme positions noted in the dialectical discussion (I.2–4), namely, that the soul is a certain sort of body, like fire or round atoms (I.2, 403b31–404a9) or that it is indifferent to the sort of body it is in or is identified with. (I.3, 407b13–26; I.4, 409a25–27; I.5, 410b7–10). By saying the soul is the form of the living body he can say the soul is not a body other than the living body and yet is something of the living body. Moreover, the soul will go where the body goes, and so will be moved only accidentally, as he suggested earlier. I.4, 408a29–34.

34   Cf. I.3, 407b13–26.

35   II.2, 413b32–414a3.

36   See also II.2, 413b13–24.

37   III.12, 434b18–24.

38   II.10.

39   III.3, 427b14–429a9; III.11, 433b31–434a21.

40   *De Cael.* II.12, 292a14–22; *Meta.* XIII.7, 1073a23–24. Once again, though he thinks there are separated substances which are intellects, Aristotle speaks of the human intellect as being only a power of a soul, not a substance in itself.

41   Cf. I.1, 402b1–9. It seems Aristotle has a definition which applies to every sort of soul (except one which is not at all the act of a material) because all mortal living things have the vegetative functions, in virtue of which he originally distinguished life (II.1, 412a14–15; II.2, 413b1–2). Since the power of the vegetative soul is in all mortal living things, this power is used to give a generic definition of the soul. If there were a living thing that had the power of sensation, say, but without the vegetative powers, it would be called living and would have a "soul" only equivocally. For the soul is defined by its powers (see II.1, 412a14–15; II.2, 413a20–25; 413b1–2; 413b11–13). But the vegetative power and its principle are potentially present in all other souls ("potentially," because it is not actually divided from the other powers – see II.2, 413b13–414a3).

  Aristotle likens the series of souls to a series of rectilinear figures: The triangle is potentially in all other figures (Euclid, *Elements* VI, 20) and the vegetative soul is in all other souls. The generic definition of figure applies to triangle and to all subsequent figures such as quadrilaterals, pentagons, hexagons, etc., and the first in the series, the triangle, is in the quadrilateral in potency, the quadrilateral in the pentagon, etc. So too does the generic definition of the soul apply to all kinds of soul, and these are arranged in a series such that the first sort, the vegetative, is in the sensitive potentially, and the sensitive in the rational.

42 Cf. I.1, 402b1–3.

43 III.12, 434b21–29.

44 For the "different account" of the intellect, see III.4–8.

45 Cf. I.1, 402b9–16. The powers are defined by their operations, and the operations by their objects, as sight is defined by the act of seeing, and the act of seeing by color.

46 That is, generated not from parents but from some rotting stuff. Cf. *Hist. An.* V.1, 539a21–26; *Gen. An.* III.11, 761a13–762a32.

47 That is, the good sought and the one for whom it is sought, e.g., the house and one who wants a house. Aristotle is perhaps thinking that the good sought in generation is the off-spring while the one for whom that is sought, at least as understood in the next sentence, is the parent, for it is the parent which is granted a sort of extension of existence through the off-spring. Cf. *Pol.* I.2, 1252a26–30.

48 "One in number" means a single, individual thing; "one in species" means that the things in question are exactly the same kind of thing. (Similarly, one can speak of "one in genus" and "one by analogy." Cf. *Meta.* V.6, 1016b31–1017a3) Here a good sought by nature is said to go beyond the good of the individual thing (which is what was emphasized in *Phys.* II.8) to a common good of the species, the survival of the species. The individual of a species seeks its own good in seeking to reproduce, for then it continues to exist even after its own death, in a way, through its offspring, insofar as it and its offspring are of the same species. The good of the species is common to all members of the species.

49 *Phys.* II.3, 194b16–195a3; *Meta.* V.2, 1013a24–b4.

50 "Substance" here means form or species. Cf. II.1, 412a6–9.

51 Presumably, the thing in potency here is the naturally organized body. Cf. II.1, 412a27–28; 412b4–6. "Account" {λόγος} is identified with "species" {εἶδος} and "form"{μορφή} at II.2, 414a9. (These words do not always carry such identical or at least very proximate meanings.)

52 This will be qualified in II.5, 417a21–b16.

53 Cf. I.3, 406a27–29. If the orientations of the organs of animals and plants depend on their functions, that orientation can hardly be explained merely by what is natural to the inorganic things of which those organs are composed.

54 Having pointed out that the nature of the components of living things is not a likely source of a complete explanation, Aristotle here indicates that they do have a subordinate role.

55 The power to cause growth acts on a material (food) so as to increase the bulk of the various parts of the living thing; the power to cause generation also acts on food to form an organized body of determinate size; it is plausible, then, to identify the two powers. Cf. *Gen. An.* II.4, 740b25–741a3.

56 II.4, 416a21–22.

57 The act of nutrition is already a step above the mere interaction of material bodies. This sort of "suffering" will be further elucidated at II.5, 416b32–417b16.

58 That an agent and a patient at first have opposed qualities and later, after the agent has affected the patient, are alike, is discussed at greater length and in a more general way at *De Gen.* I.7, 323b1–324a24.

59 Food is defined in terms of what feeds on it.

60 It seems that food is a remote source of reproduction, as the parents must part with some of their matter for the reproduction to occur. Is this incidental to being food? If the "most natural work" of the living is reproduction (II.4, 415a26–b1) and, of living functions, the vegetative functions transcend nature least, it would seem these activities are oriented to the natural goal of reproduction. This would make food oriented to reproduction. It is worth noting that all the functions of the vegetative soul are ordered to the substance of the living thing, whether by maintaining it (nutrition), bringing it to its full size (growth), or making another like it (reproduction – a sort of extreme version of self-maintenance and growth). See Appendix 3, *The Reproductive (or Vegetative) Soul.*

61 "First" here indicates that we are speaking of the vegetative soul, which is called "first" because it is before the other sorts insofar as it can be without them, but they cannot be without it. II.3, 414b33–415a12.

62 In certain of the biological works which follow upon the *De Anima*, in particular, *Generation of Animals* and *Parts of Animals.*

63 Aristotle is moving on to consider what is peculiar to the souls of sensitive living bodies, i.e., animals.

64 I.5, 410a22–26; II.4, 415b23–25; but cf. below, II.5, 418a1–3.

65 Cf. *De Gen.* I.7, 323b1–324a24.

66 The natural bodies are sensible *per se* in the sense that what has the cause of some character that it possesses within itself has that character through itself or *per se* (see *Po. An.* I.4, 73b10–16), but *per accidens* in the sense explained in II.6, 418b20–5. At II.7, 418a29–30, Aristotle says the subject of color is visible *per se* in the former sense. He seems to think, then, that both sensible substances and their sensible qualities are sensible *per se*, but not in the same sense of *per se*.

67 If we can see fire, e.g., and fire is inside the eye, why don't we see our own eyes? This unexpected problem leads to the realization that the senses are passive powers, i.e., powers which depend upon an object to bring them into act.

68 Cf. II.1, 412a10–11. One might wonder whether the word translated "sensing" in the last sentence should be replaced by one meaning "the sensed [object]," on the grounds that otherwise Aristotle seems to be simply repeating himself. Cf. Ross, *ad loc.*

69 *Phys.* III.2, 201b31–32; *Meta.* IX.6, 1048b28–36. Motion is an imperfect act because, while it is an actuality, it is an actuality of what is still in potency to the actuality defining that same potency. So when a thing is in motion, it does not have the term of the motion. Still, there is a kind of reality or actuality here, and that act is even in a sense an imperfect version of the term – the becoming is an inchoate being. Aristotle here justifies the use of the word "act" to speak of a "suffering" or "undergoing."

70 II.4, 416a29–b9.

71 We come to possess knowledge of a science by often going from ignorance (or even error) to a correct consideration, but we use our already possessed habitual knowledge simply by willing to do so, if there are no impediments present (such as hunger or disease).

72 "Suffering" (or "undergoing") and "altering" seem to imply in their first uses that what suffers or alters loses something or is harmed. But when one changes from

ignorance to knowledge, there is no harm done, nor is any done when one goes from having knowledge habitually to using it. It rather seems that the thing which "suffers" or "alters" in these cases is perfected.

73   Using one's knowledge is not properly an "alteration" because one does not come to be "other" through such use but rather comes to be more perfectly what one already is. ("Alter" is Latin for "other"; the Greek word here is also derived from a word meaning "other").

74   The change to the privative state is the loss of the quality had before the change, e.g., forgetting something; the change to a state and nature is rather the acquisition of a quality in place of a mere privation, e.g., learning something. In cases of "suffering" properly so called, some quality possessed at the beginning of the change is lost, so Aristotle calls this a change "to the privative dispositions."

75   Presumably, Aristotle means that one cannot have a science of sensible things, such as physics or chemistry, unless one can sense those things (*Phys.* II.1, 193a3–9); once the science is possessed, one need not refer over and over to actual sensation but can instead use the images those things cause in us (i.e., the phantasms). See III.7, 431a14–b19; III.8, 432a3–11.

76   II.5, 417a29–b5.

77   II.5, 417a17–20.

78   Although the sense power suffers when unlike the sensible and, under the influence of the latter, comes to be like it, the reception of the form of the other does not destroy some form which had been present, but simply perfects the power. This is a new sort of activity, unlike what we see in the transformations of matter which go on in the inanimate world, where agents, in acting on patients, destroy their forms by introducing their own likenesses to the patient's matter. This difference could be part of the reason that Aristotle returns three times in this chapter to the theme of the like and the unlike in interactions. See 416b35–417a2; 417a14–17; 418a5–6. This mode of alteration also contrasts with the transformation of matter which we saw in the case of the vegetative powers. There the food was unlike until it was acted upon by the living being and became like that being. The food was other and the otherness was overcome by the living thing acting on the food so as to effect the actual transformation of the food into the substance of the living thing or into its off-spring. But here in the case of sensation we have the other, the sensible object, acting on the living thing and making the living thing become like itself, but without the sensible object losing its identity in the process. The living thing takes on the form of the other without destroying it and without itself being destroyed. We are already on the track toward the notion of immaterial reception. See II.12, 424a17–24.

79   In this chapter, Aristotle will distinguish three ways of being an object of sense; in II.7–11 he will discuss the proper object of each of the five external sense powers and those powers themselves. This chapter will help him determine how to approach each of these five senses.

80   Speaking of the senses erring or not seems to go along with speaking of them as true or false, and Aristotle will later speak in this way (see III.3, 428b17–19). Elsewhere he says that truth and falsity are found in composition and division of subjects and predicates (e.g., *Cat.* 4, 2a7–10; III.6, 430a26–28). While the latter sort of truth is more properly called truth, the senses can be called true because they correspond to the way things are. If, when I see a wall as white, the wall I see is really white, then

my eye is conformed to the way things are. On the multitude of objects of touch, see II.11, 422b17–423a21.

81 Does Aristotle mean that we are sure that we sense a certain sort of object, e.g., color, or that we are sure that we sense the color correctly, e.g., that when we sense red the thing sensed really is red? He seems to say the former, but that would not make the relation of the sense to the proper sensible any different from its relation to the common sensibles (magnitude, number, etc.). In both cases we are sure that we are sensing this or that sort of sensible, whether color or shape. He must, despite appearances, be saying the latter, if, as seems to be the case, he is noting a difference between our sensations of the proper and of the common sensibles. One might argue as follows: We saw at II.5, 416b31–34, that senses are passive to their objects; the sense receives from the sensible a form and it is due to this reception that it is aware of the object. But the sense is so made that it receives a certain sort of form (the eye color, the ear sound). The sense does not receive anything from the sensible except the form which the sensible by its activity imposes on the sense, and the sense is naturally apt to receive that sort of form, so it does so and is aware of the sort of sensible which has that form. Moreover, the sense undergoes no harm in so receiving. Thus, the sense receives the sensible form just insofar as it is a sense and without being harmed. There is therefore no impediment to the reception of the form of the sensible; consequently it is received, under proper conditions, perfectly, and the awareness of the sensible, which follows upon the presence of the form of the sensible, is accurate. (Cf. Polansky 2007, p. 15.) Of course, none of this implies that a defective organ or medium might not cause an imperfect reception and a consequently inaccurate awareness. The inerrancy of the senses is also briefly addressed at III.3, 428b17–429a1, where Aristotle seems to concede that there is some room for error even among the proper sensibles.

82 It seems that it would be more precise to say that some are perceived by all the senses, and some by fewer but by more than one. Shape, for example, does not seem to be discernable by smell. See *De Sens*. 4, 442b4–11.

83 This is the criterion according to which we decide whether something is sensed *per se* or *per accidens*. For example, whereas both the white and the size of the white surface directly affect the sense power, the paper that the white surface is in does not. See also III.1, 425a14–b4.

84 The proper sensibles, being peculiar each one to a distinct sense power, must be definitive of those powers, whereas the common and the accidental are not thus definitive. Note too that both the common and the proper sensibles directly impact the sensation, whereas the accidental sensibles do not. Whether the white is in the surface of snow or of paper does not affect the sensation, whereas whether it is white or not and whether it is a large surface or not does. Between these two sensibles, the proper and the common, which is that in virtue of which we should define each sense? Clearly the proper, as we just saw. We might also recognize a sign of this: We are readily mistaken about the common sensibles, but nigh to infallible about the proper. If the sense powers are naturally apt to receive some sensible, it is certainly reasonable that the sensible in question be the one about which the power is not apt to go astray.

85 Having explained what is common to sensation, Aristotle, as is his custom, goes on to discuss the particulars which fall under that commonality. He deals with sight,

hearing, smelling, taste, and touch, in that order, in Chapters 7–11, before returning in 12 to a common discussion.

86   Cf. II.7, 419a1–7.

87   Cf. *Po. An.* I.4, 73a34–b16. There it is said that "in virtue of itself" or "*per se*" can mean one of four things: that the predicate is in the definition of the subject (as "number" in "three"), that the subject in the definition of the predicate (as "number" in the definition of "odd"), that a thing is a being on its own (that is, individual substances like Socrates are said to be *per se*), and finally, that two things are causally connected, as opposed to being accidentally connected (that it should thunder when I take a walk is a coincidence, but that my shoes wear out as I walk is not a coincidence but is *per se*). This last sense seems to be what Aristotle has in mind here.

88   We see through the transparent up to the opaque or colored. (Elsewhere, Aristotle even defines color as "the limit of the transparent." *De Sens.* 3, 439b11–12.) We see the transparent through an extraneous color somewhat as we hear a musical interval by hearing the notes. Since the color is what we see, the color must do something to the transparent body between our eyes and the color in order for our eyes to be affected by it.

89   See *De Sens.* 3, 439a18–b16. If, as argued in the *Physics*, there is no empty space, when we see a thing at a distance, there must be a body between us and it, and that body is obviously, then, transparent. *Phys.* IV.4, 211b14–20; IV.6–9; Coughlin 2005, Appendices 7–8, pp. 253–265. Aristotle argues for the existence of a fifth element (in addition to earth, water, air, and fire), which he called the "ether," and of which the eternal heavenly bodies were formed. See *De Cael.* I.2–3, 268b11–270b31.

90   If the body between us and a color is sometimes able to be seen through and sometimes not, i.e., is sometimes actually transparent and sometimes only potentially transparent, there must be some difference between the two states. This is called "light," so light must be some new reality or "actuality" of the body which can be transparent. This view seems to be compatible with saying that light is a wave, for a wave is a sort of actuality of a medium.

91   The position that light is an effluence from bodies was held by Empedocles. See *De Sens.* 2, 437b23–438a5; Plato, *Meno*, 87b–e.

92   Aristotle seems to be thinking of the fact that the west lights up the instant the sun rises in the east. Descartes (1596–1650) used a similar argument, based on the eclipses of the moon, to argue that light "travelled" instantaneously. Not until Roemer (1644–1710) observed apparent anomalies in the periods of the moons of Jupiter was the speed of light determined to be finite. Cf. also *De Sens.* 6, 446a20–447a11.

93   Cf. II.7, 418a26–28.

94   Fire, or any other source of light, actualizes the medium through which color is seen, while other sorts of objects of sight require a source of light independent of themselves.

95   II.11, 422b34–423b26.

96   II.9, 421b13–422a6.

97   Aristotle does not believe there are actually voids in the world; here he is speaking to the point that air, which some think is void, carries sound. Cf. *Phys.* IV.6–9, especially IV.6, 213a22–31.

98   II.8, 419b4–18.

99 A quickly vibrating string produces a high note; a slow one, a low note.

100 *De Juv.* 14–16.

101 *De Juv.* 15–16; *PA* III.6, 669a2–5.

102 Aristotle includes in this category crayfish, some crustacea and insects, and lizards. Cf. Ross 1961, *ad loc.*

103 Ross amends the text here so as to have it mean that the names of the scents are taken from the things that have the scents, rather than that the names are taken from the flavors, as the manuscripts seem to say. The text does go on in the following sentence to say that we name these odors from things. It seems that we actually do both: We can say that an odor is "sweet" or that it is "honey-scented." Cf. Ross 1961, *ad loc.*

104 Aristotle is raising a difficulty. Men smell only when breathing in, but some animals, like fish, appear to smell even though they do not breath. Do they, then, have some other sense? As he goes on to argue, the power is defined by its object, here, the sense of smell by odor, so that what senses odor must have the sense of smell. And the odors which are harmful to men also are harmful to these other animals, which implies that they sense what we sense. The explanation is given by way of an analogy to eyes. As hard-eyed animals have no eyelids, and so see whatever is before them, while men have eyelids which must be opened in order to see, so men also have a sort of covering on the sense organ of smell, which needs to be removed in order to smell, but cannot be removed while breathing. Fishes have no such covering.

105 Since the sense of smell is a sort of receptivity (to odor), the sense of smell must be able to receive odor and so cannot be already of itself odorous. This principle, namely, that the knowing power, because it is a receiver, cannot already have what it is going to receive is general in the discussion of the knowing powers of the soul. The knowing power must not have its *per se* object by nature, though it must be capable of receiving that object. Cf. I.5, 409b24–410a23–26; II.5, 416b33–417a9, 417a17–20; II.10, 422b3–5, 15–16; II.11, 424a7–10; III.4, 429a13–21.

106 Aristotle says "extraneous" because he does think flesh is a medium for taste and touch, but not one external to the living body. Cf. II.11, 423b1–26.

107 Aristotle links taste and touch again at III.12, 434b18–24.

108 II.7, 418b13–17.

109 Taste, unlike sight, requires contact with the sensible in order to operate. So were we to taste something placed in water, we would taste it because it is mixed with the water, not because the water is a medium, as the transparent is a medium for color. The flavor would come to us by being mixed with the water or by streaming off from the water to our tongues, which is not the mode of action of a color in the transparent. Still, the color and the flavor are alike proper objects of their respective senses.

110 Another application of the principle that the sense must be receptive of but not have by nature its object.

111 The first question is whether the sense of touch is really one, for it seems to have many proper objects (hot and cold, hard and soft, wet and dry – and modern thinkers might add many more candidates to this array); the second is whether there is a medium for the sense of touch.

112 As to the second question raised at the beginning of the chapter, one might think that

the fact that we immediately sense what touches our skin shows that the flesh is itself the organ of touch. But this does not follow, as the illustration of the membrane shows.

113 If air were organically attached to us in a sort of bubble, we might fall into the error of thinking that the hearing, sight, and smell are one sense, since they are all through the same "organ." But really, there would just be one medium, not one sense power, and that a medium attached to and surrounding us. This is the situation with regard to flesh and touch. So Aristotle suggests that this fact explains why we tend to identify so many apparently disparate sensibles as the objects of touch.

114 Perhaps the argument is something like this: Every animal body must be made of, among the other elements, earth, since only earth has the solidity requisite for the endurance of the body of the animal. But if the body must have the ability to sense by contact (cf. III.12, 434a30–b24), that which makes the contact on the side of the animal will have to remain with the animal and so form something one with it; otherwise what contacts the sensible might become separated from the animal, rendering it useless for the animal. It must be, then, a conjoined sense organ or the conjoined medium of such an organ and form part of the substance of the animal, and so it must be earthy. This earthy part of us is flesh. But if flesh is itself the sense organ, then there would only be one set of tangible sensibles – and yet there are many, as experience teaches us. Therefore, flesh is only the medium of touch, not the organ, and there can be many objects of the sense of touch. The two questions raised at the beginning of the chapter are not independent, for the answer to the first provides evidence bearing on the second.

115 The concern is lest all sensation, including touch, turn out to be through the media of air and water.

116 Aristotle does, then, think that there is always an extraneous medium in sensation, even in the case of touch and taste. But he goes on to distinguish how this happens in the different cases.

117 II.11, 422b34–423a6.

118 This seems to be another argument that flesh is the medium of touch. In the clearer cases, if we place a sensible directly upon the organ of sensation, sensation does not occur; but if we place a sensible object on the skin, we do sense it; so, if this case is like the others, the flesh cannot itself be the sense organ.

119 De Gen. II.3, 330a30–b7.

120 An excess of light destroys the eye (sometimes permanently, sometimes temporarily) and an excess of the tangibles (at least some of them, like heat and coldness) destroys the sense of touch, whether permanently or not. Because the animal must have the sense of touch to be an animal at all, what destroys the sense of touch is also destructive of the animal. Cf. also II.12, 424a27–32; III.2, 426a27–b7; III.12, 434b9–24.

121 For a discussion of this passage, see Appendix 4, The Sensing Soul.

122 The power of a sense organ is in the sense organ, which itself is a bodily, dimensional object, but the power itself is not such. It is a "ratio" or something given in an account, something more formal than material.

123 In saying the sense is a "ratio" {λόγος}, Aristotle may simply mean it is formal, it is what defines the subject that has it, as sight defines the eye. The present sentence, though, might incline us to think of it more particularly as a proportion of elements or parts, a proportion which might be severely disturbed by overpowering sensible objects.

124 Cf. II.11, 424a2–10.

125 A question perhaps motivated by the previous remark that plants are affected by tangible things even though they do not have the sense of touch. Can other sensibles also affect things that do not have sensation?

126 Aristotle considers flavor to be a kind of tangible object. Cf. III.12, 434b18–24.

127 It seems that all physical change occurs due to sensible qualities having to do with touch, like hardness, sharpness, dryness, heat, weight, etc. Cf. *De Gen.* II.3, 330a30–b7.

128 Some bodies, like air and water, are affected by odor and sound, but this is a reception into material, as opposed to the immaterial reception found in sensation. The air does not smell the smell it receives, it simply becomes smelly. This last part of the chapter may look like an aside, but it does bring to the fore the distinction between the ways the sensitive and the non-sensitive receive.

Endnotes to Book III

1   Having discussed each of the five external senses in II.7–11, Aristotle is now trying to show that his account of the exterior senses is complete. After this argument that we have covered all the possible proper senses, he goes on to argue that there is no sense power of which the proper object is the common sensibles, (425a14–b4), then that there is a sense power common to all the senses (III.2) and finally, before going on to the intellect in III.4–8, that the imagination and the intellect are distinct powers. (III.3)

2   The text here seems to contradict what was said in II.6, 418a7–25 and implied just below at III.1, 425a27–8. The Greek manuscripts read as I have translated them, but the mediaeval Latin translation by William of Moerbeke, a translation of noteworthy literalness, does have the word "not" and so would be translated, "by each sense not accidentally," agreeing with the other passages. On the other hand, one might think Aristotle here responds to someone who erroneously thinks that there is a proper organ for the common sensibles, and draws out the result, namely, that then the common sensibles would be sensed accidentally, contrary to fact.

3   Does he mean "by motion" as by something perceived or as by an alteration in the sense organ? Both Simplicius and St. Thomas Aquinas take him to mean the latter. Cf. Simplicius 2000, p. 34; Thomas Aquinas, 1984, L. III, l. 1.

4   Cf. II.6, 418a20–24.

5   The external sense powers do not sense each other's proper objects except accidentally. The eye does not see the sweet, nor is it directly affected by the sweet, but it does perceive what is sweet when it perceives the color of what is sweet, e.g., the whiteness of sugar. The quality sensed is joined with another quality which is sensed by another sense power, but the objects of the two senses do not directly affect each other's proper senses. These sensible qualities are therefore sensed accidentally by each other's sense powers. If, then, there were a proper sense power for the common sensibles, the latter would be only accidentally sensed by the five proper senses we have already distinguished. But this is false; therefore there is no such proper sense power for the common sensibles.

6   Because there is no sense of yellow and bitter as one object, we easily are deceived, judging when we see one of the two that the other must be present; but this is not so.

7   Here Aristotle uses a final cause to explain something common to many species, namely, that many kinds of animals have more than one sort of sense power. Such generic or specific characteristics (such as having both sight and touch) can be explained by a final cause, whereas mere individual traits (such as having blue eyes) are explained by material and efficient causes. Cf. *Gen. An.* V.1, 778a30–b19.

8   That we sense that we sense is indicated by the fact that we can, for example, drive

a car without being aware of our travel (when the road is very familiar) and by the phenomenon of blindsight, a condition in which a person who is not conscious of their sight will still be able to respond to visual stimuli. Though the person can actually see, he is not aware of his seeing; this seems odd because most of us do sense our sensing. And the fact that we are aware of the individual act of sensing indicates that it is an object of sense, not of intellect, if the mind is of universals and the sense of particulars. Cf. II.5, 417b22–23.

9   The sense by which we sense our seeing either is the same power as that by which we sense colors outside of ourselves or is a different power. However we settle that issue, the power that sees our seeing must see both the seeing and also the object of the seeing (i.e., the color). This power, then, sees color. But if the senses are defined through their objects, and the power in question sees color, then that power must be the sight by which we see the colors outside of ourselves. Consequently, the power by which we sense sensing and by which we sense the exterior sensible is the same power. The following sentence will, as the first word indicates, give another argument to the same effect. But after that, Aristotle begins to argue that a different power is needed, and this will be his final position. Cf. *Somn.* 2, 455a14–26.

10   If I see my seeing, my sight must be colored, contrary to what was said above. Cf. II.11 424a7–10.

11   We can recognize that we are not seeing when it is dark; we do this by "sight," or some sense power, for we are aware of it in the particular. So in some way we do not need color to see. But the eye is not seeing when this happens. So the power by which we see our seeing is not the power by which we see exterior colors.

12   Because the sense power is moved by the sensible, it receives what that agent has to give it, e.g., color. So when it senses, the sight is colored, but not in the way the exterior body is, because it receives the sensible without the matter. Cf. II.12, 424a17–24 and Appendix 4, *The Sensing Soul.*

13   III.2, 426a15–19.

14   *Phys.* III.3, 202a13–21.

15   The fact that the motion is in the mobile and not in the moving cause shows that it is not necessary that the mover be in motion simply because it causes motion, though in the cases we see around us this is always the case: If I put a piece of lighted coal into a bucket of cold water, the water will be heated but it will also cool the coal. That the moving cause need not be moved by a prior moving cause is shown at *Phys.* VIII.5, 256b3–257a33.

16   Because the acts of the sensible and of the sensitive are in the sensitive, and the act of the sensible is sound or color, the sensitive power must in some way possess sound or color.

17   That is, they are one in subject but two in definition, as a curved line is one and is both concave and convex, even though to be concave is not to be convex.

18   Cf. *Phys.* II.3, 195b16–21.

19   Perhaps Aristotle means Protagoras (cf. *Meta.* IX.3, 1047a4–7) or Democritus (cf. Fr. 125).

20   Cf. II.12, 424a24–32.

21   By "the ultimate sense organ" Aristotle seems to mean the organ of the common sense, and the common sense, being able to sense everything sensible, seems to be a fundamental root of sensibility. We might think this is flesh since flesh is the organ

or medium of touch and every sensitive thing must have touch. (Cf. II.11, 422b32–423a21; III.12, 434b11–18) But if this were so, we could distinguish all sorts of sensibles from each other merely by touching them; in fact, we could not distinguish them without touching them, if flesh operates as an organ or medium by being in contact.

22   The power by which the sensibles sensed by each of the five exterior sense powers are distinguished is called the "common sense."

23   The problem (426b29–427a1) is that a thing cannot undergo contrary movements at once or be subject to contrary qualities at once, but the sense power that discerns the difference between black and white must do so. The first response (427a2–5) is that the power is one but it is in potency to these contraries. This is insufficient (427a5–9) because it must have these contraries in act when it tells them apart, so it must have the contraries together not only in potency but in act. Aristotle suggests (427a9–16) a likeness to a point: A point which divides a line is one point but has two actual (not merely potential) aspects, it is the end of one part and the beginning of the other. The sense that distinguishes different sensibles must be like that. Cf. also De Sens. 7, 449a5–20; Somn. 2, 455a12–27.

24   Aristotle will now move on to the consideration of another aspect of the soul. What he does in fact is discuss imagination next (III.3), distinguishing it from the exterior senses and from intellect, and then go on to intellect. (III.4–8)

25   Cf. I.2, 403b24–27, 405b11–12.

26   Empedocles, Fr. 106.

27   Empedocles, Fr. 108.

28   The complete sentence in Homer reads: "For the mind of earthy men is such as the day the father of men and gods may bring forth." Odyssey XVIII, 136–7.

29   Cf. I.5, 409b26–28. Aristotle does not simply reject this view, but qualifies it. Whereas Empedocles holds that what is known must be in the knower in the same way as it is in the exterior world, for which reasons Aristotle criticizes him (cf. I.5, 409b23–410a22), Aristotle holds that the sense is potentially like the sensible and that the sensible is not received by the sense in a material but in an immaterial way. See II.5, 416b32–417b16; II.12, 424a17–24; and Appendix 4, The Sensing Soul.

30   Necessary, that is, if knowing is the touching of like by like. The idea that knowing is a sort of contact or touching of the knower and the known was introduced at I.3, 407a10–18 and is implicit in some later texts, e.g., II.5, 416b33–35 and III.2, 426a2–11. It seems correct to speak this way insofar as awareness of an object is a way of its being present to our knowing power.

31   Democritus; cf. I.2, 404a27–31.

32   Because our awareness is the contact of the like in us with what is like it outside of us, and this is knowing, whatever awareness we have is in fact correct, even if different persons have different perceptions. This possibility, that all appearances are true, is not criticized here, but is taken up in Meta. IV.5, 1010b1–1011a2.

33   For example, we know sickness by the knowledge we have of health, darkness by the knowledge of light, etc.

34   This argument makes no assumption to the effect that understanding or judging is proper to human beings, only that some animals have sense without judgment or understanding.

35   II.6, 418a11–12; III.3, 428b18–19.

36 We can call up any images we please but we cannot form opinions as we please – we are constrained by what we think is true.

37 Cf. *Nic. Eth.* VI.3–11.

38 Here Aristotle treats belief and imagination as species of understanding. He will treat imagination in the present chapter and the power of belief (of forming and adhering to propositions) in III.4–8, 429a10–432a14. These two powers are often identified, as for example by Hume and the other Empiricists, and not without cause, though, if Aristotle is right, erroneously. The noun νοῦς (which corresponds to the articular infinitive τὸ νοεῖν used here) is sometimes translated "mind," as this English word seems to include both intellect and imagination (as well as memory and any other interior knowing powers). When taken more narrowly, it (and its cognates) can refer to the intellect as opposed to the imagination or sense and even to the particular act and the particular habit of the intellect by which it grasps the first principles of thought.

39 Perhaps Aristotle means that all animals have the power of sensation, but not all have imagination. See the next sentence, where he moves on, seemingly in contrast to the present sentence, to oppose imagination with actual sensation.

40 Aristotle attributes a kind of prudence, and so, it would seem, imagination, to ants and bees; see *Meta.* I.1, 980b22–25; *PA* II.2, 648a5–8; *PA* II.4, 650b18–27. He attributes to some imperfect animals, among which he may include worms, only an "indeterminate" imagination. See III.11, 433b31–434a5.

41 Senses are true in that they correspond to their objects, but the imagination represents things which are not real, and so is in a sense false. Cf. II.6, 418a12.

42 The Greek verb has the same root as the noun translated by "imagination."

43 Here the word translated "understanding" stands in contrast to "imagination," whereas before at III.3, 427b27–28 it was used as a sort of genus of imagination and belief and at 428a5 the question posed was whether or not it *should* be contrasted with understanding or intellect. Having shown that imagination is not sensation, he goes on to two of the other possibilities mentioned at III.3, 428a1–5.

44 The final possibility mentioned at III.3, 428a1–5.

45 In this, it is like imagination and unlike sensation, science, and understanding.

46 Cf. Plato, *Sophist*, 264b.

47 If I have a true opinion about the real size of the sun, my opinion can only become false if I change my mind or forget my opinion, or else if the thing itself changes. Suppose the thing does not change and I do not forget or change my opinion, and suppose that imagination is the interweaving of opinion and sense. The sense is wrong about the size of the sun – it looks like it is a foot across. So if I maintain my true opinion and then look at the sun, my imagination will be both true and false.

48 Having said what imagination is not, Aristotle now goes on to say what it is.

49 Aristotle is thinking of something like a hand moving a stick which in turn moves a stone.

50 By saying imagination is a "certain motion," Aristotle seems to mean that it is some sort of alteration of an organ or power. Cf. III.1, 425a16–21.

51 The motion in question is the alteration of the imagination.

52 Which characteristics does Aristotle have in mind? Presumably being derived from sensations and so being present only in what has sensation and being of what has already been sensed (in the sense that the components of imaginations are things

that have been sensed), and being able to be wrong in the absence of sense. That animals do many things because of imagination is another property of imagination explained by its being an alteration derived from sense, as Aristotle says immediately hereafter. The argument here, then, is from properties to definition.

53 Cf. I.1, 403a10–15; II.2, 413b13–27. Having dealt with the imagination in the previous chapter, Aristotle now goes on to treat the intellect or mind, which he here identifies with judging and knowing, and earlier had apparently identified with the power which gives rise to opinion. (III.3, 427b27–29) The word translated "separable" could also be translated "separated," a fact which might lead one to think Aristotle believes the intellect to be simply a separate being from the body and from the soul. So it is important to note that he refers explicitly here to "the *part of the soul* by which it both knows and judges." The intellect is not some being other than the soul, but is a "part" (or power) of it. Earlier too, he had spoken of the powers of the soul, including the intellect, as its "parts." (Cf., e.g., I.1, 402b9–16; II.2, 413b7–15; II.11, 423a17–18; II.12, 424a32–34.) Note too, that he subordinates the question of the intellect's separability to the question of its nature and operation. This is in accord with the criterion of separability given earlier, at I.1, 403b10–11. Cf. also Appendix 5, *Intellect in the De Anima.*

54 The fact that many people confuse understanding and sensing, at least to the extent that they think understanding is the same as imagination, points to the likeness Aristotle is interested in here. Both sensing and understanding are forms of awareness of the world and are brought into actuality from potency by the action of the object of knowledge upon the knowing power. Cf. II.5, 416b33–35, 417b2–16.

55 That the understanding is "impassible" {ἀπαθές} but still a kind of "suffering" {πάσχειν} and "receptive of the species" {δεκτικόν τοῦ εἴδους} is recognized by the comparison with sensation. That these predicates are not contradictory is due to the equivocation explained at II.5, 416b32–417b16. There Aristotle argued that to receive something in the way an inanimate body does involves losing a characteristic and so "suffering;" but to receive something in sensation or intellection does not involve loss, but only fulfillment of a potency. (Cf. also II.12, 424a17–24.) Sensation and intellection therefore involve "suffering" only if said equivocally, and are "impassible" because they receive without the destruction which usually attends reception of a form.

56 Anaxagoras, Fr. 12. While it is true that the ruler must be separate from the ruled in order to command, it is more pertinent to Aristotle's consideration that the knower must be separate from what it knows, otherwise it could hardly receive it.

57 Since knowing is by way of reception, and one cannot receive what one already has, the presence within a knowing power of any particular quality would prevent that power from perceiving the quality, as our hands do not feel their own temperature. It is also possible to translate the sentence, "For what appears within hinders and screens what is outside." In either case, the sense is that, if the intellect had some physical nature (like flesh or coldness), it would be by that fact prevented from perceiving correctly what is outside, e.g., we do not feel temperatures correctly when our hands are too hot or cold.

58 Since the mind can know the natures of all sensible things, it cannot have the form of any sensible thing before receiving a form from an intelligible, natural thing, such as it would necessarily have if it had a corporeal organ. So it has no nature but to be

in potency to such intelligible forms. The natures of other things, i.e., immaterial things, if there are any, are known only by way of arguments from what we know about the sensible world. (In fact, this chapter contains just such an argument that the intellect is not a material, sensible thing.)

59   Aristotle may make this qualification to indicate that he is not speaking of the divine intellect, which never has to go through any process but is purely actual. Cf. *Meta.* XII.6, 1071b19–20; *Meta.* XII.7, 1072a24–26.

60   Consequently, the intellect cannot be a body or a form of a body, but must be an immaterial power. At I.1, 403b10–11, Aristotle had said if there is an operation of the soul which is not the operation of an organ, then the part of the soul which performs that operation would be independent of matter. Here Aristotle has argued, based on its object, to the immateriality of the intellect. Note, too, that Aristotle emphasizes that he is speaking here of the intellect of the soul, not of some other intellect, perhaps because he has just mentioned Anaxagoras' "Mind," which Anaxagoras took to be the first principle of the universe.

61   Cf. the notes to the previous four sentences. Note that, while the senses lack what they receive, the intellect, because it is not receptive of merely one sort of sensible object, e.g., color or sound, but of all natural forms, must be not only lacking this or that sort of natural form, but every sort, and so must be incorporeal.

62   Perhaps a reference to Plato, *Parmenides*, 132b.

63   When the intellect has learned something but is not actually considering what it knows, it is still in potency to that actual consideration. Cf. II.5, 417a22–29. In such a condition, it can be brought into operation at will, just as a piano player can play at will by actualizing his habitual ability. So too the geometer can consider his knowledge whenever he pleases.

64   Because the intellect is a pure potency, and potency can only be known through act, the intellect can only be known after it has taken on some form by way of an encounter with external reality. The human mind is therefore only known by reflection on its habits and operations of knowing other things. I may know my own act of knowing, but that act cannot itself be the knowledge of another act of knowing, and so on forever – there must be at the origin a knowing of something else. (I have retained here the reading of the manuscripts; some translators alter the text so as to have the sentence end, "...understand through itself.")

65   Having shown that the intellect is immaterial from the fact that any material thing can be an object of the intellect, Aristotle now goes on to specify that object more completely. For though all natural things are knowable by the intellect, it knows them first and foremost under a certain aspect or formality, namely, as to *what* they are. This need not mean perfect knowledge of what they are, of course; as *Phys.* I.1 argues, our initial knowledge is very vague and confused.

66   Material things like horses are combinations of form and matter, and what they are is not identical to the one they are, as this horse Trigger is not simply what a horse is, otherwise every horse would be that horse. Similarly, to be a circle is not to be this circle, so there can be many circles. Aristotle uses two natural examples (water and flesh) and one mathematical example (magnitude) to indicate that in the cases of these two sort of things, what a thing is and which one it is are not the same. (The present paragraph emphasizes the natural; the subsequent, the mathematical.) But things that are not combinations of form and matter, but are instead purely immaterial

substances, are the same as what they are. Cf. *Meta.* VII.6, 1031a15–1032a11; VII.11, 1037a29–b6. Cf. also I.1, 403b7–16. These are not proper objects of the human intellect because they cannot be perceived by way of separating their essences from phantasms. Cf. Appendix 5, *Intellect in the De Anima* ; *DA* III.8, 432a3–10; *De Mem.* 1, 449b30–450a25.

67   The expressions "to be flesh," "to be water," etc., signify the whatness or essence of a thing, while the expressions "flesh," "water," etc., signify individual things that have those natures. Because these are different objects of knowledge there must be some difference in the powers by which they are known (cf. I.1, 402b9–16 and II.4, 415a16–22), or else the same power must know both but in somehow different ways. The understanding can know what things are but the senses cannot; to know this particular thing just as a thing with this or that essence, then, the intellect must come into play and so too must that which grasps the particular, i.e., sensation or imagination. So the mind sees its own object, what a thing is, as it were directly, but sees that this thing in front of it is an instance of a certain sort of thing by reflecting back on the origin of its knowledge of the essence in the exterior thing or its image in the imagination. (This relation to the imagination will be clarified below at III.7, 431a14–b2.) It seems that the intellect, because it knows that the universal is not the particular, must know both in some way, just as sense must know both white and sweet in order to tell them apart. II.2, 426b12–29.

68   The word translated "abstraction" {ἀφαίρεσις} is not used by Aristotle for the grasping of a universal but for that separation of form from matter which we encounter in mathematical reasoning. In the English philosophical tradition it is also used of the abstraction of a universal from particulars. In this translation, and the one of the *Physics* (Coughlin 2005), I only and always use the English "abstraction" to translate this word. I do not observe this restriction in the notes and appendices, however, as the English is open to the other meaning.

69   Here the "continuous" is the homogeneous extension of mathematics.

70   A common expression in Aristotle for the nature or essence or whatness of a thing.

71   As he often does, Aristotle uses as an example not his own opinion but that of some other philosopher. He probably has the Pythagoreans in mind. Cf. *Meta.* VII.11, 1036b12–13.

72   Aristotle seems to be making the same point about mathematical objects as he made in the previous paragraph about sensible ones. The intellect grasps the essence of mathematical objects but it is the imagination that perceives the particular instance of a line; the intellect sees that nature in the particular line by looking back to the source of its knowledge. Cf. also *Po. An.* II.19, 99b32–100a5.

73   Because the essence or whatness of even a sensible thing is removed from the particular matter that embodies it (as what a horse is is common to all horses and does not involve the particular flesh and bones of this or that horse), and the proper object of the intellect is the essence, the mind seems to be related to things in so far as they are universal and removed from matter. Still, the precise object of the intellect is not the universal as such, but the whatness of a material thing.

Aristotle does not consider here the way the mind seizes upon purely immaterial things, which are formally treated in metaphysics, presumably because they are not seized through experience, as are, each in their own way, the objects of natural philosophy and of mathematics. It is a question whether there is any philosophy beyond natural philosophy; this is answered when we prove the existence of some immaterial thing. Cf. *Meta.* VI.1, 1026a27–32.

74   The reason one thinks there must be something common to the thing that acts and the thing it acts upon is that they share material of some sort: When a warm rock heats water, the material of the water must be capable of taking on the form which is in the material of the rock, so those two materials must be of the same sort – especially if the action is reciprocal (as when the water cools the rock in return). Cf. *De Gen.* I.7, 323b1–324a9.

75   If the intellect understands itself, it does so either through itself or through another. If through itself and not by something added to it, while "to be intelligible" means one thing (or "is one in species"), and other things (like flesh and line) are also intelligible, they must be the same sorts of things as the mind. If, on the other hand, the intellect understands itself through another, by "something mixed with it," while "to be intelligible" again means one thing, the other things too, since they are also intelligible, must be such as the mind is when that other factor is added to it.

76   Aristotle answers the first question. "Suffering" {τὸ πάσχειν} is equivocal, as was noted earlier. (II.5, 417b2–7) When the intellect learns, it does not suffer in the sense that it is damaged or loses any positive quality. It may accidentally lose something, e.g., an erroneous opinion, but this is not necessary to learning. So the commonness expected between agent and patient (here, intelligible and intellect) is not like that found in physical changes, a commonness of matter, but is only of what is in potency to the form, in the one case in an immaterial way, in the other, in a material way.

77   Aristotle answers the second question. The actually intelligible is indeed one sort of thing: It is the presence of a intelligible object (a whatness) to the intellect. The intellect, to be in act, needs to have the intelligible added to it (because it is in itself only a potency or a "blank slate"), but when it is in act it is intelligible as are other things, namely by being the intelligible object immaterially. If we actually know things, they themselves, and not just their likenesses, must be present in our minds; if not, we will never be able to get from the thing present in our mind to the thing which we know, as the history of modern philosophy since Descartes indicates. But, as we saw in criticizing Empedocles, the things known cannot be in the intellect materially, as if we had little horses in our heads when we know what a horse is (see I.5, 410a10–13). Instead, Aristotle says, we have the nature or whatness of horse in our head, but this does not include the matter by which a horse is this or that horse, so we have universal knowledge of the whatness of material things. Aristotle thus preserves the important insight of Empedocles while rejecting the imprecision which makes the position impossible. Cf. III.3, 425b22–426a15.

78   If possessing the form of the intelligible is the ground of intelligibility, why shouldn't everything, e.g., trees, understand? They are united to their own forms, after all, and this so long as they exist. But they have them in the material way, and knowing is the immaterial possession of a form. (Cf. II.12, 424a17–24 and Appendices 4 and 5). A question then arises: How can the form of a material object come to be in the intellect in an immaterial way? This question is addressed in the next chapter. Some commentators think that the "agent intellect" of III.5 is superfluous for Aristotle's account. See Caston 1999, pp. 199–205. This is far from the case. Rather, without the agent intellect, the possible intellect could never come into act because the potentially intelligible objects found in the material world are just

that, potentially intelligible; they cannot bring themselves into actuality, nor, which amounts to the same thing, can they of themselves act on the possible intellect.

79   Where there are things which are sometimes in potency and sometimes in act, there must be both a thing which can become each of those things in act (something potential) and also something which can actualize that potential (an agent, which is something in act). Cf. III.7, 431a1–4; *Meta.* IX.8, 1049b17–29.

80   The so–called "possible intellect" (III.4, 429a21–22) was discussed in the previous chapter. Note that the intelligible species come to be in this power. ("Possible intel-lect," "agent intellect," and "intelligible species" are names used by the later Aristotelian tradition, but not by Aristotle himself, though he does use very similar expressions.)

81   The active principle spoken of here (the agent intellect) is like light because it illu-minates the phantasms in the imagination. The "possible intellect" is like the eye and the phantasms are like the colors, as will be clearer later. (III.7, 431a14–15, 431b2) It seems that, just as the light and the color do not see, so neither this active principle nor the phantasm knows. The "intelligible species" comes to be in the pos-sible intellect, and when that species is actually present, there follows in the possible intellect the operation of knowing. III.4, 429b5–7.

82   Aristotle argued in the previous chapter that the possible intellect (spoken of here as "material") is separate from body, impassible, and unmixed (III.4, 429a18, 429a24–25, 429b4–5, 23–24); the agent intellect is just that, a sort of agent, so it must be more perfect or actual than what is potential (since nothing which is only able to be, as such, can do anything. *Meta.* IX.8, 1049b24–26) Here Aristotle expresses this by saying it is "in substance act" and "more honorable." Since it is more actual, it is even less tied up with the potency of material than is the possible intellect, so that the agent intellect too must be separate from body, impassible, and unmixed. But this of course in no way undoes the argument of the previous chapter to the effect that the possible intellect is unmixed and impassible and separate from body; rather the argument of this chapter uses that claim as a premise.

83   Here Aristotle shifts from speaking of the powers of mind (agent and possible intel-lects) to their actuality, "science according to act." That science in act is the same as the thing known was advanced in the previous chapter and will be returned to short-ly. Cf. III.4, 430a4–5; III.7, 431a14–15. The actual presence of the known in the knower is knowledge. Before the agent intellect has acted to make the form of the knowable immaterially present to the possible intellect, there is only potential knowledge.

84   Each human mind goes from being able to know, i.e., being able to receive the form of the intelligible object, to knowing actually, i.e., actually having that form. Yet an actually knowing mind always exists before the mind which comes to know, either a human teacher, or at least the first principle of the universe, which Aristotle argues is an intellect. This first intellect ultimately accounts for the intelligibility of the uni-verse. Cf. *Po. An.* I.1, 71a1–11; *Meta.* IX.8, 1049b5–25; *Meta.* XII.7, 1072a26–b14. Some translators excise this and the previous sentence, though they are found in all the manuscripts. They are repeated at III.7, 431a1–3, leading them to think the pres-ent occurrence may be an error of transcription.

85   To have the operation of knowledge (as opposed to the mere power or habit), no actuality beyond that furnished by the agent intellect (i.e., the illumination of the

phantasms and the consequent presence of the species in the possible intellect) is required. When this situation obtains, there is always knowing in act. Some read this sentence as referring to the divine mind discussed in *Meta.* XII.7–10. The previous sentences clearly refer to the operation of a mind which can go from potency to act, however, and it seems that such a mind should be understood as the unstated subject of this sentence.

86 When the mind is separated, it still exists. It is immortal and eternal. Some thinkers take this sentence to refer only to the agent intellect, and, further, take that agent intellect to be the divine mind. The "this" in the sentence cannot refer only to the agent or only to the possible intellect, because both have been seen to be immaterial and therefore not subject to corruption. (*Phys.* I.7, 190b10–17) The premise for this conclusion seems to be that if a thing has an operation separate from body, then it can be without body. (I.1, 403a10–11) The various hints that the intellect might be separable from the body have now found their resolution in this claim of the immateriality and thus the eternality of the intellect. Aristotle does not go back on his definition of the soul as the form of an organized body, so that this thinking soul, which at least human beings have, is at once the form of a body and separable from the body. It is the form of a body, but not *only* the form of a body. When he says it is eternal, then, he may mean either that it preexists the body but comes to be united to a body as its form, or that it begins to be with the body of which it is the form (as do other forms), but can maintain its existence afterwards. The former position would contradict and the latter agree, however, with what he says about the relation of form and matter, and in particular about reason, in *Meta.* XII.3, 1070a21–26.

87 The last two sentences each have a "this." It seems only natural to say that they refer to the "this" of the previous sentence and so to the whole intellect, or perhaps to the soul that has the powers of intellect. The question is, if the mind is separable, can it understand after death? Aristotle seems to say that it cannot, at least in the same way as it does while the human being is alive, because the human depends on "the mind which is able to suffer" {παθετικος} in order to understand, and this can be destroyed. This cannot, though, refer to the "possible" {δυνατον} intellect of the previous chapter, which was said to be separable from the body, that is, immaterial; if it is such, it cannot be destroyed. (*Phys.* I.7, 190b10–17) It has to refer, then, to something destructible but able to be called "intellect" or "νοῦς;" that can only be the imagination. See III.3, 427b27–29; 433a9–10.

88 While the intellect does not operate through a bodily organ, it still learns through the body by feeding off the senses; later, Aristotle will say the intellect must use phantasms (images in the imagination, though not necessarily visual or simple images) to think. (III.7, 431a14–15) This explains why the intellect, even though it is itself immaterial, can be affected by problems in the imagination or the sense organs. The sentence could also be translated: "Without this, nothing thinks."

89 Aristotle here goes on to speak of the way the intellect grasps complex objects. The fact that he here speaks about how the intellect works, which seems to be a continuation of III.4, is a problem for those who wish to say that III.5 is an excursus about the divine intellect or some other non-human and purely immaterial substance. It would make more sense to interpret III.5 as part of that project. Cf. Gerson 2004, n. 2.

90 Empedocles, Fr. 57.

91   Empedocles, Fr. 20.

92   In III.4–5, Aristotle restricted his considerations to our knowledge of simple ideas abstracted directly from experience. Here he speaks of the combination of such concepts into propositions, wherein truth and falsity primarily reside. Cf. *Cat.* 4, 2a4–10; *De Int.* 1, 16a9–18.

93   That is, whatever can be affirmed can also be denied. Or the sentence may be translated, "One can call all of these 'division' as well." When we predicate one thing of another, one can consider either the division of the subject and predicate from each other or else their combination into one statement.

94   Aristotle qualifies the claim that statements about the future are always true or false in *De Int.*, 9, 18a28–19b4.

95   It is odd that Aristotle compares the mind's work of combining simple ideas into sentences with Empedocles' notion of Love and Strife mindlessly combining parts of animals into wholes. Perhaps he means to point out that simple notions do not of themselves always fit together well, so that we easily have statements combining predicates and subjects which ought not to be together, resulting in false statements, somewhat as Empedocles speaks of the heads of men being put onto the bodies of oxen, resulting in beasts which cannot survive. (Empedocles, Fr. 61) This contrasts with the truth of what is apprehended simply. III.6, 430a26–28, 430b26–30.

96   Having introduced indivisible objects of thought and unions of such indivisibles into statements, Aristotle is now concerned to show how the mind grasps these composites.

97   A line, for example, is a whole composed of parts. How can we think that? As a whole, it must be grasped by a single thought; as having parts, the parts must each be grasped separately, which seems to divide thought and the time of thought. (He is not, as he was above, thinking of the tense of the verb in a statement, but of the time taken to think a statement.) If we think the whole, we think the parts only in potency and do so in a unified time; but if we think the parts as actually separated, we think them in separated times. So too, a statement insofar as it is thought of as a complete statement must be thought in a unified time, but if we consider the subject and predicate apart from each other, then they are thought in separate times. Cf. III.2, 426b12–29.

98   Some editors move this sentence to 430b20; I have kept the manuscripts' reading.

99   There are things which are one by continuity, like a line or a stretch of time, and things which are one by having one species or notion, like an animal or a house. Even the line and the stretch of time, though, are one in species. In either case, then, the mind can grasp by a simple apprehension what these things are, and in an indivisible time. If the species cannot be separated in reality from the particular animal or the particular line, it is still not the same as these and can be grasped separately. Insofar as the predicate of a statement is a light in virtue of which we understand the subject, the unity of the predicate with the subject is akin to the unity of the species with the particular animal or line and can be grasped separately as well as in its unity with the subject. To form the statement, both the subject and predicate must be grasped, and they must also be compared in a single act of the mind. Cf. III.2, 436b12–29.

100 A privation, like blindness, is only known by knowing the opposed state, in this case, sight. So too, what is indivisible in the sense that it cannot have division is

knowable only by knowing the opposed divisible thing, as we know a point by what has parts. (Euclid, *Elements* I, Def. 1: "A point is that which has no parts.") In knowing one thing through another, there is something of potency in the act of knowing, since the first thing known is a principle from which the other comes to be known. If, then, there is something which does not know opposites in this way, it would be a knower without potency. Such is the first principle of the universe in Aristotle's view. (Cf. *Meta.* XII.6, 1071b19–22; 7, 1072b26–30) Since our minds know by gathering from sensation and piecing together the notions so gathered, our knowing is not like this, but is such as has been described in the previous two paragraphs.

101 For the comparison to sense, cf. II.6, 4181a11–17; III.3, 428b18–22. Aristotle said earlier that truth and falsity are only in combinations. (Cf. III.6, 430a26–31) Here he grants a sort of truth to simple sensible and simple intellectual apprehension on the grounds that the sense or the mind is in conformity with the way things are, as the eye seeing a color properly sees the color that is there and the mind thinking of "triangle" thinks a real nature. When we combine thoughts, though, we can go astray, as, e.g., when we think the white thing we see is a man whereas it is really a mannequin.

102 Either Aristotle means to say that immaterial things do not know by combinations of thoughts, so they do not go astray, or else that if an immaterial thing were to be understood, the knower could not go astray in knowing it. Cf. *Meta.* IX.10, 1051b17–32.

103 Cf. III.2, 425b26–28; 426a15–19; III.5, 430a19–21.

104 How is the second sentence a premise for the first? Maybe Aristotle means that because the sense power is not really altered by the sensible object (II.5, 417b2–12), it is *only* brought from potency to act and not from one act to another.

105 *Phys.* III.2, 201b27–32; *Meta.* IX.6, 1048b17–36. When the act of physical motion is occurring, the subject of the motion is still in potency to the term of the motion and so is still imperfect; when that term is realized, the motion is over. Sensation and intellection, on the other hand, maintain while knowing a steady gaze upon their objects and do not tend to any term beyond what is seen in that gaze; instead, they already possess perfectly the act which the object induces in them.

106 II.11, 424a5–10; III.2, 426b3–7.

107 This seems to mean that there is no separate organ or power of appetite beyond the sensitive organ or power, but that there is still a difference in definition between the power or organ as perceiving and as desiring. Aristotle starts with pleasure and pain and desire in the sensitive appetites in order to pave the way to an understanding of the relation of the intellect to the phantasms. As the senses detect objects which please or pain them, and desire or aversion follows upon this, so the intellect recognizes things, in some cases as good or bad for us, and then, in these cases, pursues or avoids those things.

108 Thus, the intellect sees, as it were, its intelligible object by looking to the phantasms. As in the analogy in III.5, the agent intellect is like a light shining on a color which the eye sees; here, we are further told that the object of the intellect is seen in the phantasms of the imagination.

109 The intellect recognizes an object as good, and some desire follows upon this recognition. But without a particular object, no actual action could follow. The mind must be seeing this goodness in the particular which ends up being pursued. Since all this

can take place in the absence of actual sensation, e.g., in dreams, the particular object must be presented to the intellect by some power which recognizes the particular and can still present the particular even when it is absent. That is the imagination. (Cf. III.2, 425b22–24; III.3, 428a5–8, 429a4–8) So Aristotle says that, due to these facts, the intellect must see its objects in the phantasms of the imagination.

110 Cf. III.2, 426b17–19, 427a2–5. These two sentences might read more naturally as a longer but incomplete sentence. It would then read, "As the air made the pupil of a certain sort, while the pupil [made] another [of a certain sort] (and so too in hearing), while the extreme [of the senses] is one and is one mean, though its being is many...."

111 III.2, 426b12–427a14.

112 Cf. *De Sens.* 7, 448b17–449a20. This paragraph presents many problems and there are many interpretations of it. The following is an interpretation in seven parts. (1) The first three sentences refer to the common sense as a single term of sensation and notes that that term is one in number but many in being or definition. (III.2, 427a2–5) Aristotle says we have to speak of this power again. Why? Sandwiched as this paragraph is between texts which indicate that the intellect "sees" its objects in the phantasms (431a14–17 and 431b2–5), it seems likely that Aristotle is thinking of some parallel between the way the intellect and the common sense relate to their respective objects. (2) The sweet and the hot are one in number (in one subject) and one by proportion (because they are to the powers of taste and touch in the same way); it (the power of common sense) relates to sweet and hot as sweet is related to hot – the perception of sweet is to the perception of hot as sweet is to hot. (3) He says the situation with the proper sensibles of one sense is explained in the same way and (presumably because it is more obvious that they are judged by one power) he uses the objects of one sense, white and black, to make his point. (4) Thus, A : B :: C : D, that is, white is to black as the perception of white is to the perception of black. So, alternately, white is to the perception of white as black is to the perception of black. (5) So the perceptions of white and of black are to the power that distinguishes them, sight or the common sense, as white is to black; although in exterior reality these cannot be in one subject (in one part, anyway), they can and must be in one part in the power that distinguishes them. (III.2, 426b17–23) (6) And "that other," the power of intellect, is so related to the perceptions of the sensibles and to their remnants, the phantasms (III.2, 425b23–25; III.3, 428b10–17) as the exterior sense powers are related to their various objects. (7) Finally, we could have said similar things using not various objects of one sense but objects of various senses, e.g., sweet and white.

The upshot of the paragraph may be that the intellect has to compare things which are distinct in knowledge (when, e.g., it compares subjects and predicates in a statement) and to do so it must both be able to perceive them each and to perceive them together. This is like what the proper senses do with regard to their own objects and what the common sense does with regard to all the objects of the senses. But for the intellect to do this, it must have presented to it separately the things to be compared, just as the eye needs to see the black and the white in different places or the common sense needs to have hot and sweet presented to it by different senses. Since we come to know from sensation, the natures we grasp when we know must be presented to us by sensation and its more flexible cousin, imagination. The natures we compare are presented in different phantasms or images; the phantasms are then necessary for our knowing.

113 The common what? It would seem that Aristotle means the common sense (the Greek noun for which is feminine, and so would agree with the grammar here), but earlier Aristotle had said there is no common sense for the common sensibles like motion. (III.1, 425a14–b4) Even then, he did say that "we already have common sensation, not accidentally, of the common sensibles." (III.1, 425a27–28) Here, then, he may be referring to the common sense as the root of all sensing. Cf. *Somn.* 2, 455a12–26.

114 As we compare the commotion we sense and the flame we see in the present, and so take action, so we can compare the things we see to things imagined and so deliberate about future action.

115 So in the absence of actual sensation, we still take action. This must be because of the presence of images of the good and bad in our imaginations. See III.2, 425b22–25; III.3, 429a4–8.

116 Aristotle is here expanding his discussion from practical intellect, which has to do with human activity, to speculative intellect, which has to do with simply knowing the truth. He is not saying that good and bad or truth and falsity are genera strictly speaking, for his ultimate genera are the ten spoken of at *Cat.* 4, 1b25–27. Rather, he is saying that the intelligibility of the true and the good are of a kind: When we see that something is good, we do so by recognizing the truth about what sort of thing it is and what sort of thing we are, e.g., that this action is a just one, that justice is a good thing for the city and the citizen, and that we are citizens. This implies knowing what justice is, what goodness is, what a city is, and what a citizen is. The intellect can grasp all these sorts of things and relate them to ourselves and our situations, i.e., by considering them "in relation to someone." So practical intellect presupposes speculative intellect, for we choose what to do based on knowledge of who and what we are and what is good for us. (Of course, this knowledge need not be precise, and sometimes we might have error instead of truth about things.) Moreover, as he will say later (III.9, 432b29–433a1), the intellect can consider what might be objects of the practical intellect simply speculatively, as someone might think about how to heal a certain disease even if he has no intention of actually doing anything. And as the intellect can grasp things which enter into our fields of choice, so can it grasp things which do not, about which we can do nothing, e.g., what motion is, what a cause is, what the heavens are, what God is, etc. Aristotle leads us in this chapter from pursuit and avoidance on the level of sensation, to pursuit and avoidance on the level of intellect, and finally to the level of pure, speculative intellect.

117 The "abstract" things are the mathematicals, like number and line and surface. Here Aristotle expands his discussion again to include these sorts of things. Cf. *Phys.* II.2, 193b22–194a12.

118 Cf. 431a1–2; III.4, 430a3–5; III.7, 431a1–2; III.8, 431b21–23.

119 Having argued that our mind can only grasp things when looking at a phantasm, Aristotle raises the question of whether we can think of things (like the gods) other than those of which we have phantasms. (Aristotle held that the first principles or "gods" of the universe were immaterial "intelligences"; cf. *Meta.* XII.6–10.) He never explicitly addresses the question in the extant works, but we can divine some

of what he might have said. First of all, he already has said that the intellect can know itself once it has been informed by the species of a material thing, even though it is itself immaterial. (III.4, 429b5–9) Since the intellect in act and the intelligible in act are one thing, as he just said, knowing anything is a doorway to knowing the mind, which is immaterial and of which there can therefore be no phantasm. And one can know a thing not directly by a phantasm of that thing, but by seeing the implication of things which we do have phantasms of. For example, the ultimate matter is knowable only by proportion: "For as bronze is to statue or as timber is to bed or as material and the formless before it takes on form is to whatever else has form, so is this underlying nature to substance and 'this something' and a being." (*Phys*. I.7, 191a7–12) So too, we can know immaterial things by way of arguments which start from the things we sense and of which we have phantasms. Presumably, the arguments of the *Physics*, which lead to the first mover (*Phys*. VIII.1–10, especially 267b17–26) and of the *Metaphysics* (*Meta*. VII–XII, especially 1071b12–22, 1073a3–13) are examples of such procedures.

120 This chapter sums up what has been said about the knowing powers; the next chapter will go on to speak of the powers that cause the motions of animals. Cf. I.2, 403b25–27; III.2, 427a17–22; III.9, 432a15–17.

121 The very first thing Aristotle says in his discussion of sensation and of intellection is that these powers are moved by their objects. (II.5, 416b33–34; III.4, 429a13–18) It is this fact that allows him to draw the conclusion that the intellect is immaterial – because the intellect can know all natural things, and it knows by receiving a form from its object, it must beforehand not have that form or any other, so it must not be a body. (Cf. II.5, 416b33–34; III.4, 429a13–15) After having been affected, they are one with the thing known. Cf. III.2, 425b26–426a26; III.4, 430a2–5; III.7, 431b17.

122 This recalls the considerations of Book I, where Aristotle treated the position that the soul is composed of the elements of physical things because it knows them. Cf. I.5, 409b23–26.

123 Cf. *Part. An*. IV.10, 687a16–b7.

124 Aristotle clearly believes there are intelligible things beyond those found in the physical world, as he proves the existence of an immaterial first mover at the end of the *Physics* (*Phys*. VIII.10, 267b25–26) and has even shown the intellect itself to be immaterial earlier in this work (III.4, 429a24–27; III.5, 430a17–18); moreover, he states that metaphysics is about such things, at least in part. (*Meta*. VI.1, 1026a10–18) Here, when he says "it seems" that there are no things beyond the sensibles and mathematicals (which latter are themselves in some way found in the sensibles), the implication is perhaps that this is the opinion of others, or that this is how things look to the untutored mind. The first things encountered as intelligible are, in fact, the sensible things around us and the mathematicals. Thus, when he introduced the proper object of the intellect in III.4, 429b10–22, he mentioned sensible things and mathematical things, and did not bring up the possibility of separate intelligibles (except obliquely, insofar as he spoke of how the mind knows itself – see III.4, 29b5–9). Just as we see everything we see (horses, shapes, motion, etc.) by seeing the proper object of sight, namely, color, so we know everything we know by knowing the proper object of the mind, the "what it is" of material things. Immaterial things are only known to exist and to be immaterial by arguments and their propositional conclusions which are finally traced back to the

individual terms of the premises, which, in the end, express the "whatnesses" of material things. (Aristotle has spoken of the mind's putting together simple thought at III.6, 430a26–b6.) Cf. *Po. An.* II.19, 99b15–100b17 and *Meta.* I.1, 980a21–981a12.

125　While the intellect depends on imagination for the presentation of its object, the forming of propositions goes beyond the capacity of the imagination. The statement, "a triangle is a figure" is not simply a phantasm, though it cannot occur without phantasms.

126　Even if thinking does find its objects in the phantasms illumined by the agent intellect, the simple thoughts which are combined to make statements are not themselves merely phantasms. (Cf. III.5, 430a10–17 and III.7, 431b2) What the intellect sees first of all is *what* things are (III.4, 429b10–22), while the imagination can never do more than present instances of things. Cf. III.3, 429a4–8.

127　Cf. I.2, 404a25–27; III.3, 427a17–19.

128　Cf. II.2, 413b13–27. To be separate in magnitude or place is to be in a different physical organ, to be separate in account is only to have a different definition.

129　The question of how (or even whether) to divide the soul into "parts" (the word is equivalent to "powers" in this context) came up earlier, at I.1, 402b1–10, I.5, 411a24–b30, and II.2, 413b11–414a3. Why does it come up here particularly? Hasn't Aristotle already made certain divisions and even said about the intellect that it is not only separate in account but even in magnitude? The power of locomotion seems to pose a particular challenge because, whereas in seeing the eyes alone are affected, in locomotion, it is the whole animal that moves, so that the power might seem to be the whole soul or all the powers combined. On the other hand, we move locally to pursue the good or pleasant and to avoid the evil or painful, so it seems that the principle of locomotion is what is aware of pleasure and pain, of good and evil, i.e., the principle seems to be either sensation or intellect. In short, while the other powers were not too difficult to distinguish, the power of locomotion seems more mixed up with the other powers and with the whole soul.

130　Cf. Plato, *Republic* IV, 434d–441c.

131　Cf. *Nic. Eth.* I.13, 1102a26–28.

132　The imagination (III.3, 427a17–429a9) can look very much like both the sensitive and the rational parts. In English we often use the word 'mind' to include the imagination and memory and the intellect. And, at III.3, 427b27–29, Aristotle includes imagination as a kind of understanding {νοῦς}, though he also, in the same text, distinguishes imagination from the rational power. (III.3, 428a16–b9) But, on the other hand, the imagination seems to be a sort of remnant of the alteration of the exterior senses. III.3, 428b10–429a2.

133　In the *Nic. Eth.* I.13, 1102b13–1103a3, Aristotle distinguishes a power of the soul which is in a way rational and in a way irrational, namely, appetite. It is irrational in the sense that it is not itself a sort of reason, but rational insofar as it can obey reason.

134　Cf. II.3, 414b2.

135　Aristotle wrote separate treatises on these: *On Respiration* (really part of a larger treatise, *On Youth and Old Age*) and *On Sleep and Waking*.

136　Cf. II.3, 414a29–32. In this chapter and the following two, Aristotle will treat of the powers of locomotion and of appetite.

137 Aristotle addresses the relations of appetite, imagination, sensation, and locomotion
    in several places: II.2, 413b21–24; II.3, 414b1–6, 415a8–11; III.3, 428a8–9; III.9,
    432b19–21; III.10, 433b27–30; III.11, 433b31–434a5. He is not denying that plants
    move for an end, but only noting that motion for an end is in the most clear cases
    always accompanied by knowledge of the end, desire, and self-direction, as the lion
    chases the antelope guided by sense knowledge, instinct, and the desire to eat.

138 Plants do, of course, have a kind of self-motion (cf. Appendix 3, *The Reproductive
    (or Vegetative) Soul*) but they do not cause locomotion; instead they are rooted to a
    particular place.

139 Cf. I.5, 410b19–21.

140 III.4, 415b16–17; III.12, 434a31; *De Cael.*, I.4, 271a33. That nature acts for an end
    is argued at *Phys.* II.8, 191a23–b34.

141 Cf. *MA* 6, 700b17–20. At III.3, 427b27–29, Aristotle indicated earlier that imagina-
    tion can be considered as a sort of mind. In the previous chapter, Aristotle argued
    against both appetite and intellect as being the movers. Here he says it is apparent
    that they are the movers we seek. Because the other candidates, sensation and veg-
    etation, are also found in things that cannot move, we know with certainty that they
    are not the movers. And we see in our experience that we move because we want
    things and that we want things we don't have and move towards them because we
    think or imagine that they are good. (Imagination and intellect both are able to pres-
    ent to the appetite goods which are not possessed, and so provoke a desire which
    leads to motion.) Because Aristotle is now considering imagination as a sort of
    νοῦς, I have translated this word by "mind" for the remainder of the book.

142 Cf. *Nic. Eth.* VI.2, 1139a21–31.

143 That is, the last thing the intellect comes to in thinking about how to attain the object
    of its desire is the first thing to be done; e.g., if I want a house, I might think about
    how to build it and come to see that I must start with the foundation; the foundation,
    then, is the beginning of the action but the end of the deliberation. Cf. *Nic. Eth*, III.3,
    1112b11–31.

144 That is, good is the principle of the practical intellect.

145 Alternative manuscripts read "the appetible power."

146 The two powers would only produce a single effect to the extent that they form some
    sort of joint cause.

147 Translating βούλησις by "will" may be considered unorthodox. Some think that
    the word "will" has too many connotations to fairly translate Aristotle's word. But
    if we think of the will simply as an appetite that follows upon reason, which is, I
    think, the fundamental notion, the notion which anyone who speaks about the will,
    even if only to disagree, has in mind in when he uses the word in the first place, then
    such concerns are misplaced. That Aristotle thought there was such an appetite is
    apparent from this text.

148 Appetite {ὄρεξις} includes desire {ἐπιθυμία} and will {βούλησις}, desire being
    appetite for pleasure (II.3, 414b2–6), the will for good (*Rh.* I.10, 1369a3).
    Elsewhere, Aristotle also names anger as a sort of appetite. Cf. *Rh.* II.2, 1378a30;
    DA I.1, 403a30–31.

149 Here "understanding" {νοῦς} might be taken as the habit of knowing the first prin-
    ciples, such as "the whole is greater than the part." Cf. *Po. An.* II.19, 100b5–15. Cf.
    also *Nic. Eth.* VI.6, 1141a3–8. On the other hand, maybe Aristotle implicitly means

"understanding simply," i.e., not adulterated by the influence of imagination or appetite, is always right.

150 To bring us to act, it is enough that we think a thing good even if it is not; moreover, we might think a thing is good and it might still not move us to action, if it is a good for another (as I don't desire to eat alfalfa even if I see that alfalfa is good for horses) or if it is a good for me but one about which I cannot do anything (as I might hope my favorite team wins a game, but there is nothing I can do about it).

151 No one deliberates or takes action about what cannot be otherwise, e.g., about the sum of the angles of a triangle equaling two right angles; of course, not everything that can be otherwise is a subject for deliberation and action either: No one deliberates or takes action about whether there will be an earthquake tomorrow.

152 Aristotle is implicitly criticizing Plato's division of the soul. Cf. Plato, *Republic* IV, 436a–c.

153 Cf. Plato, *Protagoras*, 353c–357b.

154 Aristotle earlier showed concern over dividing the appetitive power into parts (III.9, 432b4–5); here he affirms a sort of unity to the cause of animal motion, namely, the unity of the desired object. But there are many of these, though they all move insofar as they share one notion, that of the good, so they are, in a way, one in species. Perhaps he also has in mind, when he says the movers are many, that there is a moved mover in the animal as well, namely the appetite, as he immediately goes on to say. 433b13–18.

155 On the bodily organs of movement, cf. *MA* 7, 701b1–32; *IA* 6, 706b15–23.

156 At *Phys.* VII.2, 243a23–25, Aristotle says all locomotions occur by pushing, pulling, carrying, or whirling, but he reduces these to pushing and pulling at VII.2, 243a15–17 and VII.2, 243b16–244a4 (in the alternative text VII.2, 243a28–b23 and VII.2, 244a15–16).

157 Cf. *MA* 1, 698a15–b6; 4, 700a7–11; 8, 702a22–33; *PA* III.3, 665a10, 654a33–b2.

158 III.10, 433a21, 433b13–18.

159 Aristotle discusses the division of imagination into rational (called "deliberative") and sensitive in the next chapter. Cf. III.11, 434a5–12.

160 Cf. III.9, 432b21–26.

161 Some animals do not form distinct images of things they desire or wish to avoid, but they do move in an indeterminate way, flinching from what is painful and clinging to what is pleasurable. So they would seem to have an indefinite imagination to go along with this. Cf. III.3, 428a8–11.

162 Human beings can choose among options, so they must be able to form a multitude of images and compare them according to some standard measure. All these images, and the standard, must enter into a whole which presents to the appetite some particular course of action as desirable. The ability to form such complex images for presentation to the appetite is what Aristotle calls here "deliberative" imagination. "Sensitive" imagination, on the other hand, is in all animals and issues immediately in desire and action.

163 The word "syllogism" has a particular meaning in logic, being a kind of rational argument (Cf. *Pr. An.* I.1, 24b17–24), but etymologically and more commonly simply means a reckoning or, even more primitively, a gathering together.

164 The Greek text here simply says "this has that," and both pronouns are feminine. The only feminine nouns mentioned in the previous sentences are "opinion" and

"imagination" (whether qualified as deliberative or sensitive). It is questionable
what is meant here; some scholars, including Ross, remove the offending words and
use them to replace "the will" in the next sentence. Cf. Ross 1961, *ad loc.*

165 Deliberation belongs rather to imagination and reason.

166 One might take the sentence to speak of one ball moving another, as in billiards, so
that the meaning is that the appetites conflict and push each other out of their proper
paths, or, on the other hand, one might think he is speaking of the motion of a limb
which depends upon a ball and socket joint. The former seems more naturally to fit
with what he goes on to say, that this happens in the case of a lack of self-control.
However, as he goes on to speak of the higher naturally moving the lower, one might
be tempted to think of the heavenly spheres, with the motion of the same and the
other and the consequent complex motion. Cf. Plato, *Timaeus*, 37c–40d.

167 The various appetites, for the political good, for food, for society, etc., can come into
conflict, but the virtuous man will control his appetites in the light of reason, the
highest and ruling power of the soul. Cf. *Nic. Eth.* I.7 1097b33–1098a20; I.8,
1099a7–16.

168 The speculative intellect, as opposed to the practical, is not a mover but a pure
observer, and its premises and conclusions are necessary and so timeless. Cf. III.10,
433a14–15; *Po. An.* I.1, 71b12; I.4, 73a21–25.

169 The universal statement, "helping the poor is good," is not enough to cause us to
actually do anything; we need the additional, more particular statement, "these people here in front of me are poor" for action to occur. The former does not move without the latter and either the latter is what moves us or both statements do, the former
as a sort of unmoved mover, the latter as a sort of moved mover. Perhaps most properly, the appetite following upon the conclusion that it is good to help these people
in front of me is the interior mover, while the good to be achieved in the world is
the ultimate mover. Cf. *Nic. Eth.* VII.3, 1147a25–31 and III.3, 1113a2–5.

170 Having dealt with the definition of the soul (II.1–2), the "parts" or powers of the
soul (II.3), i.e., the nutritive (II.4), the sensitive (II.5–III.3), the intellectual (III.4–
8), and the appetitive (III.9–11), Aristotle completes his discussion of the soul by
treating the relations of these powers to each other in the last two chapters. Cf. II.2,
413a31–b10, 413b32–414a3; II.3, 414a29–415a1.

171 Cf. II.12, 424a17–b3; III.2, 425b23–24.

172 Cf. *Phys.* II.8, 198b10–199b33.

173 The senses, including touch, are ratios, that is, peculiar combinations of elements
which permit a being to receive the sensible qualities immaterially. Since a simple
body has no ratio of elements, it cannot be a sensible body. Cf. II.12, 424a24–28;
III.13, 435a11–b3.

174 The sensible qualities like hot and cold, wet and dry, hard and soft, which the sense
of touch is aware of, are those which determine generation and corruption. (Cf.
II.11, 423b27–424a10 and *Phys.* VII.3, 245b19–248b28 or, in the alternative text,
VII.3, 245b3–248a9). The body of the animal is itself subject to generation and corruption due to such tangible qualities. Whence, if the animal did not have touch, it
would not recognize those very attributes of the bodies around it in virtue of which
it might be preserved or destroyed. Cf. also *Somn.* 2, 455a12–27.

175 Cf. III.13, 435a12–18, 435b4–19.

176 Some animals may have senses beyond taste and touch, but only those which can move about in place must have these further senses in order to survive.

177 Cf. *Phys.* VIII.10, 266b27–267a2.

178 Cf. Plato, *Timaeus*, 45b–46c and *DA* II.8, 419b18–420a4.

179 III.12, 434b9–24.

180 Cf. II.11, 423b1–26.

181 I.5, 410a30–b1.

182 So the sense of touch is convertible with animality.

183 III.12, 434b9–18.

184 III.12, 434b22–27; *De Sens.* 1, 436b13–437a17.

185 At III.12, 434b20–24, Aristotle spoke of taste as absolutely necessary for an animal, but here he speaks of it as only for the well-being of the animal; there, he was considering it as a sort of touch, here, as aware of flavors and determining for the animal what is nutritious and what is harmful.

186 Cf. II.8, 420b13–22. The tongue is, of course, not a sense organ insofar as it speaks, but Aristotle perhaps ends with the animal's ability to signify to others by means of the tongue both in order to indicate the coherence of the animal's bodily organization and to signify an opening to further inquiry, especially moral inquiry. Cf. *Pol.* I.2, 1253a7–18.

Appendix 1
Dialectic in Book I of the De Anima

The first book of the *De Anima* is divided into a first part (Chapter 1) outlining the subject of the book and some problems that arise concerning it, and a second part (Chapters 2–5) reviewing and rebutting the views of Aristotle's predecessors. While all grant that this section is of historical interest, especially as some of the positions discussed are not recorded elsewhere, few think it merits a philosophical discussion. To my mind this is based on an error about how philosophical thought begins, the view that a philosophically interesting position must be sophisticated and that such sophistication is available even without the dialectical consideration of elementary or even simplistic positions. Aristotle, however, affirms the importance of this dialectical part when he writes, "It is necessary to take along with us the opinions of those who went before us, that we might grasp what has been well said, but if something was not well [said], that we might beware of it."[1] In this essay, I will illustrate how some of the problems and refutations presented here are preparatory to the reading of the rest of the *De Anima*. I will focus on the questions of vital motion, sensation and thought, and the definition of the soul.

Before looking at the text of the *De Anima*, though, we should say something about dialectic, the process by which we think problems through on the basis of the opinions of the majority of people, or of the wise, or of the very wise.[2]

Aristotle contends that dialectics is the road to science.[3] For example, in the *Physics*, in considering the principles of change, he considers the positions of his philosophical forebears before he determines the truth.[4] He notes that they all agree that the principles of motion are contraries before he goes on to determine this with certainty and to refine the claim, arguing in his own voice and from the experience of change. In later parts of the work, Aristotle will frequently refer to the principles, matter and form, which in the first book were initially uncovered by dialectic. Dialectic prepares the way for the philosopher to recognize the principles of his science, to grasp them, and to isolate the problems to which his subject gives rise.

But can a process based on opinion do this? Insofar as it is based on opinion, it is opposed to certitude. Yet among the statements to which the uneducated give credence, there must be those which are expressions of knowledge, if there is to be any development of knowledge at all.[5] How can anyone learn anything beyond what he already thinks if he does not use the thoughts he already has as a beginning, however tentatively? There can be no philosophy at all, if that name indicates actual knowledge and not just sophisticated opinion, unless it begins with what everyone already knows. The philosopher may surpass the common man, but only by building on the knowledge which the common man actually possesses, and certainly not by having contempt for his ideas.

A model of the use of dialectic is in the *Meno*: Socrates teaches a slave boy how to double a square, using only obvious facts known by everyone.[6] Socrates is strong in his grasp of the order of the required propositions, so he can ask questions in the right order and thus bring to the slave boy's mind, in the right order, premises which the slave boy already knows. The fundamental point here is that our developed knowledge is exactly that, a development of the knowledge which we had before our inquiry even began.[7] The latter is mixed up with error and is out of order, but is nonetheless knowledge. One job of dialectic is to separate the error from the knowledge and to put the knowledge into order, at least tentatively. Socrates shows the slave boy that he does not know how to double the area of a square, though he thought he knew. Socrates does this precisely by showing the boy that his opinion about how to double the area conflicts with other claims about which he is more certain (for example, with the claim that two times two equals four). He thus separates what the boy knows from what he does not know, so that the boy knows what he can rely on and what remains a subject of inquiry. This gives the boy a beginning and an end, thus defining his task and even suggesting how to achieve it. Although dialectic is a discipline which begins with the opinions of the interlocutors or of those they respect, it is necessary for philosophy because it carries us from indistinct knowledge which is mixed up with error to consciousness of our ignorance and, more positively, consciousness of our most basic knowledge. It will also, evidently, bring to light different opinions and likely arguments for and against them.

The science of dialectic is taught in the *Topics*, and discussions of its uses are found there and in the *Metaphysics*.[8] Among these are the discovery of the principles of the sciences – not of their truth, but of the fact that they are principles, that they come before the other claims in the science, as the slave boy sees that "two times two equals four" is more of a foundation than is "building a square on the diagonal of the original square will result in a square twice the size of the original square." Dialectic also places before our minds opposed views and difficulties with them; this puts us in a better position to judge them, lets us see what problems we ought to focus on, and helps us see which opinions the opposed philosophers share and which they disagree about and so come to some judgment about which claims are more fundamental. Finally, having seen the problems with different positions, we are better able to recognize when we have sufficiently answered those problems. The first book of *De Anima* does all these things, as I will here attempt to indicate, not exhaustively, but, I hope, persuasively.

Chapter 2 begins with the claim that those who study the soul always do so from one of two points of view: either as a principle of motion (primarily motion according to place) or as a principle of sensing.[9] It is through these activities that we recognize the presence of soul. Everyone agrees that trees are alive, and also that this fact is not as obvious as that cats or, even better, we ourselves are alive. This is because trees do not sense or move around. "The life of plants is hidden."[10] Aristotle has here given us a good beginning, one which he found by looking at what everyone thinks about life. Despite the superficial differences in their opinions, the philosophers betray a fundamental agreement not only among themselves but even with the majority of people. Aristotle has used a principle he often avails himself of, namely, that what is always or for the most part is natural. If all or most people think a certain thing is true, it must be natural to think so, and what it is natural to think is unlikely to be too far wrong.

Aristotle begins to look into the first of these two beginnings of the inquiry into life immediately in Chapter Two.[11] Those who look at the soul by way of motion are convinced, one and all, that what is in motion is either in motion in virtue of itself or is in motion due to something else which is in motion in virtue of itself. This is reasonable enough: When we see a train moving we attribute the motion of the cars to the motion of the engine, which has an intrinsic principle of motion, whereas the cars do not have such an intrinsic principle. Most of us believe that a gas heats up because the kinetic energy of its particles is increased, i.e., the particles of the gas, which are always in motion and seem to be so of themselves, cause the motion of heating. So too the early philosophers of Greece thought that what causes the motion of living bodies, the soul, must be something which is in motion of itself. And what is in motion, whether in virtue of itself or not, must be a body. So, it seems, the soul must be a certain kind of body, one which is in motion in virtue of itself (or "*per se*").

At this point, then, the search is on for what that self-moving body is, and the answers given vary based on what different thinkers think is likely to be such a body: Some choose fire, some air, some water – though no one chooses earth except those who think there are four elements and who, for other reasons,[12] think all the elements must be found in the soul. A more modern version of this position would hold that the functions of life are explained entirely in terms of the smaller, seemingly self-moving bodies inside our animated bodies: cells, e.g., or amino acids and proteins, or electrons and other elementary bodies, or quarks, or some combination of these.

In Chapter Three, Aristotle advances at least six arguments against the position.[13] His objections, generally, take the form of "reductions to the absurd."[14] For this reason, we have to accept that the absurdity adduced is in fact absurd and therefore that its contradictory is better known than the position being refuted. Certain of these absurdities are only problems for the ones who hold the position Aristotle is refuting, but often a position is seen to be absurd because of our own basic knowledge of life. The arguments, then, do more than simply negate the position; they also point to a better approach. For example, he begins with the challenging suggestion that "perhaps it is not only false that its [the soul's] substance is as some say, that it is a self-mover or a thing able to move [another], but it is even an impossibility that motion should belong to it."[15] He then distinguishes being in motion by another and being in motion *per se*, as he had already done in the *Physics*,[16] and suggests we look into whether motion can belong to the soul *per se*.[17] Difficulties with the claim that the soul is in motion *per se* will point us toward thinking it must be in motion *per accidens*.

Aristotle first points out that if the soul is itself in motion *per se*, it will have its place.[18] It is not entirely clear why this is absurd. Aristotle may be thinking that if the soul has its own place, then it cannot also be in the same place as the body which it moves. (This is at least a plausible reading; he must think the absurdity is rooted in something which belongs to being in place.) If the soul is in its own place, then, it could not exist where the living body exists, that is, it could not coincide with the living body. The body we thought was alive would only be in reality an inanimate container of what is truly self-moving, the soul. The living being we started out trying to understand turns out to be more like a hamster wheel, while the soul is the hamster – the living being. Thinking that we can account for life in this way is like thinking that milk actually makes the glass which contains it white. The life of the living body, which we experience in ourselves,[19] turns out to be an illusion.

The next few arguments pile on the problems. We were concerned that the soul is not, in fact, animating a body but is merely contained by one; now we will see that the soul, conceived of as a small, mobile body, cannot explain the vital motions which we see animated bodies have. If the soul moves the body because it has of itself a natural motion, then it could also have a forced motion and rest – but when an animal moves, unless something pushes it, it moves where it wills and stops when it wants. These are voluntary, not forced motions.[20] The soul must be a principle of motion that transcends the limitations of simple natures, that goes beyond what an elementary body with its extreme determination can accomplish. Further, if the soul were fire (or earth), it would be against the animal's nature to go downstairs (or up). But we do not find the motions of animals to be against nature in this way; rather, motions in all directions are voluntarily undertaken by animals. Besides, if the soul can move locally the way the body containing it does, it might leave the body altogether and then reenter it, causing dead animals to resurrect. But we do not see that; the soul must be not only in the body, but so fixed to it that it cannot come and go. It seems to exist in some way *by being in* a body, but not in the sense, as we have seen, of being contained by it. Next, if the soul is in motion through its nature, then, being moved by another would be more or less accidental to it. Yet the soul is moved by the sensible goods and evils surrounding the animal (it chases prey and flees predators, for example), and this not adventitiously, but by nature. So the soul must be something moved not inexorably, as earth always tends downward, but by seeking fulfillment in whatever direction seems right.[21] Finally, if we take "by nature" to mean "in its very substance or nature," then the nature of the soul would be to move out of its own nature, destroying itself in fulfilling itself, for what moves moves away from what is present at the beginning of the motion.

What can we gather from this set of arguments? Obviously, we are led to see the problems with the position being refuted, and are closer to the truth to the extent that we now suspect that a certain position is false. We are also shown propositions to which we are more inclined than we are to the position being refuted; otherwise, the "reductions" would fail in their basic task.[22] We see not only that the soul cannot be a little body that moves of itself, we also see that it must have certain attributes: It must be present in the very stuff of the living and be closely linked in its nature to that stuff; it must produce motions that are not merely natural but voluntary and determined not because the animal cannot help moving left or right, but because the animal desires to do so; and the soul must be understood to be itself completed, not destroyed, by the motions to which it gives rise.

These pointers are aimed at positions which Aristotle formulates throughout the second and third books. If the soul is in the category of substance (and the determination of genus is usually the first thing to do in defining something), then it will not be a body in that category, but either an incorporeal substance or something in the genus of substance in a more removed way, as, for example, the point is in the genus of quantity not as a species of quantity but only as a principle of quantity. If the soul permeates the stuff of a living body and cannot be detached and then again reattached, it seems unlikely that it would be a separate incorporeal substance. So our dialectic has led us to think the soul must be something intrinsic to an animal, a thing which is not isolated from the body but coexists with it. We might also add that if the soul has functions like moving the animal and sensing, which are peculiar to the sort of thing that has it, it must not be purely material (since matter is only passive) but must be something actual. Already, in the space of just over one page of text, we are very close to Aristotle's idea of the soul, the substantial form of a living body.[23]

A more summary account of the rest of the first book will support the claim that these arguments are not just of historical value, but are part of Aristotle's strategy for leading the student to the truth.

Aristotle turns to the *Timaeus* in which Plato presents the view that the soul is a magnitude. The reason for holding this is a little obscure, but it is clear that Aristotle takes Timaeus, the main character of the dialogue, to think he can explain the soul's intellectual functions through his theory. In particular, Timaeus seems to understand thinking as a kind of motion.[24] (This is probably why the position is treated here, with the arguments about the soul causing motion, and not with the later discussion of sensation and thought.[25])

Note, first, that this part is reasonably placed after the discussion of the soul as a body because the arguments against that position show us that the soul must be *of* a body but not *be* a body and that it must be wherever the body is. Saying the soul is a sort of dimension might well seem to satisfy these criteria, as dimensions are properties of bodies and exist exactly where the body is; in fact, it is its dimensions which determine where the body is to begin with.

Secondly, the arguments against the position, like those we saw earlier, do more than refute; they also direct our minds to phenomena critical to our inquiry by bringing them forth as facts opposed to the consequences of the theory. For example, thought is understood here to be discrete – there is no continuum between the premises of an argument – but the motion of magnitudes is contin- uous, so thought cannot be the motion of a magnitude, and neither, then, can the soul be a magnitude.[26] This argument grants that thought is somehow discrete. We must wonder how thought can be a sort of motion if it occurs by discrete jumps – yet it certainly does seems to be a sort of motion and to be performed in "steps," not by continuous motion. Moreover, though thought is composed of discrete steps, we can rest in contemplation on these various steps – we can think, in a sense, even without the motion called discourse.[27] So thought cannot be motion as defined in the *Physics*. In some ways it seems more like rest, a rest we can take at any step in our argument.[28] This should open us up to the possi- bility that the soul, at least one which thinks, is somehow more perfect than are bodies and their motions, for its "motion" has a kind of finished character in every part.[29]

This section also emphasizes "contact" or "touching."[30] Timaeus apparently thinks of thinking as a kind of contact between the mind and the intelligible object. He takes this, or at least Aristotle treats him as taking this, literally: The magnitude which is the soul sidles up to something intelligible and this contact is knowing. This sounds strange, but it is not entirely unjustified: Whenever we think, we must have the thing we think of in mind, so it must somehow be in contact with our mind. And, if we do really know something outside our minds, we must not only have contact with a likeness of the thing, but with the thing itself. How this can happen is something Aristotle is especially concerned with in Book III,[31] but here he contents himself with showing us that Timaeus' very literal idea will not work. As in other cases, though, his argument points us in a certain direction: The intelligible has to come into contact somehow with our minds, but not in the way that two bodies come into contact.

Some of the other arguments in this section similarly underline experiences or positions Aristotle takes to be fundamental. For example, the theory gives no explanation of why this or that sort of body has a soul, and yet it seems that the soul, as a mover, and the body, as a mobile, must be fitted for each other. Magnitudes, as such, are homogeneous and so not fitted to move each other – difference is necessary for a mover to act on a mobile. This problem of the ade- quation of the soul and the body is not one which the earlier thinkers addressed, but Aristotle points out, tellingly, that "each [body] has its proper species and form."[32] What is the species and form of the living body? It will be shown in Book II that it is the soul.[33]

Chapter Four takes up two main positions: first, that the soul is a harmony, a position he says is convincing to many[34]; second, that the soul is a self-moving number, a position he says is by far the most unreasonable one of all.[35]

The view that the soul is a harmony was not mentioned in Chapter Two, when he was reviewing the opinions of others. Here he gives an incomplete argument for the view. Filling it out a bit, we might say that the soul, whatever it is, is the principle of life – this is just what we mean by the term 'soul.' The principle of life, however, is what makes a body alive, and what makes a body a living body is a mixing and composition of contraries. (Here Aristotle calls such a body simply, 'the body.') So the soul is a harmony.[36]

Having argued in the previous chapter that it is a fault not to consider how the soul and the body are proportioned to each other, he now cites a position that seems diametrically opposed: The soul is precisely the organization or articulation of the living body. The position is significant: It seems to explain death,[37] thus getting at something essential to life, and it moves us toward the view that soul is something like a form. A sign that Aristotle thinks the position has some serious merit is that after attacking it, he still defends it.[38]

His counter-arguments focus on three problems. The harmony is either the composed thing considered as composed or the ratio of the composition.[39] The former, the composed thing, cannot be the soul because it is the living being which we are trying to understand by speaking about the soul to begin with, and the latter is an accidental attribute, because it is the organization of already existent things.[40] This last implies that the soul is more likely something in the genus of substance. This is confirmed by his next argument, that the soul is a cause of motion but a harmony is not,[41] for a harmony is more something changed when other things change, as the violin goes out of tune when a string is stretched.[42] This seems to indicate that a harmony is not a principle. The soul, however, is a principle and mover and such things are substances, even if they need certain accidents to actually do anything (as water must be hot to heat something else, and being hot is accidental to water). The idea of harmony fits better with health,[43] which is an accident,[44] for it can come and go while we continue to live.

The position that the soul is a harmony is attractive because it fits with our experience that life needs a body containing certain kinds of parts in a certain order and that disturbing that order too severely can result in death. Harmony also seems to be the sort of thing that makes things be what they are – something formal – as a machine is the sort of machine that it is because of how it is put together and is no longer that sort of machine if you alter the organization too much. But the view fails because it cannot explain motion and this because it makes the soul accidental. Aristotle, at least, will conclude in Book II that the soul is somehow in the category substance because the living thing is a different kind of thing from the inanimate.[45] He takes as given that we and other living things have a nature and are some *sort* of thing, not a mere collection of atoms or cells or what have you, that our life is not an accidental outcome of some more basic processes nor our being an accident of some more substantial being.[46] The consideration and refutation of idea that the soul is a harmony thus brings to the fore the substantiality of the soul.

The order up to now has been that of the *Categories*, Chapters 5–7, which deal with substance, then quantity, then relation.[47] These line up with saying the soul is a body, a magnitude, and a harmony. Alternatively, one could say that the view that the soul is a harmony is putting it in the genus of quality, for disposition is a species of quality. If we take harmony to be in the genus of relation, then we would wonder whether quality could be the genus – Aristotle at least mentioned quality when pointing out that we need to determine the genus.[48] As it turns out, though, we have already been led to suspect that the soul is not an accident at all and have dialectically placed the soul in the genus substance.

Besides, in some way it is true that the soul is a quality, if the word is taken broadly. In the *Categories*, Aristotle does take the word very broadly: Second substances, i.e., the genus and species of first substances, "signify the quality that something has. … They do not, however, signify qualification simply, as does 'white.' For 'white' signifies nothing other than a qualification, but species and genus mark out a qualification about substance. For they signify a certain substance as to its qualification."[49] Generally, a quality says how a thing is, and the genera and species of first substances name how they are, for they distinguish *these* first substances from *those* by determining them qualitatively. The name "horse," for example, names a kind of thing, differentiating it from a dog, e.g., and so it "qualifies" the notion of substance. The soul is not a genus or a difference of a primary substance but, like them, is in the genus substance on the side of form, i.e., as determining what a thing is.[50] Aristotle does not leave aside quality altogether, but either considers it when considering harmony, or reserves it, in this extended sense, for Book II.

The soul, then, is not able to be in motion and so, *a fortiori*, cannot be moved by itself.[51] But for some reason, there is one more position to take on, that the soul is a self-moving number. This, "[t]he most unreasonable [position] by far,"[52] is treated at surprising length, especially given that, as Aristotle immediately points out, we already know it is false because we know the soul cannot be in motion *per se*.[53] As in the other cases, at least some of the counter-arguments point us towards something valuable.

The very first argument[54] recalls a teaching from the *Physics*: Every self-mover has parts, one a mover, the other a mobile.[55] If we recall one of the reasons for this fact, namely, that the mobile must be, as such, in potency, whereas the mover must be, as such, in actuality,[56] we are immediately led to suspect that the soul, the mover, stands to the body, the mobile, as actuality to potency, as in fact Aristotle will conclude when he determines his own view.[57] Another argument emphasizes that the soul and body must be distinct though not external to each other because the body is sensitive and the soul is the principle of sensitivity.[58] This again shows that the soul must be precisely where the body is, so it must be something of a living body, though not a living body.

In the last part of Book I,[59] Aristotle turns to the second phenomenon associated with life, sense and thought.[60] The claim made by earlier philosophers,[61] that "like is known by like," is not overtly rejected, and this because it is in a sense true. When we see red, e.g., it is our eye that does the seeing, and the red we see, the red in the stop sign, must somehow be present as an object to the eye. It is not enough that we have an image of the red sign in our eye, or that we have in our eye an effect of the electromagnetic radiation which emanates from the red object, or that we have an encoded signal which our brain interprets as "red" – if we are going to see real things (and Aristotle never questions whether we do so or not, under normal circumstances), we need the actual object to be present to our eyes. Knowing does involve some sort of contact or presence of the object to our knowing power; in some sense the object must be "in" our knowing power. Empedocles takes this literally to mean that we know or sense fire because our knowing power is made of fire, earth because it is made of earth, etc. So, since the soul can know all things, it must be made of all the elements.

Aristotle attacks this position with a number of arguments, some of which set for us something of an agenda for our discussion of knowing and sensing. First, he points out that it is not the case that we really can know only the elements; rather, we also know composites of the elements, like horses and horseflesh. Merely knowing the elements of these will not get us knowledge of the composites, so, if "like is known by like" is understood as Empedocles understands it, even little bits of horseflesh and little horses must be in our minds.[62] Moreover, there are many things known which are not even substances, such the colors, relations, sizes, etc. Are these elements of the soul? For, because there are no principles common to all the genera, we cannot retreat to say it isn't really *all* things but is only whatever their common principles might be – there are no common principles.[63] Yet if the principles of all the genera are actually in the soul, it will itself be in all the genera. But how could anything be everything?[64]

Accepting the notion that in some way the known is in the knower, these arguments lead us to say that that presence cannot be the kind of physical presence we normally think of. The next argument starts to hint at how we should think of the presence of the known in the knower. When we sense, we are being affected in some way by the sensible, but, if we say with Empedocles that we sense because the sensible is already in us just as it is in the real world, then we must explain how what is like can be affected by what is like.[65] Hot water does not heat equally hot water but cold water, and vice-versa. Some difference is necessary between the cause and the material it works on if there is to be any activity.[66] What is affected must lack exactly that property which is the principle of its being acted upon, a fact which militates against the claim that like knows like. How can we reconcile the passivity of our knowing with the need to have the object of knowledge present in the knowing power? The object must be present in the power only *after* the power is affected by the object.[67] Even then it cannot be present in the material way already deemed so ridiculous as not to provoke refutation.[68] We begin to see that the known is in the knower in some other way.[69] And so another question arises: What other way is there?[70]

In his last argument of this section, Aristotle says that we do not need all the elements in order to know all things, because opposites manifest each other: We know disease by health and the curved by the straight. So it is sufficient that we have one of the opposed elements in order to know the other. This too points to a remarkable difference between the way a thing is in our mind and the way it is in reality, for in material things opposites cannot coexist, but in the mind the thought of one opposite is the very principle by which the other opposite is known. The difference between these two modes of being, that in the mind and that in reality, must be such that the former permits coexistence of the opposites but the latter excludes it. Again we are led to think of the mind as somehow immaterial, since when matter receives an opposite, the other pole of the opposition is excluded. For example, if a piece of clay has a flat surface, it cannot also have a curved one in the same place. But things known are distinguished from each other and so must be "in the same place;" if not, how could one power recognize both so as to say they are distinct? Furthermore, if we know one opposite by another, we must surely have to qualify the statement that "like is known by like." For here it is known by what is precisely *unlike*. The mind comes into contact in these cases by way of the presence to it of what is not merely different from but is incompatible with the material existence of the thing known. No mere material process or reception would seem adequate to this odd situation.

Empedocles' position also raises questions about the unity of the animated body. If the soul is made of the four elements, what holds these together as a soul? The soul, and especially the mind, should be the ruler of the body and so should be prior, a principle of the body, but according to Empedocles, the elements are the first principles.[71]

Aristotle also notes that his predecessors consider the soul in a very limited way, focusing on one sort of operation, for the most part on the locomotion of animals or on knowing. Experience teaches us, though, that there are animals that can feel but have no power to change places, that plants can feed, grow, and reproduce and cannot sense, and some animals, namely, human beings, can do everything the other living things do and can also think.[72] The implication of Aristotle's text is that the study of the soul requires more latitude, that the limited success of the theories of his predecessors may be due to their having confined their attention to only a few vital phenomena. Broadening our scope may lead to more satisfying explanations. But it is likely, too, that when we seek a more universal cause, we will be led beyond the sorts of simple, material explanations offered hitherto. If there is one soul in an animal that allows it to move and to sense and to feed, that soul is a very different sort of thing from a bit of fire or a circle.

Book I ends with concerns about the unity of the animal and its soul, something Aristotle's predecessors hardly seem to have put their minds on. Aristotle thus asks two questions in his own name, introducing dialectical inquiries beyond those of the wise men he has consulted hitherto. Does the soul have parts which perform the different vital functions or does one soul do all these things? And secondly, does a thing live in virtue of one of the parts? Or are all equally "vital?" Or is living actually due to something else altogether?[73]

Some have said that the soul itself is divided into parts, and that it thinks with one part and desires with another, etc.[74] Aristotle offers three arguments against this. First, if the soul is itself divided into parts, what holds it together? Not the body – if anything, the reverse, for when the soul leaves, the body rots. If some other principle holds it together, this other principle would be the soul, so we might as well say immediately that the soul is a unity.[75] This argument adds more weight to the claim made above that the soul is going to have to be something that can explain a wide variety of operations from a single root. It will have to be quite different from the basic natural bodies and the entities studied by mathematics, like circles and numbers.

Secondly, if the soul holds the whole body together, it seems the parts of the soul would hold together the parts of the body, sight the eye, e.g., and hearing the ear. But the mind is held out as exceptional: What part it holds together cannot be imagined. Aristotle offers no reason for saying this, though his earlier arguments might indicate the reason. He argued that the intellect knows not only the elements but composites, not only substances but accidents, and sometimes knows one thing through its opposite. If like is known by like, all these phenomena indicate that the mind must receive in a way very unlike material bodies. How could such a thing as mind, then, hold a material part together?

Finally, Aristotle points out that when some plants and insects are divided, the parts continue to live with all or at least many of their powers intact. This implies that the whole soul is a single principle of many operations, that it is present in every part, and, as its operations transcend the simple operations inanimate bodies perform, it must itself transcend their principles of operation, i.e., their species or forms.[76]

At the beginning of Book II, Aristotle moves on to determine the truth about the soul, starting with the definition and then going on to the various sorts of souls: the vegetative, the sensitive, and the rational, ending the entire book with a discussion of the motive power of animals. What has he gained by his dialectical review? Has he just embarrassed his forebears, or has he learned from them, even from those who may seem not just wrong but primitive?[77]

The dialectic of this book leads us away from error and also towards the truth. We now suspect that the soul is in the genus of substance, not of any accident.

Moreover, it is not a body, but something which permeates and is somehow affixed to certain very peculiar sorts of bodies, and which makes those bodies be what they are and do what they do; that is, it is something formal, not material. Further, if it is not an accident, it cannot be a harmony, though it is like a harmony in being formal and organizational and in supplying unity. The harmony of the parts of the body seems rather to be an effect of some sort; at least, such harmony is present so long as the soul is present and leaves with the soul. As such, the soul seems to be something which rules the body and allows the living thing to do all the things it does.

A thing like this cannot be a mere element or even any sort of purely "natural" entity, if that means a thing always inclined to act in the same way, as fire always goes up. For animals and even plants transcend such determination, since they have a multitude of functions, a fact not accounted for by those who make the soul a simple body or group of bodies.

Furthermore, some of their particular operations are significantly beyond anything an inanimate body could manage. Animals, at any rate, move not by innate impulse but by appetite, motivated by desire and aversion for the things of which they are aware. Sensation, too, and much more so intellect, has properties which force us to consider the soul as something which is not simply material. It knows by having the known present within it, but when it does so it does not become the thing known in a physical way – we have little horses in our heads neither before nor after we learn what horses are. And our knowledge is not limited to a few things: We can know all things – but how can the soul receive and so be all things? This obviously cannot happen to a material thing. We even know one contrary by another, so that one is present to us *because* the other contrary is: an impossibility for material things. Nor is the process of thought like a material process, for we move from premises to conclusions not by sliding from one to the other, but by a step-wise or discrete process, a process, moreover, in which we are free to pause at any time to contemplate, to think without discourse (i.e., without motion), whichever premise or term we might fancy.

Thus, the dialectic of Book I has paid off. We are prepared for the discussions of the definition of the soul, of sensation, of intellection, and of movement. Dialectic has brought us to the verge of knowledge.

Endnotes to Appendix 1

1   I.2, 403b21–24.
2   *Topics* I.1, 100a18–24; 100b21–23.
3   *Topics* I.2, 101a36–b4.
4   *Phys.* I.4–7, 187a12–191a22.
5   *Po. An.* I.1, 71a1–9.
6   Plato, *Meno* 82a–85d. I have had students claim that Socrates is really telling the slave boy the answer, even though he never makes any statement except to tell the slave boy the name of a certain line in the figure ("diagonal"). The slave boy learns because he puts into proper order, under the pressure of Socrates' questioning, the knowledge he already had. He has learned something he really did not know based on knowledge he, and everyone else, already had from experience; no esoteric or sophisticated knowledge was required. The dialectician can perform this service for us in other areas as well, particularly in philosophy.

    One might question whether the slave boy passage is an example of dialectic; I have called it a model, not an example, because we see in it how a dialectician can use one's own opinion to lead one into contradiction or into truth, not because all the marks of dialectic are present here.
7   How this preexistent knowledge is acquired is the subject of *Po. An.* II.19.
8   *Topics* I.2, 101a25–b4; *Meta.* III.1, 995a24–b4.
9   I.2, 403b24–27.
10 *De Plantis* I.1, 815a10–13. This work is, according to the scholars, not actually by Aristotle; the statement quoted is in his spirit.
11 I.2 403b28 ff.
12 I.2, 404b13–15; I.5, 409b23–25.
13 I.3, 406a12–b15.
14 A *reductio ad absurdum* is an argument which proceeds by showing that if a certain claim were true, something false would follow, so that the original claim cannot be true. If the earth were flat, we could not come back to our starting point by travelling constantly in one direction, but we can; therefore, the earth is not flat.
15 I.3, 405b31–406a2.
16 I.3, 406a4–10; *Phys.* IV.4, 211a17–23.
17 I.3, 406a11–12.
18 I.3, 406a12–22.
19 See the *Introduction*.
20 I am using "voluntary" to mean "proceeding from desire," not necessarily rationally determined. Cf. *Nic. Eth.* III.1, 1111a22–b3.
21 This difference between elemental and living bodies will come to the fore again in the distinction Aristotle makes in II.1 between first and second act. Cf. Appendix 2, *The Definition of the Soul*.

22   See note 14.
23   II.1, 412a19–21; Aristotle will be much more explicit at I.3, 407b23–24.
24   I.3, 407a2–6.
25   I.5, 409b18–411a7.
26   I.3, 407a2–10.
27   I.3, 407a32–34.
28   *Phys.* III.2, 201b27–202a2.
29   Cf. II.5, 178b2–16.
30   I.3, 407a10–18.
31   III.4, 429a13–18; 429b22–29.
32   I.3, 407b13–26; II.1, 412a15–22.
33   II.1, 412a6–b4; II.2, 414a14–19.
34   I.4, 407b27–408a28. Cf. also Plato, *Phaedo*, 85e–86d, 91c–95a.
35   I.4, 408b31–409a30.
36   I.4, 407b30–32.
37   I.4, 408a24–28.
38   Ibid.
39   I.4, 408a5–9; Aristotle says that the first of these meanings is the chief one.
40   Aristotle only says that the soul cannot be a harmony in either of the two senses. I
     have tried to fill out the argument partly by looking to the rest of this section.
41   I.4, 407b34–408a1.
42   Cf. Plato, *Phaedo*, 92e–93a.
43   Cf. *Phys.* VII.3, 246a21–b14 (or, in the alternate text, *Phys.* VII.3, 246b3–10).
44   *Cat.* 8, 8b35–37.
45   II.1, 412a11–15.
46   Cf. the *Introduction* for a more complete treatment of this issue.
47   *Cat.* 5–7, 1b11–8b24.
48   I.1, 402a23–25.
49   *Cat.* 5, 3b15–21.
50   Ibid.
51   While Aristotle makes a further suggestion about how the soul can be in motion,
     namely, by being angry or fearful and so on, his response does not so much refute
     that claim as indicate that it is not necessarily true. I.4, 408b4–31.
52   I.4, 408b32–33.
53   At I.2, 404b21–30 Aristotle makes it clear that those who hold this do so because
     the soul must account for both the motion of living things and their thought, and
     thought is largely explained by the principle, "like is known by like." (I.2, 404b17–
     18; I.5, 409b26–27) Since some think that numbers are the principles of all things
     (I.2, 404b24–25), some of these go even further and make the soul a self-moving
     number.
54   I.4, 409a1–3.
55   *Phys.* VIII.5, 258a20–25.
56   *Phys.* VIII.5, 257b6–12.
57   II.1, 412b4–6.
58   I.5, 409b2–4.
59   I.5, 409b19–411a5.
60   I.2, 403b25–27.

61   1.5, 409b26–27.
62   I.5, 409b31–410a13.
63   Cf. *Meta.* III.3, 998b14–999a23.
64   Cf. III.8, 431b21.
65   I.5, 410a23–26.
66   *Phys.* VIII.5, 257a33–b13.
67   II.5, 416b35–417a20; III.4, 429a13–18; III.4, 429b22–26.
68   I.5, 410a10–11.
69   Cf. II.12, 424a17–24; III.4, 429a13–27; III.5, 430a17–18.
70   Cf. III.4–5, 430a5–17.
71   I.5, 410b10–15.
72   I.5, 410b16–411a2.
73   I.5, 411a26–b5.
74   Plato, *Republic*, 435e–441c.
75   I.5, 411b6–14.
76   Cf., e.g., II.4, 416a13–18.
77   Cf. *Meta.* II.1, 993b11–19.

Appendix 2
The Definition of the Soul

In the first chapter of the *de Anima*, when discussing the various issues to be dealt with in a study of the soul, Aristotle lists first the determination of the definition.[1] This accords well with the description of a strictly scientific study as outlined in the *Posterior Analytics*, where we are told that a science shows that its subject has certain characteristics because of what that subject is, as, in mathematics, we see that it follows from what a triangle is that its three angles are equal to two right angles.[2] The latter predicate is not what a triangle is, yet it is true of every triangle at all times, for it follows from what a triangle is. Doubtless the perfection of mathematical science cannot often be expected in natural philosophy, yet our nearer approach to such perfection will be guaranteed by possession of the definition of the soul.

How, then, does Aristotle determine what the soul is? We notice immediately that he says we should start *as if* from the beginning, indicating both a significant past and a new approach.[3] That past can only be the discussions of Book I, which, as we have seen, prepare us for the study of the soul, including the determination of the definition. There Aristotle argued dialectically that the soul is in the genus of substance, not by being a body, but by being something of a body, something on the side of actuality, not of potency, and, moreover, something proportional to different sorts of bodies so as to be the mover of those bodies. In accordance with this, he also argued that the soul is able to be in motion *per accidens* though not *per se*, and is a principle of those motions or operations recognized as vital. Finally, he argued that the soul is what unites the disparate abilities of living bodies so that they are single things with a multitude of operations and not just an amalgam of powers.[4]

Besides having uncovered some likely positions in Book I, we also know from the *Physics* that changeable things (including, then, living bodies) are composed of form and matter.[5] This is true of things which change accidentally, as when a child learns grammar, as well as of things which change substantially, as when a child is conceived. The "matter" of a change is what persists through the change and what underlies the new aspect in which the change terminates; the "form" is that new aspect. In every changeable thing, then, we find matter and form, and so we know that there are substantial forms and a correlative matter in the genus of "substance," because many (if not all) substances are generable. The Aristotelian tradition, though not Aristotle himself, calls the matter of substances, "prime matter." Because this form and this matter are principles of substance, we can reasonably extend the word "substance" to them. They are not *species* of substance, but are called "substance" by an extension of the word.[6]

With this background, we are better able to inquire as to what the soul, this principle of those living operations with which we are so familiar, is.[7] It cannot be an accident; it must be in the genus substance. But it is not the living thing itself, which is a kind of substance. The living thing is what has a "soul" as a principle, it is not itself that principle. So it must be either material or form.

Of these two principles, the form is actuality and the material is potency. The latter receives the former so that together, as joint causes, they produce the composite being which we experience.[8]

Aristotle quickly dismisses the idea that the soul could be the material element, the body:

> But since it {the living thing} is also a body of a certain sort (for it is one which has life), the soul could not be the body. For the body is not among things which belong to an underlying, but rather is itself something which underlies and is material [for another].[9]

The implication of this text is that the soul belongs to an underlying matter. Certainly, when we understand the soul to be the principle of life, we mean it to be the principle of life for living bodies.[10] It is due to the soul that the body is alive, so the soul cannot be the body or material element, but that which the body receives so as to be alive. As being received by the body to make of it a certain sort of body, the soul must be what makes the living thing be what it is, and what makes it able to perform the operations peculiar to life. As such, it must be the form of the living thing.

For forms, even accidental ones, are responsible for making a thing be a certain sort of thing and do certain sorts of things: A wheel is a wheel because it is round and that form is what makes it roll so well, a car is a car because the parts are arranged in a certain way and this arrangement is what makes the car capable of forward motion. Substantial forms do the same for substances. When water is broken down into its elements, hydrogen and oxygen, we have new things with new properties. If we synthesize water from hydrogen and oxygen, we again have a new thing with new properties. In either case, what comes to be is composed of a material which pre-existed and a "form" which did not pre-exist. That new form must be what makes the product different from what had been there at the start of the change, and the new activities and attributes which the new thing has must be due to this new form. When an animal or a plant is generated, there is (much more obviously) at the end of the process a new thing with a new definition and a set of properties and powers proper to the living. Since the form is what is new and accounts for the new powers and properties of the generated thing, the form of the generated living thing must be the soul, for by "soul" we mean nothing other than the principle of the living thing and its vital activities.

But a puzzle arises here. Like accidents, substantial forms are not complete beings, and so must include in their definitions something extraneous to their essences.[11] A shape must include in its notion the material it shapes, but that material is not part of what the shape is. So too, substantial forms must be understood to be in the matter they inform. And yet, saying the soul is the act of prime matter would not go any distance toward distinguishing the soul from the forms of inanimate substances like water or gold, since these too have substantial forms which are the forms of prime matter.

Consequently, we must use a subject in our definition but we cannot use the ultimate subject, prime matter. So we must use matter as already formed in some way. Yet we cannot say that the soul comes to a matter already formed by a different form, because then the soul would be an accidental form. Whatever form first is given to prime matter must make it actual, and there can be no actual being before the substantial one. Thus, we must somehow account for the soul by a subject, but not a subject other than the one which the soul itself informs.

As a first attempt, we might say that the soul is the form of the living being considered as a composite of matter and form, saying that the soul is the substantial form of the organism, for example. But this would include in the definition what is being defined. For the living being is nothing other than the composite of form and matter and so includes the form which we are trying to define. Still, even if the composite living thing cannot be put into a perfect definition, it can be put into a helpful description, as we might say that the form of *The David* is the form *of the marble* or we might say it is the form *of the statue*. This latter expression can be helpful because the composite is something better known to us, being directly experienced.

Another way to understand the subject of the soul is to say that, when Aristotle refers to that subject as "a natural body having life potentially,"[12] he is speaking not of the composite substance precisely as composed of body and soul, but of whatever is able to operate as a living thing operates. Read in this way, the statement that the soul is "substance as the species of natural body having life potentially," defines the soul through its subject's having certain abilities, rather than a certain formation. This avoids the circularity of the definition and respects a fundamental fact, one which comes into more precise focus in II.2, namely, that the soul is recognized by its operations. For we know these operations better than we know the soul and in a way even better than we know the composite – at least, the composite is seen as living because it displays the operations of life.

It is not clear, though, that this is exactly what Aristotle himself intends by his definition of the soul. He did say that "by life we mean self-nutrition and growth and diminution,"[13] and these are operations; when he then goes on only a couple of lines later to say that the soul is "the substance as species of what has life potentially,"[14] it is not unnatural to read him as meaning that what has a soul has the *operations* of life potentially. Further, one can look to this claim: "It is not what has lost its soul which exists in potency so as to live, but what has [a soul]."[15] Here Aristotle says that what has a soul is still in potency to life, so the actuality which fulfills that potency cannot be the addition of the soul, but must be an actuality over and above what is possessed by the completed composite. Such further actualities are accidents, and here in particular, operations.

But the text seems to indicate that we should contrast the soul and body as two components of what is alive: "For the body is not among things which belong to an underlying, but rather is itself something which underlies and is material."[16] We often speak of a person as "made from body and soul" and we often refer to survival as "keeping body and soul together." The body is the subject or what underlies the soul, as he immediately goes on to say: "Therefore, it is necessary that the soul be substance as the species of a natural body having life potentially. Substance, however, is actuality. Therefore, it is the actuality of such a body."[17] A later text, in which Aristotle compares the soul to the power of sight, also seems to imply that a formed matter in proximate potency to the fully formed thing with ability to operate is what Aristotle is considering as the material for the soul: "... the eye is the material of sight, and if sight is left out, the eye is no longer an eye, except equivocally, like a stone eye or a painted eye. So one must grasp what is said in the case of the part about the whole living body."[18] Here the eye is the subject of the power of sight; it is understood as a material which underlies or is the subject of that power, and the power is understood as the final form which makes that subject actually be an eye. This implies articulation because the eye is able to receive the power of sight only when it is formed into a lens, a retina, etc.

Note that Aristotle begins here by taking "body" as a genus, but moves to consider it as the underlying of the soul.[19] This requires some explanation: "Whence every natural body which shares in life will be a substance – substance, however, in this way, as composite."[20] Here "body" is the genus of composite natural bodies: It is said in answer to the question "what is it" of many differing in species,[21] as of animals and plants and rocks. Aristotle treats "natural" here as a specific difference, and under "natural" we would have animate and inanimate, etc. Now, the genus must name the whole nature, even if it does so in a way that is open to further specification. For the part of a thing cannot be predicated of it, since the whole is not the part. I cannot say, "George is his hand" or "the dog is his tooth." Consequently, when Aristotle shifts from speaking of "body" as composite and as being a genus of natural body to "body" as one part of the composite of body and soul, he is shifting the meaning of the word "body" from meaning a genus to meaning a part.[22]

On this understanding of the text, "body," the subject already formed by the soul, is also understood to be that which is in potency to the soul as actuality. In the first two readings of lines 412a15–22, we understood the subject of the soul to be a fully formed substance, either simply the composite or the composite as in potency to the operations of life. But we can also understand that subject to be imperfectly formed by the soul. For the one substantial form gives many degrees of perfection: It makes the matter be, be a substance, be a body, be a living body, be a sensitive living body, be a human being. All these perfections are received by the matter through the soul, but they come to the matter in an order, for to be substance presupposes being, to be a body presupposes being a substance, etc. The earlier perfections are in potency to the later ones. We can understand the soul, then, as giving the finishing touches to a subject, the body, understood as not fully formed.

When we say that a man is composed of body and soul, this seems to be what we intend. We are not thinking of a body as the whole man (for then it would not need to be combined with anything else to compose the man). Rather, we seem to be thinking of the body as the receiver of another thing, the soul, and therefore as lacking at least something of what the soul brings to it. But because it is already thought of as a body, we must be thinking of it as already formed by a form. As we saw above, that form cannot be some form other than the soul, because then the body would already be a substance and the additional form, the soul, would necessarily be an accidental form, contrary to what we uncovered in the dialectical discussion and to our own intimate experience of being one living thing.[23]

All three of these readings have something to be said for them. It seems clear, though, that one can fuse the second and third and that the resulting reading is faithful to the text. For Aristotle overtly claims that the body is the subject of the soul, which can really only be taken as the third reading takes it (unless we are willing to accept the first reading and its imperfection), and he also is quite clear that "potentially living" refers to the potential for the operations of life. It is best to say, then, that the soul is the form or species of the body, which body is understood as able to be further formed by the very soul that made it be imperfectly formed to begin with, and that we know the nature of the formation given by the soul as such by way of the ability of the living thing to operate. This fits well, too, with the substitution of "composed of tools" for "natural body having life potentially."[24] It is the body which is articulated into tools or "organs" that is in proximate potency to life and living activities.

So far, so good. Aristotle does not stay with the language of form, species, and actuality, however, but switches to "first actuality."[25] The actuality of a thing is opposed to its potency. The English word "act" is derived from the Latin, "ago," which first meant to impel something, in particular, to drive cattle.[26] The things called "activities" (derived from the same word) are fulfillments of our powers, of our potentials to perform whatever operations we might be capable of. This is the first imposition of the word.[27] Because the operation stands to the ability to operate as the form of a thing stands to its material, insofar as the form fulfills the matter's ability, the form, too, can be called "act" or "actuality." So while actually playing the violin is an actuality insofar as it fulfills the habit of playing the violin, the habit of playing the violin is also an actuality, not of the ability to play but of the person who has an ability to develop that habit. As such, the habit can also be called an "actuality" of the ability to develop that habit. The fulfillment of the ability for operation, the ability to play the violin, say, is called "second actuality" and the fulfillment of the ability for that ability, the development of the habits involved in playing violin, is called "first actuality." So too, the substantial form of a thing is an actuality, and might be called "first" because it is contrasted with the second actuality, operation.

The question remains: Why does Aristotle switch from calling the soul "species and form" to calling it "first act?"[28] Perhaps because of the possible confusion of these in the case of inanimate things.[29] At the very least, form and first act in elemental bodies seem always to be together with second act or operation. Fire always burns and rocks always fall, etc., their second act always following immediately upon their first act, unless impeded from without. What is purely natural is determined to one operation at all times, because nature is a principle of motion and rest, and the more natural a thing is, the more it depends only on that one principle and so the more it is oriented in only one way. Living things, on the contrary, do not always perform their vital operations in the same way, or even perform them at all, despite the presence of the right conditions. They do not keep growing as long as food and energy for its conversion is available to them, or run until they fall over from exhaustion. The performance of vital operations is regulated from within; it is neither simply the effect of external agents nor the pre-determined result of the possession of a particular kind of power. By using the expression "first actuality" for the soul, Aristotle suggests that we attend to the distinct way in which a living thing has its first actuality as a possession to be deployed in bringing about operations and not as an uncontrolled urge.

Finally, as we saw above, Aristotle modifies his description of the subject of the soul, from "a natural body having life potentially" to "a natural body composed of tools." The natural body having life potentially can be understood, we saw, as the body formed to the degree that is in immediate potency to the presence of life (and that this degree of formation is bestowed on the subject of the soul by the same soul which endows it with life). We could go further to delineate the formation which it is necessary to have in order to be in that immediate potency. Describing that degree of formation in any detail is not the work of the *De Anima*, which looks only to what is common to living things. Moreover, even if there are formations of this sort which are common to all species of living being (as RNA and amino acids are common to all known life forms), the discovery and description of these forms is not the concern of the initial, general, and abstract part of biology, but of the more particular and concrete parts of biology.

We can say something, however, based on experience and on some considerations made in the *Physics*, and connected, too, with that unique relation, already mentioned, between first and second act found in living things. Aristotle had argued in Book VIII of the *Physics* that a self-mover must be divided into parts, one of which moves the other. It seems that these parts are as act and potency, for Aristotle argues to the division of the self-mover precisely on the ground that a mover must be in act but a thing moved must be in potency, and a thing cannot be both in potency and in act with respect to the same thing and at the same time, since potency implies privation and act implies possession.[30] In the end we should understand the mover of an animal to be the soul, a part of the composite organism together with the body,[31] but Aristotle had also argued earlier in the same work that a homogeneous whole, like an elemental body, cannot be a self-mover; there must be some difference between the mover and the moved for motion to occur.[32] Not only does the soul move the body, but it does so by using one part to move another. Living things, then, must have some part or parts by which they move other parts, as the muscles move the bones, and all these parts will have the character of tools by which living things accomplish their works, i.e., they will be organs and the living things will be "organic."[33] Because the soul is able, under the influence of desire, to move these parts in different ways at different times, the living thing can move itself from first to second act. And since what is moved is part of the living thing, the living thing is always affecting itself and so causes immanent and not only transitive motion.[34] There are also immanent motions of a more subtle sort, as are sensing, thinking, and desiring, for these activities, too, do not produce some external effect but terminate in the living being itself. As we know from experience, these operations also require peculiar formations in the body, and the parts which are so formed are called "organs" because they are instruments of the soul.

Aristotle thus gives his completed definition: "If, then, one must say something common about all souls, it would be the first actuality of a natural body composed of tools {of an organic natural body}."[35]

So Aristotle seems to be done with the definition, but, surprisingly, starts all over again in Chapter 2. The reason he gives for doing so is that we should start "from what is unclear but more apparent,"[36] and that a definition should not only say that a thing is defined in this or that way, but also give the reason. His example is "squaring," which he defines as "making an equilateral rectangle equal to an oblong rectangle," i.e., making a square equal to a given rectangle. He goes on: "Such a term {definition} has the account of a conclusion. But he who says that squaring is the finding of a mean proportional says the cause of the thing."[37] The implication is that the definition of the soul given in II.1 is like a conclusion and that it does not give the cause. A better account would give a reason and, one supposes, conclude to the definition given in Chapter 1. And this is just what Aristotle goes on to give us. Of course, he does not give us the cause of the soul itself, but of our thinking that the definition of the soul is what he says it is. While in the example of squaring the middle term is the cause of the thing we are speaking of, in the example of the soul it is not the cause of what the soul is but is only that better known object which we use in coming to the definition, i.e., it is the cause of *our knowing* what the soul is. In fact, the second actualities of the soul are these better known phenomena from which we begin and they are caused by the soul rather than being its causes.[38]

The processes of coming to a definition are discussed in the *Posterior Analytics*. Aristotle offers two paths: the comparison of things which display the characteristic to be defined and the continuous division of the genus into which it fits.[39] We might try to define courage, e.g., by comparing many cases of courageous action or else we might try to define it by dividing qualities into habits and its other species,[40] then habits into long-lasting and more transient ones, until we finally get to something like moral habits and intellectual habits and, subdividing moral habits in some way, locate courage. We would then gather the various divisions into which courage falls and so produce a definition.

While in the *Prior* and the *Posterior Analytics* he criticizes the method of "division" (though not unqualifiedly), he does use it in *De Anima* II.1 and elsewhere.[41] But in II.2, Aristotle demonstrates his definition as a conclusion from another definition.[42] The essential argument of II.2 may be summarized thus:

The principle of vital operations is the first act of the living body;

The soul is the principle of vital operations;

Therefore, the soul is the first act of the living body.[43]

The minor premise is the primitive definition of the soul. We should not think this is a weak beginning. If we are going to have any grasp on the way things are, we have to start with such definitions. For example, if I wish to study biology, I have to have already recognized something as my subject, namely, living things. This implies some grasp, even if only an imperfect and pre-scientific one, of what life is. It may be mixed with error or confused, and so I may need dialectic to remove the dross from the silver, but I either start with this or I start with nothing. There is nothing else to start with, and when I have achieved something in the way of science, its touchstone is that first understanding – life as first experienced is what I am trying to understand. In fact, if my elaborated understanding undercuts my initial knowledge, I have not explained life but explained it away, rejected the very thing I knew better than all my theories. This is why Aristotle says that "the beginning of the inquiry" is to divide the living from the non-living by the operations of life.[44]

Thus, all the thinkers whose positions we reviewed in the first book held that some things were alive and some were not, and they named whatever it was that caused that distinction, "the soul." And all of us can agree that we are alive and that there must be something that causes that fact. Not everything, after all, is alive, so there must be some distinguishing factor. We agree to call it "soul."

Aristotle discusses this minor premise by pointing out the kinds of operations he has in mind when we speak of life. More is included here than had been in II.1: "understanding, sensation, motion and standing according to place, moreover, motion according to nutrition, and both diminution and growth."[45] The soul, he says, "is defined {ὥρισται} by these: by the power of nutrition, of sensation, of thinking, and of motion."[46] He then goes on to discuss how these living powers are arranged in a series and how they are related to the body.[47]

By including more operations, he is preparing for a more perfect grasp on the soul (especially with regard to its unity in the higher living things), as well as for the division of the kinds of soul based on their powers. For the division of a species ought to be by differences which touch upon what the genus expresses. For example, we divide triangles by the ratios of the sides or by the quantity of the angles, the former rendering "equilateral," "isosceles," and "scalene" triangles, the latter, "acute," "right," and "obtuse" triangles. We do this because the divisions must be *per se* divisions of the genus, i.e., differences of what is included in the understanding of the genus. Thus, in our example of the triangle, sides and angles are included in the general idea of triangle. Accidental differences do not divide the genus into *kinds* of things, e.g., dividing triangles into red, white, and blue triangles would not give us different kinds of triangles because color has nothing to do with what is in the general definition of triangles. So, since the soul is the principle of the operations of life, different sorts of operations (nutrition, sensation, and thinking) make for different sorts of living things.

Secondly, the serial arrangement of the powers of life points to the unity of the soul. The higher living things have all the powers of the soul, while lower ones have fewer: sensation without intellect, or touch without the other senses, or even nutritive functions without any others at all, as in plants.[48] But we who read Aristotle are privileged to be among those who can do all these things, and we are aware in our own lives of the unity of our being. We know that we are the ones who think, sense, and feed, that we were smaller when we were children and are now larger, that we see and hear, and that we reflect on all this. Whatever we say about other beings, we are not amalgamations of powers or of pieces of matter, but have unified selves. By reviewing the powers and their serial arrangement, Aristotle puts us in mind of this central fact of our experience, a fact which is a powerful indicator of what he will say in the major premise, that the operations of life are due to the form that makes this body of ours able to do the things we do. We are not primarily acted upon or subject to unseeing forces, but act from ourselves in an organized and purposeful way. The serial arrangement of the powers of the soul indicates that the rarer powers are always added to the more common ones but not accidentally; rather, they are perfections of the one living being as such.

The major premise is the heart of the argument. It is here that the link is made between our initial grasp of the soul and the definition which tells what the soul essentially is. The claim it makes, that the principle of the operations of life is the first act of the living body, is an application of a more general principle, that the principle of operation is a form or first actuality. The principle cannot be the second actuality, certainly, since that is the very thing for which we seek a principle. Our only other options for the principle are the matter and the form of the thing which operates. For these are the principles of the substance which is operating, and so must be, finally, the principles of the activities of that substance.

Aristotle provides two examples, health and science, to help us see which of the two principles is the one we should call the soul.[49] We are called "healthy" both by the body and by the form of health (whatever that is exactly), and we are called "knowing" both by the soul and by the form of knowledge, for example, by the habit of geometry. As the body receives health so the soul receives the habit of geometry. The body and the soul, in these two examples, are both as matter, while health and knowledge are both as forms. We can multiply examples of this sort: We know an argument by our mind and by the premises of the argument. Here the mind is like material which receives the argument and the premises are like the form received by the mind. We see by the eye as by matter and by the power of sight as by a form.

So, since we know that the soul is that by which we first live, the only question is, by which of the two principles do we first live? If we look at the examples, our own and Aristotle's, we see that it is the formal element in every case that is the first principle of the effect in question. We are healthy by the body, but not until the form of health is added, so we are healthy first of all by the form of health. We know by the mind, but not until the habit of geometry is present, so we know first of all by the habit. So too, we know the conclusion primarily by the premises and we see primarily by sight. In each case, we are thinking of the first principle as that which, being present, causes the effect to be present, i.e., that before the presence of which the effect is not found. We can have a body and not be healthy, but we cannot have health and not be healthy, and so too in the other cases. Thus, that by which we first have an effect is the formal element, not the material. This is a more general version of the major premise of the demonstration. In the demonstration as Aristotle presents it, "live and sense and think"[50] is the effect which occurs in the presence of the form.

Perhaps to support this claim, Aristotle mentions the fact that the act of an agent is in some material, as the fire heats wood and the teacher teaches a student: In each case the "material" is "formed" by the agent after its own likeness. But the material is only passive to the agent until it has received the form, after which it is able to act, as the ignited wood can heat another piece of wood and the student, become a knower, can teach. The activity, then, follows upon the reception of the form and is not present given only the receptive matter. Since the soul is the first principle of the operations of life, it must be the form of the body, where "body" is once again taken as was explained above, namely, as the material counterpart of the soul. The body only lives when it has received the soul.

What have we gained by this approach from what is clearer to us to what is clearer by nature? We have tied the phenomena which lead us to see the existence of life to the form of living things as to their principle. In the first definition, this link was present, but only implicitly. We proceeded "from above," as it were, and how we knew where to put the soul in each set of divisions or how we knew which divisions to make in the first place was unclear. Here in the second chapter, we proceed from our experience of the activities of living things to see that the soul must be the principle of those activities and that to be so it must be the form of the living body.[51] What was the purpose of the definition as given in the first chapter, then? We saw above that we can see from the first chapter, with some reflection, that the definition is a good one. Having that definition as a target for the second discussion, we were able to follow a more direct and certain route to the definition.

It is instructive, too, to compare the approach of Aristotle with that of the earlier philosophers. For some the soul was fire, for some a harmony of bodily parts, for some, the four elements, for some, a self-moving number. But these positions, as varied and as odd as they sometimes are, are all attempts to grasp what the soul, the principle of life, really is. The approach of these early thinkers is more or less hypothetical: If the soul were X (fire or harmony or the elements), we could explain this or that vital operation (motion or conformity with the body or thought). The line of argument is like that found in some parts of modern science and ancient astronomy: If such and such a particle, with these or those properties, were to be postulated, we could explain this or that phenomenon. If the planets move on epicycles of such and such a size at such and such a speed, we can explain the motion of Venus.[52] Other hypotheses lurk in the wings awaiting their role in the drama of scientific advance. One of these hypotheses may take over center stage for a long time, because of its greater explanatory power or because we have discovered other phenomena which it can explain. But the initial move, at any rate, does not give us certitude beyond that of the detective who guesses at possible explanations.

Aristotle's argument in the second chapter is not such a hypothetical postulate but is a demonstration of the definition of the soul based on the initial grasp of the soul which all have and the certitude of which cannot be seriously doubted. The divisions, too, upon which the approach in the first chapter is based, though they are not self-evidently the right divisions to make, are still divisions which are obvious from experience or else from earlier studies. Aristotle, in short, proceeds from the known to the unknown, from experience or commonly understood truths accessible to all, to something most people get wrong, the nature of the soul. The earlier philosophers did not so much proceed from the known to the unknown as make an imaginative leap from the phenomena to be explained to a guess, more or less probable. None actually argue from what is given in experience to their views, they only say, in effect, "*if* this were what the soul is, *then* this or that operation would be (more or less) intelligible." In other words, Aristotle is the only one who gives us the thread by which we can actually come to know what the soul is, starting from what we already know just in virtue of the analysis of change in the *Physics* and the experience of being alive.

Endnotes to Appendix 2

1 I.1, 402a10–22.
2 *Po. An.* I.6, 74b5–12; Euclid, *Elements* I, Propositions 1–32.
3 II.1, 412a2.
4 See Appendix 1, *Dialectic in Book I of the De Anima.*
5 *Phys.* I.7, 190b17–20.
6 It should not be thought that every genus name is extended to the principles of that genus; e.g., points are in the genus quantity as principles of magnitude, but are not *called* "quantity." It is a matter of convention, at least in part, which genus-names will be extended to the principles of the things in that genus: In contrast to the point, we do often call one a "number," even though it is not a "multitude composed of units," but only a principle of such a multitude. Cf. Euclid, *Elements* VII, Definitions 1 and 2. Note too, that when I say that form is not a species of substance, I am not denying that the form is also called "species." The latter is a name of the form as it is a principle of the thing's intelligibility, since "species" names originally the "look" of a thing and is then extended to mean the "look" things have to the mind.
7 For a discussion of the certitude of our knowledge of the soul and of the experiences upon which that certitude depends, cf. the *Introduction.*
8 *Phys.* I.9. 192a13–14.
9 II.1, 412a16–19.
10 I.1, 403a3–28. If there are non-bodily living things, they are not part of the study of natural science, within which falls the study of the soul. See I.1, 403b15–16 and *Meta.* VI.1, 1025b34–1026a6. Nevertheless, that study which does treat of them might presuppose the study of the soul.
11 *Meta.* VII.4–5, 1030a17–1031a15.
12 II.1, 412a20–21.
13 II.1, 412a14–15.
14 II.1, 412a19–21.
15 II.1, 412b25–26.
16 II.1, 412a17–19.
17 II.1, 412a19–22.
18 II.1, 412b20–23.
19 II.1, 412a14–22.
20 II.1, 412a15–16.
21 Cf. Porphyry, *Isagoge*, Ch. 2.
22 II.1, 412a11–22. The genus is material with respect to the difference, since it is in potency to being perfected by different specific differences, and so is in that way like, though not the same as, the matter of the composite.
23 On the living experience of being one thing, see the *Introduction.*

24 II.1, 412a20–21; 412a27–b6. The Greek word, ὄργανον, from which we derive the English "organ" first of all means a tool. It is itself derived from the same root as ἐνέργεια (which I translate "act"), namely, ἔργον, which means "deed," "action," or "work," and is in fact cognate with the latter. "Composed of tools" seems to get at what Aristotle intends here, especially as the English word "organ" is not, for most of us, associated any longer with the notion of a tool.

25 See *Glossary,* "Actuality."

26 Cf. Ernout 2001, entry "ago."

27 Aristotle claims the Greek equivalent is also used first to name motions. *Meta.* IX.3, 1047a30–32.

28 II.1, 412a19–28.

29 Cajetanus1939, pp. 18–29.

30 *Phys.* VIII.5, 257b6–12.

31 II.4, 415b21–22.

32 *Phys.* VIII.4, 255a12–18..

33 Cf. *Movement of Animals* and *Progression of Animals.*

34 See the *Introduction* for this distinction.

35 II.1, 412b4–6.

36 II.2, 413a11–13.

37 II.2, 413a13–20.

38 One might say that the argument is from the final cause to the formal cause because Aristotle proceeds from the operations, which have the character of an end. But when Aristotle says we should proceed from what is more apparent to what is more known according to account, he is thinking of the argument as going from what is posterior to what is prior, and so not from final to formal cause but from effect to cause.

39 *Po. An.* II.13–17, 96a20–99b7.

40 *Cat.* 8, 8b26–9a4.

41 Aristotle also addresses the way of division in *Pr. An.* I.31, 46a32–b30. The definitions of motion and nature are seen by divisions. Cf. *Phys.* II.1 192b8–23; *Phys.* III.1 200b–26–201a11.

42 Other cases of the demonstration of definitions are that of happiness in *Nic. Eth.* I.7, 1097b22–1098a18 and the definition of the demonstration itself in *Po. An.* I.2, 71b9–72a7. In both cases, Aristotle moves from a definition along the lines of final cause to one along the lines of material cause.

43 II.2, 414a4–19.

44 II.2, 413a20–21. See also the *Introduction.*

45 II.2, 413a23–25. In I.1, he had only mentioned nutrition and growth and diminution. Cf. I.1, 412a14–15.

46 II.2, 413b11–13.

47 II.2, 413b13–414a3.

48 Or so it seems. If one were to argue that some or even all plants have some sort of sensory awareness, this would simply mean that Aristotle would call them animals, not that his general theory was misconceived.

49 II.2, 414a4–12.

50 II.2, 414a12–132.

51 Note that this is an application of the principle presented at *Po. An.* II.8, 93a28–29,

namely, that our path to "what a thing is" is more or less secure to the degree that our knowledge "that the thing is" is secure. The better we see why we think that a thing exists, the more able we are to see what it is. For the reason that we think it exists is that we see something of it, even if only its effects, and this is the only link we have to it. Other examples are the discussions of place and time in the *Physics*, in which Aristotle argues to what place and time are from the fact that we know place exists because we know change of place exists and that we know time exists because we experience it in the experience of motion. Cf. *Phys.* IV.4, 211a12–b6; *Phys.* IV.11, 219a2–b2.

52 Ancient astronomy explained the appearance of the motions of the planets, such as Venus, largely by assuming that the planets were borne upon circles (called "epicy-cles") the centers of which were themselves thought of as being borne upon larger circles (called "deferents"). Cf. Ptolemy, *Almagest*, III.3.

Appendix 3
The Reproductive (or Vegetative) Soul

"Life is found in animals and plants; but while in animals it is clear and evident, in plants it is hidden and not apparent."[1] Even in ourselves, the least evidently vital of our operations are those associated with the vegetative functions, i.e., feeding, growth, and reproduction.[2] We are almost completely unaware of our digestion and growth unless something goes wrong and, while some of our reproductive activities are hard to miss, in this and in the cases of the other vegetative functions, we are aware of them only to the extent that they impinge on sensation or have some result which we can sense, like off-spring or greater weight. A sign that the vegetative life is the least obvious sort of life is that the earlier philosophers seemed to have had very little to say about it. They discussed life in terms of motion, mostly locomotion, and sensation.[3] One might even wonder why we think that growth and feeding should be categorized as vital operations along with sensation and reasoning. Everyone does so, but why should they? And why does Aristotle begin with these, if they are the least apparent vital operations?[4]

We might argue that Aristotle does, in fact, begin with the more obvious sort of life when, in Book I, he reviews the positions of his predecessors, for they followed the road to the soul from sensation and motion. In any case, we come to see that the vegetative operations are in fact vital by comparing them to more obviously vital operations. The common element in virtue of which we realize that these various sorts of operations are indicators of life is a sort of self-motion, and consequently, a kind of immanent operation. When we eat or grow or sense or think or desire, our operation has completion within ourselves, even if it also has a natural tendency outward.[5] For example, the act of seeing, even if it depends on something outside ourselves and is ordered to knowing that thing, is still an activity within our eyes. Further, we recognize death, in animals and plants, by the absence of such operations, especially locomotion, breathing, the beating of the heart, and, in a medical setting, brainwaves or other more subtle motions.[6]

These operations, then, are all forms of self-motion, as we noted in the *Introduction*, and the living things that have such operations are "self-movers." Such movers, Aristotle argued in the *Physics*, are necessarily made of parts, some of which move and others of which are moved.[7] This mover is, in the end, the soul, but it moves the body by using organs to work against each other.[8] The living is composed of dissimilar parts which the animal uses as tools or organs. The animal uses its muscles to move its legs, so that one part moves another, and the part moved is a part of the animal itself; the motion of the legs, of course, results in the further motion of the whole animal in reference to the space around it. Thus, the vital operations are those which are immanent, having some term within the mover itself; this is implicit in calling living things "self-movers." But the plant lacks many of these motions and those it does have are not so obviously instances of self-motion. To see that they are, in fact, self-motions, we need to recognize these vegetative operations in ourselves first, even if those functions, when found in non-human organisms, are sometimes so differently instantiated as to be barely recognizable.[9]

We know, then, that we take in food and use it to power our activities, activities that belong to the one substance each of us is. In feeding, we already recognize ourselves as agents that act on the world by means of tools built into our bodies (e.g., teeth, tongues, stomachs, intestines, etc.), turning some portion of the world into food to be used as fuel by ourselves and for ourselves: Without food, our vital operations quickly come to an end in death. We work on a material which is, to the extent it is called "food," defined in relation to ourselves (or other organisms). When we see that plants too have organs by which they turn exterior material, even sunlight, into fuel for their activities, we see how they have a vital operation like our own, and it is due to this (and other vegetative activities) that we call plants "living."[10]

But we do not only use food for fuel, we also use it to add to our bulk. Who does not remember being too small to see over the kitchen table and then later being proud of having grown to the point where he could inform the world about this signal feat? Where did that extra height come from? It came from the food we ate, which was transformed into our own substance and added bulk to it. We are well aware that the additional length in our arms and legs belongs to us, and, while the process of the addition of the digested stuff to our substance is not something we directly experience, the result, our survival and increased bulk, is directly experienced.[11]

Feeding and growth, like sitting and standing, show that each of us is one substance, one real thing underlying the shifts in stuff and size and position. I am immediately aware that the one who stands and sits is myself, that I am not a new man or a new sort of animal when I cross my arms; and also that I am the same one who feeds and whose body is fed, who lives as a body fed by the food I eat. In order to endure, I metabolize food, and to do that I must be composed of organs differentiated in kind but working together harmoniously to produce an effect which is the very continued existence of the substance that performs these operations to begin with. I am not what I eat; rather, what I eat I transform into myself, a highly articulated organism which endures by metabolizing food into its own organs, even into its own organs of eating. No machine produces its own body, but the organism does: It is its own purpose and even its own agent (after its parents), because it forms out of the food it eats the organs which it is uses to eat and to perform its other vital activities. The organism is thus a substance which outlasts the material it consumes, forming always anew its own body. The thing that survives this unending regeneration is the organism, a substance, separated from its surroundings and taking advantage of them, maintaining itself and its kind through endless changes. While the inanimate merely lasts, doing nothing to achieve its longevity, the animate works to survive, "to keep body and soul together," to maintain its self-identity as a being separate from the world and occupied in turning that world, or at least the part called food, into itself.[12]

The third operation of the vegetative soul, reproduction, is the one Aristotle says most perfectly attains the fulfillment of this sort of soul.[13] Even in reproduction (which obviously ends in an external product), food is instrumental, since it is first turned into gametes, spores, cell walls, etc., which have an innate ability to become or to be some principle of a new individual, produced out of the old one in one way or another, so that reproduction, too, is a process that is in a sense immanent: Though the final product is external, the off-spring is an out-growth of the innate principles of the parent and is actually formed out of the very substance of the parent.[14] The new organism is the most complete result of the organism's impulse to continue living and to bring matter under its own form.

Inanimate "reproduction" or "growth" (e.g., the growth of a fire or its generating a new fire by leaping across a fire break) differs in principle from the reproduction or growth of the living.[15] With the inanimate, there is no strong unity in either the new individual or in the old – a fire can grow simply by finding more fuel and can become two fires by having a middle section extinguished. Moreover, the fire does not use tools or organs to grow or reproduce; it just spreads out. The fire does not have any natural limits but burns as much as it can, whereas the vital principle of the plant, its soul, informs a determinate size of body and, when its body is fully developed, brings about another such organism, another thing that will use food to survive and grow until it, in turn, comes to full size and then to produce another like itself.

Having seen that the operations of the vegetative soul are vital, we still might wonder why Aristotle begins with them, as they are the most difficult to see as vital activities. They are the most common vital operations, and this is why Aristotle treats them first despite their being less known to us. In presenting the unity of the definition of the soul, he focuses on the fact that the sensitive soul includes the vegetative soul in potency and the intellectual includes both the sensitive and the vegetative souls.[16] The vegetative is "present" in the other souls. The other souls, then, stand to it as further perfections to something relatively imperfect and material, something that can be further formed by these further powers. The commonality of the vegetative powers is thus the basis for a "generic" definition of the soul.

Why is there so little said in the *De Anima* about the vegetative soul and its operations? Only one chapter, II.4, deals with this soul, while the sensing soul receives a total of eleven chapters (II.5–III.3) and the intellectual soul receives five chapters (III.4–8). The reason probably lies in the order peculiar to natural science. It tends from the relatively abstract to the relatively concrete. The *Physics*, for example, starts with the most general consideration of motion and its conditions, and then Aristotle descends into more concrete matters in the *De Caelo*, the *De Generatione et Corruptione*, etc. So too, the biological works descend from the relative abstraction of the *De Anima* to the more concrete considerations of the *De Sensu et Sensato*, the *De Memoria*, *De Generatione Animalium*, *Historia Animalium*, etc. Little can be said of the vegetative functions from a general point of view; it is in descending to the concrete considerations of organic chemistry and biochemistry that we can say more. Only very general claims are made at the level of the *De Anima*.

Endnotes to Appendix 3

1   *De Plantis*, I.1, 815a10–1. This text was long attributed, though falsely, to Aristotle. It is more likely by Nicolaus of Damascus (b. 64 B.C.).

2   II.4, 415a22–26, 415b27–416b31.

3   I.2, 403b25–27.

4   Aristotle discusses the vegetative soul at II.4, 415b27–416b31.

5   This issue is discussed at greater length in *The Introduction*.

6   Not all the operations of life are equally "motions," as Aristotle will argue at II.5, 417a30–b16. In the case of the feeding and growth, though, it seems the motions are motions in the sense of the definition of motion given in *Phys.* III.1, 201a10–11. Reproduction, to the extent that substantial generation falls outside of the definition, is also motion in a more removed sense (cf. *Phys.* V.2, 225a10–11), but in this case not because it is immanent. In fact, it is the most transitive of any of the vegetative operations, and we will need to think a little to see why it is considered vital at all.

7   *Phys.* VIII.5, 257a33–b12; cf. also VIII.4, 255a12–15.

8   See II.4, 415b8–28, III.10, 433b13–27, and Appendix 2, *The Definition of the Soul*.

9   Proceeding from what we know about ourselves here is essential, as we saw in the *Introduction*, even though there is a legitimate concern about anthropomorphism. But that fear, if allowed to exclude any consideration of our own experiences of the vegetative or, more generally, the vital operations, will, as we also saw there, cut us off entirely from the understanding of life, whether our own or others', whether human, animal, or plant. We cannot let the fear of error command ignorance.

10 Aristotle does not speak of food as fuel, but does note that organisms need it to keep living. II.4, 416b11–15.

11 In the text cite in note 10, Aristotle also notes that food causes growth.

12 Much of the foregoing discussion is derived from Kass 1999, pp. 21–56.

13 II.4, 415a22–b7.

14 This contrasts with other sorts of physical activities, wherein the agent gives a "form" to what it acts upon, but does not give it material (when material is given, we really have locomotion rather than causal action.)

15 Aristotle considers the view that fire grows in II.4, 416a9–18.

16 II.3, 414a32–b32.

Appendix 4
The Sensing Soul

While the life of plants is hidden from us,[1] the life of animals is not. We easily recognize animals as alive, at least those animals that, like us, move about in space. It is the presence of self-motion that defines the living,[2] and motion in place seems to be the most obvious sort of motion and the most obvious sort of self-motion. Sensation, which is even more identified with animals, is a kind of "alteration,"[3] a change from not being aware to being aware. It would be difficult not to notice that we ourselves sense the things around us and move ourselves toward objects of desire and away from objects of aversion; less difficult but still outlandish to think that the dogs, cats, and blue jays do not.[4]

What is this sensation of which we have such intimate knowledge? At the very least, it is an awareness of other things and even of ourselves. By sight we know what is around us, the walls and furniture and occupants of the room we happen to be in, and things quite far away, the moon and the sun and the stars, and even things so close as to be called not merely our own but our selves: Our arms and legs and, in mirrors at least, our faces and eyes; by touch we are aware of the things we are in immediate contact with and of our own bodies; and so for the other senses.

We seem, in fact, to have two ways of knowing ourselves, one from the inside and one from the outside. We know other things, tables and chairs, trees and flowers, cats and dogs, and even our friends and relations, by sensing them, hearing and seeing and touching them. But we know ourselves by the interior experience of being the ones who hear and see and touch. We sense all these things and are also aware that it is we ourselves who are aware of them. We also know ourselves by exterior experience, for while we can feel other things with our hands, we can also feel our hands with our hands, and see them too. This is most striking when we are anesthetized, e.g., at a dentist's office. We feel our cheek and are surprised that our hand reports the cheek as usual but our cheek does not report anything about its experience of being touched. Our cheek feels just like anyone else's cheek; it has become an object of external sensation alone.

Senses, then, make us aware of the things surrounding us as well as of our own selves, in the latter case both because we sense our bodies as we sense other bodies and because in sensing we are aware that it is we ourselves who are doing the sensing. I will consider separately these two aspects of sense, i.e., our awareness of exterior objects and our experience of ourselves as sensing.

What is this awareness we call sensation? In the case of sight, we are aware of things which are at a distance from us, greater or smaller. But the awareness itself, somehow, is in us and is nothing other than the thing's presence to our sight.

Our first thought about this presence is probably that it is some sort of mechanical interaction between the eye and its object; we might think a stream of particles or a disturbance in an electromagnetic medium causes some physical change in the eye. One might think that light affects the retina so that it in turn does something to the optic nerve, etc., and that this entire process when terminated in the brain *is* seeing.

But while these sorts of motions may be required for seeing, it is not possible that this is all that seeing really is. For, on this view, the object is not even perceived; rather, it stimulates the sense organ to produce some sort of image which may or may not be in any way a likeness of the thing we supposedly see; there is simply no way to be sure because (on this view of sensation) we never know anything about the exterior object except by this sort of process. We can, in fact, stimulate parts of the brain with electrodes so as to make a person think they are seeing things – but they are deceived; they are in fact not seeing at all. If sensation were merely this sort of response of the brain or sense organ to a stimulus, then we would have to admit that we are not really aware of the things we think we are aware of, that the world as we know it in immediate experience is nothing but a picture show with no discernable connection to the things causing it (supposing there really are things causing it). For how would we ever be able to look behind the mechanisms at the real objects causing the show except by using other sensations subject to the same difficulty? No; if there is such a thing as sensation, that is, an immediate awareness of the bodies around us and even of our own bodies, as there assuredly is, a mechanical explanation is incomplete in the most fundamental way: It misses the first point of all, namely, that sensation is an awareness of sensible things themselves. A theory which denies this denies the very phenomenon it was trying to explain in the first place.[5]

Consider, too, that the way the one body affects another in material interactions is by changing the character of the thing affected. In particular, the agent gives to the patient an actuality which displaces an earlier one and so in a sense corrupts the patient. When water is heated, it loses one temperature in gaining a new one. But in the case of sensation, the sense is not in any way corrupted by the sensible; on the contrary, it is perfected by it, brought to its own nature, fulfilled.[6] This fact points to a different sort of interaction, one in which the patient attains integrity and perfection. And the possession of the sensible, unlike the way the form given by the agent is possessed in other physical interactions, is all at once. The eye (after certain physical adjustments are made, such as altering the size of the pupil) sees its object steadily; it does not come to see it more and more the way that a body being heated takes on heat more and more. This seems to indicate that the organ of sense is in potency to the form received in a peculiar way, for normally the matter must be brought from potency to act by a continuous motion.[7]

The view we have been considering does have this in its favor: It rightly claims that the sensible object is doing something to the sense power. We are not always sensing and even if we were always sensing something, we are not always sensing everything. When we look at an apple we see red, when we go to the symphony we hear notes, but we do not see red apples at the symphony nor hear music when we gaze upon an apple. Why aren't our senses always perceiving their objects? The object must be present to do its work on the sense power.[8] This is the very first claim Aristotle makes about the sense, namely, that they are passive powers, their objects stand to them as agents to patients.[9] The sense power is one which is activated by an exterior object and which, in the absence of such an object, whether an odor or a color, etc., cannot actually function; we can only sense in the presence of the objects of sense. If we think we are sensing when the object is not present, something is amiss; we need a doctor of some sort. Sense is essentially a passive power, one activated by the sensible as by an agent.[10]

While the mechanical view of sensation fails,[11] its failure directs us to the necessary fact: Awareness is the presence, to the knowing power, of the very object about which we are aware, and this not in the way one body is present to another either in place or in physical causality. It is the object itself – color or odor or sound – of which we are aware, not some image or effect of it, even if some such thing is necessary for awareness.

This should remind us of the Empedoclean notion that "like is known by like."[12] Empedocles argued on the basis of sensation that the soul was made of the four elements (earth, water, air, and fire). Since the known must be in the knower, and the thing known, when well known, is known through its principles, to know must be due to the presence in the knower of the principles of all things – but these are the elements. Aristotle argued against Empedocles' view on several grounds.[13] One of the more damaging criticisms was that, if Empedocles is right, not only the elements but whatever it is that makes the elements be formed into this or that composite, namely, the ratio of the elements or the form, must also be present in the mind, if we are to know not only the elements but the composites. But we do know the composites, and the implication that we have little horses in our heads when we know what a horse is militates against common sense. The principle must therefore be wrong. Or is it just wrongly applied?

Empedocles' fundamental insight is doubtless right: To know a thing, it must be present in the knowing power. But, Aristotle argues, this presence is not something connatural to the organs, as Empedocles' view would indicate, for the object is received by the sense power; before that reception the sense power has the object in it only potentially. Moreover, when the sense receives the object, it is not corrupted, and when it has it, it has it in a perfect, steady way. Thus, this presence cannot be such as the thing known has in the exterior world. Yet what else is there?

Aristotle speaks of the "reception of the sensible species without the matter."[14] Just what is this "immaterial" reception?" We are apt to assume that immaterial means something completely incorporeal, but surely this cannot be what Aristotle means when he is speaking of sensation, which, as he notes,[15] always has a physical organ. What is he negating when he says that senses receive the species of the sensible "immaterially?" And what are these "species?"[16]

The word translated "species" is εἶδος which literally means "appearance" or "look."[17] It has a strong presence in all of Aristotle's works as well as in those of his master, Plato. In the latter works it is often associated with the theory of the "ideas" (from the same root as εἶδος), and in Aristotle's logical works with the most specific (again, from the Latinate root, "species") kinds of things (as opposed to generic kinds). In both cases, the likely reason for the use of this word is that it conveys the notion of how a thing looks to a knowing power. Its original use is to name the look a thing has to the knowing power that literally looks at things, namely, eyesight, and then the word is stretched out to mean the way a thing "looks" to any knowing power. It can even be used to mean the nature of a thing, since the nature is that *by which* the thing appears to the mind.[18] The species, then, is the "look" of the thing known and the sensible species is that aspect of the sensible due to which it has an appearance to a sense power: its color, sound, smell, taste, or tangible quality. This is what Aristotle says is received without matter, "immaterially." What does that mean? As a negation, it must be understood by contrast with what it negates.

Here is the text wherein Aristotle speaks of the species being immaterially received:

> ...sense is what is receptive of the sensible species without the material, as wax receives the sign of the signet ring without the iron and the gold. However, it takes on the golden or the brazen sign, but not as gold or bronze. Likewise, too, the sense of each thing suffers by what has color or flavor or sound, but not insofar as each of those things is said to be [the thing in question], but insofar as it is of such a [sensible] sort, and according to its account.[19]

Aristotle says the wax receives the sign of the ring "but not as gold or bronze." The sense organ does not take on the nature of the thing it senses, i.e., the nature of the substance the sensible qualities of which it perceives, but it takes on what the sensible substance has which is formal or definitive relative to the sense, i.e., color if it is seen, sound if it is heard, etc.

Yet this does not seem sufficient to distinguish sensation from purely natural changes. In every case of agent causality, the agent gives to the matter of the patient a form like the one it has, but the agent never gives the patient any of its own material. When that does happen, we do not have an example of an agent cause but of material cause; the matter of the "agent" actually changes place and goes into the body of the patient, as when salt makes water salty: It does not alter the water, it just breaks down into small parts which mix with the water, thus giving the water something of its material. Agent causes do not do this: When one ball hits another and gives it motion, the motion itself is not moved from one ball to the other, however much we might speak this way when, say, the motion is "transferred."

Still, it remains true that when we sense, we receive something that is in the sensible, for we sense what is present in the object, as we see the color of a wall with our eyes and that color comes to be in our eyes due to the color out there in the wall. Of course, the wall is not in our eyes, only its color is.[20] And when the color is in our eye, it does not color our eye the way it colors the wall, i.e., so as to make the eye another instance of a thing colored as the wall is colored. And if the eye did become colored as the wall is, noting that would not bring us a step closer to understanding sensation; we would simply have kicked the can down the road to ask, "how is the color of the eye seen?" Since the color stands to the wall as form to matter, we can say that in sensation, we receive the form without the matter. We receive the form of the sensible in such a way that the form remains the form of the sensible object and does not transform the sense or the organ of sense into an instance of the sort of thing sensed. It takes on the form in a different way than does the matter of the physical object of our sensation. In fact, we might go further: To the extent that the sense power receives the form but is perfected by so doing, it is not receiving as matter receives: Matter, in receiving, is perfected but also loses what it had, some previous form.[21] Even though the form of the sense organ conditions the reception, as does any form (cold water is harder to heat than hot water), yet without that form, there would be no immaterial reception at all. The reception here, then, is due to the form itself.

It is likely that all of this is intended by the negation "without matter." The illustration of the wax and the golden or brazen signet ring reflects this because the wax does not receive the form of the ring the way the gold or bronze does. The wax receives not as the material of the ring does, and this is akin to the sense receiving in a way other than does the matter of the sensible object. We can see more clearly, too, why the "alteration" which is sensation is not of the same sort as other alterations.[22]

One thing that is not intended is that the sense is itself an immaterial being; it is obvious that the senses inhabit corporeal organs and are powers of such organs. Because of this, while they receive immaterially in the sense just outlined, they still receive with certain material conditions. They receive whatever they receive as particular. The color in the wall is a particular and the color as it is in the eye is also a particular. As Aristotle says, "...sense according to act is of particulars, while science is of universals...."[23] And just as the particular color is spread out in reality across a surface, so is the color in my eye spread out: I have what can be called a "visual field." So the senses receive immaterially, but not in every meaning of the term; the negation involved must be sharply defined.

Moreover, though the sensible object acts upon the sense power and causes the form of the sensible to be in the sense power, the knowing is not merely passive. Even though some passivity is presupposed in sensation, insofar as the sensible must act on the sense power, sensing is still an activity, a "doing" of some sort, a perception or awareness; the presence of the known, the term of the operation, in the power due to its having received the form of the sensible, in an awareness, an activity. For this reason, the activity of sight is also an immanent activity, that is, unlike purely physical operations, it remains in the operator and does not go over into some material, as the activity of heating goes over into the material being heated.

Above, I mentioned a second aspect of the sensing soul, namely, its self-awareness.[24] Plants are self-contained in a way that the inanimate things are not, because their vital operations are terminated within themselves. But animals not only have the vital operations which plants have, they also have sensation, which, while it requires the presence of exterior objects, is still an activity occurring within the living being. It is this which elevates the life of animals over that of plants. Because the senses make us aware of other things, they also, by consequence, make us aware of ourselves. In sensing, the animal is not only aware of the things around it, it also places itself in opposition to them.[25]

The senses, then, make us both more part of the world and more opposed to it: We recognize ourselves as parts of the world and also as faced with it, forced to "take it into account," to use some of it as food and avoid some of it lest we become food. Moreover, this conscious interaction with the world leads to desire and fear; if we can sense, we can feel pain and pleasure, and so we have the first instances of conscious striving for goods not yet possessed.[26] While plants and inanimate bodies may act for ends, as Aristotle thinks they do,[27] they do so without any awareness of those ends. Animals, by contrast, hunt down their prey or flee from their predators or seek mates and coworkers because of desire based on knowledge: sensation and that innate knowledge called "instinct."[28] The world even accommodates these desires by providing beings which we can treat as food or as companions.

Finally, the senses, because they make us aware of ourselves as sentient beings, also lead us to see that we are individual substances. We might think of rocks and puddles as just collections of bits of matter, liquid or solid; it is not easy to think of ourselves that way. The reason it is hard is that we are aware that we are the ones who see and hear and taste. More, we not only know we have these sensations, we know that they are not the same as each other.[29] This we can only know if each one of us is some one self. If not, how could we compare the various sensations? To tell the difference, there must be one knower comparing them, just as there must be one mind knowing each of two statements in order for them to be recognized as different; if I know one statement and you know the other, neither of us will know the difference between them. Our ability to sense and to sense the difference between the objects of the various senses, then, points immediately at a unified person who is aware of the multitude of sensations. If we are aware of the differences between the sensibles due to our unified self, is there any reason to deny such unity to other animals, at least those we call "higher?" They behave, with regard to sensation, very much like ourselves. My dog does not seem to confuse seeing with hearing any more than I do.

Clearly, we can extend this argument to the rational activities of the mind as well. But note that we can also extend it in a way to the vegetative functions. The organs of sight, hearing, etc., by which I perceive the sensibles, and the organ of the common sense, by which I compare the sensibles of the various senses,[30] are all products of my growth, of my taking in food and turning it to my own advantage as fuel and as material. So, in fact, is the brain which I use when I think.[31] The one being that senses all these things is one with the one being that feeds, grows, and reproduces itself. The soul of the animal is not something added on extrinsically or accidentally to the vegetative being; it is the same soul with more powers, and so the vegetative being and the sentient being are one and the same. There is substantial unity, therefore, within ourselves and also within other living things that are like us in these regards.

The senses, then, not only make us aware of their proper objects like color and sound, they also make us recognize ourselves as part of the world and the world as something we must deal with; they also give rise to appetites and so to the first more or less conscious apprehension of good and bad things. Moreover, our senses point toward the unity of our selves and, insofar as they are in a way immaterial, begin to point to what is beyond the material world they reveal.

Endnotes to Appendix 4

1   *De Plantis*, I.1, 815a10–1. Cf. Appendix 3, *The Reproductive (or Vegetative) Soul.*

2   Cf. *Introduction*, and *Appendices 2* and *3*, *The Definition of the Soul* and *The Vegetative (or Reproductive) Soul.*

3   II.5, 417a30–b16.

4   Cf. *Introduction* for a discussion of the mechanistic view of life.

5   We might add that those who hold this view are never so critical of the experiments upon which they base their claims: When a person's brain is stimulated so that they see things, these theorists suppose they really know there are brains and electrodes and that they know that the person is not really seeing things because the things seen are not really there. But how do they know they are not there? They uncritically assume the awareness of the subjects and conditions of the experiment itself. Their interpretation of the experiment is self-refuting insofar as it does away with the reality of the experiment (and the experimenter, too).

6   II.5, 417b2–5.

7   Cf. *Meta.* IX.6, 1048b18–36.

8   II.5, 417b19–20.

9   II.5, 416b33–34. By "patients" I only mean something which undergoes something under the influence of an "agent."

10 In discussing the fact that the object of knowledge is an agent relative to the knowing power, Ronald Polansky concludes that the objectivity of knowledge is guaranteed by the fact that "the cognitive faculty takes on the object's very form." Polansky 2007, p. 15. This assessment seems right to me.

11 For further criticism of the mechanical view of life, see the *Introduction*.

12 Cf. I.5, 409b24–27.

13 I.5, 409b28–411a7.

14 II.12, 424a17–19.

15 III.1, 424b24–27.

16 II.12, 424a18 ff.

17 The Latinate word "species" has a similar ancestry, as evidenced by the cognates, "spectacle" and "specious."

18 III.4, 429b10–22.

19 II.12, 424a17–24.

20 Similar things were said earlier at I.5, 409b23–410a22.

21 II.5, 417b2–12.

22 It is more obvious in intellectual knowledge that we receive the form of the object not as our own but as of the other: I am not unjust by knowing what injustice is.

23 II.5, 417b22–23.

24 While there seem to be forms of sensation that do not involve awareness of the self, e.g., blindsight, these cases probably should be understood as falling away from the

sort of sensation we usually have, just as we understand the inanimate by how it falls away from life.

25 Aristotle discusses the way we are aware of our acts of sensing at III.2, 425b12–426a1. It is possible that there be animals which, while they sense exterior objects, are only in a very limited way aware of that fact.

26 II.3, 414a32–b6; III.11, 433b31–434a5. It is true that the "consciousness" of animals is probably quite different from our own; still, unless it is held that they do not have sensation at all, they must have awareness of sensible things and so some form of consciousness. If we hold, with Descartes, that animals other than man are mere automata, we in essence reduce them to insentient beings. For a critique of the Cartesian view, cf. Jonas,1966, p. 58–63 and the *Introduction*.

27 *Phys*. II.8.

28 Exactly what instinct is may not be entirely clear, but it seems to be something more than a mere mechanical response to stimuli. The stomach's production of acid when food is ingested is not an instinct, it is just a response; the swallow's ability to build its nest correctly seems to be more than that; it seems to be a sort of knowing. A sign of this is that instincts can be honed by learning. Cf. Gould and Marler 1987, pp. 74–85.

29 III.2, 426b12–29.

30 That the common sense is a sense, not the intellect, is indicated by the fact that it perceives the particular acts of sensation of the exterior senses, and that we need no argument or learning to become aware of what the common sense teaches us. And if we think that telling apart the proper sensibles of the exterior senses is the work of the intellect, we will have to attribute intellect to a great many animals, perhaps even all.

31 It will be clear later that the brain is not the organ of thought and also that it is necessary for thought. Cf. Appendix 5, *Intellect in the De Anima*.

Appendix 5
The Intellectual Soul

Because the intellectual soul is not obviously distinct from the sensing soul, the former must not only be explained but discovered. As Aristotle notes, the ancients did not even distinguish the power of mind[1] from the power of sensation, and so he spends some time in the *De Anima* proving they are distinct.[2] The similarity is so great that Aristotle even calls imagination, which is a kind of interior sense power, a kind of "mind."[3] This is not unreasonable: David Hume, for example, identifies thinking with imagination, with predictably unfortunate consequences like the denial of any objective causality and of the self.[4] For if to think is to imagine, and we have no sensory image of a cause or of the self, then these are by definition unthinkable. The significance of the distinction between sense and intellect is not lost on Aristotle. In the *Metaphysics*, he argues against those who, identifying sense and intellect, end by denying the principle of non-contradiction.[5]

Unfortunate consequences aside, why should we distinguish sense and thought? Do we have to accept the paradoxical results of their identity or do we have good reason (apart from the *reductios* implicit in the previous paragraph) to draw a bright, or at least visible, line between the two? For the two are much alike. Most obviously, perhaps, both are kinds of awareness or knowledge. Sometimes the word "knowledge" is used more restrictedly for universal knowledge, but it does not seem an outrage upon the word to say, "I know that Fred is seated because I see that he is seated." Generally, anyway, sense and intellect seem to be the same sorts of things.

It seems, too, that in both cases the power of knowing begins to operate because of the reception of something knowable. The senses go from potency to act, from being able to see, e.g., to actually seeing, and this under the influence of the thing seen. When the eyes are open and the lights are on, we see what is before our eyes. Our sight is, moreover, somehow caused by the visible as by an agent cause: The visible makes our eyes see it. So too, the intelligible is what causes us to understand. The object known comes before our minds and causes our understanding.[6] Both sense and intellect come to be in act under the influence of their objects as agents, which produce their effects in the knowing powers.

What is known by the two is also in some way the same: The senses and the mind both grasp the sensible things around us. What we think about is what we experience around us. So, since powers are distinguished by their objects,[7] sense and intellect might, again, appear to be the same.

Aristotle, however, takes pains to distinguish them. He points out, for example, that the senses know the particular, the mind the universal,[8] and that the senses, unlike the mind, never tell us what anything is, though they are our chief way of knowing particulars.[9] So they do seem to have somewhat different objects after all.

Moreover, the senses only operate in the presence of the sensibles, whereas the intellect can consider its object whenever it wants to. It seems in some way to contain its objects in a more permanent way than do the senses.[10] On the other hand, the imagination too retains sensible objects,[11] but, because it is so tied to the particular and does not (as mind seems to do) delve beneath the surfaces of things, it looks to be more of a sense power than a kind of mind. Still, Aristotle does call it mind.[12] In its retention of its objects, the imagination approaches the intellect, as does memory. Further, while imagination presents to us simple images and even narratives of a sort, and memory can reminisce, that is, use some memories to provoke and search for others, neither has the combining power of the statement or argument, both of which belong rather to the intellect.

Aristotle begins his discussion of the intellect by pointing to the likenesses between intellect and sense:

> If, then, understanding is like sensing, either it would be suffering some-
> thing from the intelligible, or [it would be] some other such thing. It must
> be impassible, then, but receptive of the species, and be such {the species}
> in potency though it is not this [, i.e., the species]. And it must be related in
> the same way: As the sensitive [is related] to the sensibles, so is the mind to
> the intelligibles.[13]

He had already spoken of the senses as "suffering" or "undergoing" something from the sensibles, and now he notes that the intellect too is affected by the things it knows, not being altered in the primary meaning of that term (thus, "impassible"), but altered somewhat as the senses are by the sensibles.[14] It is the sensibles and the intelligibles which cause the senses and intellect to come into operation. Here, then, the objects act upon the powers rather than, as in eating, the power acting on the object. Both the senses and the intellect are brought into actuality by their objects, the latter being to them as agent causes.

If so, then these knowing powers must receive forms or species from their objects. Every agent produces its likeness in the subject of its action: Fire is hot and produces heat in the air; a moving ball which strikes another ball produces motion in the second ball.[15] The objects of sense and intellect must give to those powers forms or species like their own. The forms received are not the same in every case: In sensation, for example, the same object may be seen and felt;

while the eyes receive the form of color, the hands receive temperature and texture.[16] Each receiver must be for some reason apt to receive this or that species.

The form received by a sense power is called "sensible" because it is a form which is sensed: The form received is exactly that aspect of the exterior thing which the sense power knows, its color, for example. Similarly, what comes to be in the intellect is called a form or species and, since when it does so the intellect understands some aspect of the object, what is received is called an "intelligible species" or "intelligible form." In this reception, the mind undergoes an alteration so as to take on the form of the thing understood, and does so because the intelligible object acts upon the intellect. So the intellect is receptive of the forms of the intelligibles as the sense is of the forms of the sensibles.

But just as the senses must not have the forms they are going to receive in sensing,[17] so the intellect must not have the forms it receives in understanding.[18] What does the intellect understand? What is its proper object or the intelligible form which it receives? It understands "all things,"[19] all bodies and all the accidents of bodies at least insofar as they are things of some sort (taken broadly enough to include not only substances like men and roses and stones, but also their colors, shapes, etc.). While our knowledge of most things is very imperfect, it is certainly about bodily things, at least at first. Nothing completely escapes the scope of the mind, it seems. The intellect, then, must lack the natures of all bodies; it is a purely "possible thing,"[20] that is, it is able to be anything, to take on any bodily form, so it cannot of itself have any bodily form. It is, in that way, like the prime matter of the *Physics*: In itself it has no nature, but it can take on all natures;[21] or like water: In itself it has no shape but it can take on the shape of any container. Consequently, Aristotle concludes, the intellect cannot be a body or have a bodily organ.[22]

As a sign of this, he notes that, whereas the senses do receive immaterially (taking this negation is a very particular way[23]), they still suffer damage from very powerful sensibles like loud explosions or intense lights. This shows that they do have some matter which is in potency to destructive transformations. In contrast, the intellect is not undone by very intelligible objects. The first and most knowable premises of all, like the principle of non-contradiction, instead make lesser intelligibles more intelligible; self-evident premises illuminate and do not obscure conclusions.

Another sign is that the senses receive things with certain conditions which we might call "conditions of matter": particularity, as we have seen, and determinate dimensions and positions.[24] Our "field of vision" contains objects with certain sizes and shapes. But our minds do not contain their objects with these conditions. There is no size to the idea of size nor is the idea of shape itself round or square. Since these quantitative aspects arise from material, we can say that the intellect is immaterial. For the objects as they exist in the world do have these aspects, so that it is not due to their natures in themselves that when we know them they do not have these conditions; it is rather that what receives them, the intellect, receives them in a way appropriate to its own immateriality.[25]

Though it is more obvious that the objects in the mind are universal than that they are the natures of the things known, the object proper of the intellect is rather what things are.[26] It knows the natures even of the objects which are proper to the sense powers and the appetites: what color or taste or the pleasant are, though vaguely, while the senses perceive the colors or tastes without knowing what they are. Aristotle gives these examples: what flesh is, what water is, and what magnitude is. The first two are subjects for natural philosophy and the last for natural philosophy or for mathematics[27]; the first two are substances, the last, an accident. It is clear enough that we know what some things are, e.g., circles or animals or color, at least in general, so there must be some power that knows *what* things are. Aristotle does not say much about why we should say this is the intellect, though it is clear that there is a different object and so there must be a different power. He may identify that with the intellect simply because we do have experience of knowing what a thing is and we tend to label the power that does that "the intellect." He may also be thinking of Socrates' insistence that we do not intellectually grasp anything, really, if we do not know the whatness of what we are talking about. Is virtue teachable, asks Meno, or how does it arise? How can I know if I don't know what virtue is, asks Socrates, and after a lengthy discussion, he returns to his first response to Meno, "...we shall have clarity about this when, before we ask in what way virtue comes to be for human beings, we ask about the very thing itself, what in the world virtue *is*."[28]

Consider also the way we proceed in argument. When we show something to be true or likely about something, we draw the conclusion from premises: If we think the premises are true and well-ordered, we accept the conclusion. How do we know the premises? We look to the predicate and the subject and, from our knowledge of what they are, we consider whether the premises are well-founded or not. So we reduce argument to statements and statements to definitions. The beginning, then, is definition, i.e., the nature of the thing we are talking about. Even in casual conversations we use persuasion of various sorts, sometimes more or less rhetorical or dialectical, but we only consent to a position when we think it follows from premises which we accept based on our notions of what the subjects and predicates are.

Nor should we think that we are then merely reducing the argument to the meanings of words and not to the natures of things. If our everyday words, which express our initial thoughts about the world and are derived immediately from experience, do not reflect the natures of the things we name, then there is no such thing as philosophy (or any other kind of real knowing). For we must proceed from the better (and so prior) known to the less known, but there is no knowledge to start from except the basic knowledge that everyone has just from the experience of living. If that knowledge is not reliable, then we have no criterion at all by which to judge our further thoughts. In fact, when we proceed dialectically, that is, from the opinions of most men or of those reputed to be wise, we are precisely testing our unexamined notions and beliefs against each other. For we easily confuse what is really better known with prejudices derived from our culture or earlier learning or mere personal dispositions, and so we need to test our opinions by making them face others. Only in this way can we see which really are derived from our experience of the world and which are only opinions grounded in human custom or learning. The touchstone of such arguments is always something derived directly from experience; we find some opinion doubtful because it seems to imply something we find more objectionable than we find the contradictory of the opinion in doubt. For example, Aristotle argues in Book I that the soul is not a harmony because, if it were, it would not be a substance or a principle of substance, but instead an accident of some substance. This only carries weight because all of us recognize on some level that we who live and argue about such things are not merely accidental wholes but are essentially living beings somehow made one even if composed of various organs.[29] We judge the validity of arguments, if we are serious thinkers, against more firmly established truths – ultimately, if we can attain science in Aristotle's very strict sense, against self-evident propositions.[30]

Even these self-evident propositions are derived from sensation, experience, and memory, as Aristotle argues.[31] If we all know them and apparently do so without effort, they must be known naturally (the effort comes when we try to use them to argue to or judge other claims) and so must be the foundations of all our further thinking. If they are wrong, we certainly will never find out, since they are the very criteria by which we judge the true and the false. But we have experience of the objectivity of truth; we know that $2 + 2 = 4$, and even if one were to argue that that is a tautology, that tautologies cannot be false is itself self-evident.

There is no escaping, then, Aristotle's claim that we have a basic knowledge of what things are, that this is the most basic knowledge we have, and that it is therefore the proper object of the intellect. For the proper object is always also the first thing a power attains. If not, it would attain something else first and would attain it not under the aspect of the proper object of the power – but then it would not be the power it is, since proper objects define the powers.

The fact that the mind alone seizes on the universal, what is neither here nor now, but is everywhere and always, might tempt us into thinking that the universal as such is the object of the intellect. The truth is that, because the nature of a thing is present in the thing and can also be received into the immaterial mind, the nature of a material thing is neither universal nor particular in itself; it is universal when in the mind (otherwise we could not understand the sentence, "all triangles are figures") and particular when in matter (otherwise the triangle ABC would be universal and so predicable of other triangles). Thus, though the intellect knows universals, it is not quite precise to say that the proper object of the intellect is the universal; the proper object is the nature and it happens to the nature to be universal when present to the intellect. The universality is an accident of the object as it exists in the mind; the nature is not the object of the mind itself insofar as it is a universal, but insofar as it is a nature.[32]

Because the intellect grasps the natures of things outside of it, it is, like the senses and much more so, a power by which we know the world as other from ourselves and ourselves as within the world and a part of it. But the intellect transcends the senses because it knows not only particular things and their exterior qualities, not only the here and now, but penetrates into the natures of things, not only of substances but even of accidents, to see what they are everywhere and always.[33] Our minds begin with this understanding of what things are and, when it manages to come to know something fully by an argument, perfects its activity by seeing that the truth we have arrived at holds because of the natures of the things we are talking about. Rarely is our knowledge so final, yet we strive for perfection precisely by trying to understand the natures of the things we are thinking about. In a way, then, grasping what things are is at both the beginning and the end of all our inquiries.

But, as Aristotle puts it, our minds start as blank slates.[34] Being in pure potency, the mind cannot at that time be known even by itself, since potency is only known through act and no act is present.[35] Consequently, it is when the mind has come to know something by being acted upon by the natures of sensible things that it can think about its own activities and mode of being, or even just be aware of itself.[36] It is self-aware by being aware of others first.

Once it is aware, though, it is not only aware *that* it is a thing in the world, but can even know *what sort* of thing it is and how that contrasts with what other things are. The senses permit at least the higher animals to hunt and flee the hunter and to mate and, it seems likely, to be in some sense aware of themselves as they do so. But they could never understand what they are doing, what they are who do it, or why they do it. For why they do it is all wrapped up in what they and other things are. Lions chase antelopes because they are lions and antelopes are antelopes, but the lion never ponders this significant (for her at any rate) truth.

The mind, then, allows a more complete awareness and self-awareness than do the senses. The former knows the body, the senses and their objects, and itself and its objects. It can, once actualized, reflect on what it knows and how it knows and even on the relations among its own ideas (which reflection would culminate in logic). Whereas the lower animals can only respond to pleasure and pain and by instinct (and, in some cases, a sort of experience) avoid things that are harmful and seek things that are helpful, human beings, by knowing what things are, can recognize what is good or bad in a universal way. We are not just compelled by nature but we can understand and deliberately conform to what is naturally good. As such, we are able to control our own lives. Even if we find ourselves determined by nature to certain ultimate goods, like society and truth, we still can choose how we attain them. Our grasp on what things are universally gives us the freedom to direct ourselves to the goods nature has ordained for us based on what we are.

Moreover, the mind also views the world in a speculative way. We want to know why hawks fly as they do or why the elements are arranged into a periodic table. Even when there is no practical concern, we want to know the truth about things, for the truth is the good of the intellect as such. The intellect has an instinct for this truth; the mind naturally grasps that the truth is a good thing for it. But once it does pursue the truth for its own sake, if Aristotle is right and the mind in question hits pay dirt, it will eventually come to see that the entire universe is the result of a good and knowing God.[37] The contemplation of the universe and its cause is, for Aristotle, the ultimate perfection of the human being.[38]

But there is a problem with Aristotle's account of how we come to know. If the intelligible nature is intelligible when received in the immaterial intellect, but in the physical world is present in only a material way and so is only potentially intelligible, how can the nature get into the intellect? How can the nature of a material thing, embedded in matter in the natural world, come to be present in the intellect? If, like Plato, Aristotle thought that the intelligible natures existed in the real world immaterially, like the Good-Itself or Justice-Itself,[39] then we would need no explanation of this; the condition of immateriality would already be satisfied. But Aristotle emphatically holds that the things we understand are not other than the things we sense but are present in them. The nature of the good is in the good things we see around us, not in a separate, non-material, purely intelligible realm. How can the forms be "dematerialized" so as to become intelligible? And if it cannot, then are we not stuck with a Humean account, in which we cannot transcend the imagination, all thinking is particular, and nothing can be known universally and necessarily?

Moreover, the human mind proceeds from potency to act. Children are not born knowing what dogs are; they have to learn this and everything else. How does the mind, which obviously starts in potency, come to be in act? It cannot be by contact with the pure intelligible forms of material things, as Plato thinks, so how does it happen? The material things which we encounter are what we understand first and so the intelligible species by which we understand those material things must themselves be something pertaining to those same material things. In order for them to act on our possible intellects (the intellect discussed in III.4), there must be something else that can make their forms, which are embedded in matter, capable of affecting the immaterial mind. Again, this points to something which can put the potentially intelligible into a more immaterial state, so as to permit it to be present to the possible intellect.

Since we do in fact know things in a universal and immaterial way, and we do in fact learn from experience, there has to be a faculty which can do this. This is the so-called "agent intellect." Aristotle argues that where something is sometimes in potency and sometimes in act, there must be, on the one hand, something which is capable of receiving new forms and, on the other, something capable of producing those forms in that matter.[40] If a house is in potency and then in act, the potency must be present in some material, wood, stone, and concrete, for example, and there must be some agent, a house-builder, capable of putting the form into that matter. Potency cannot bring itself into act because it does not have actuality to give.[41] Consequently, the possible intellect, though it is that by which the soul knows, is not sufficient; we need also an agent that brings about understanding by bringing the intelligibles into act and allowing the intelligibles to impress themselves, or else itself impressing them, on the possible intellect.

Aristotle explains the working of the agent intellect by saying it is like light. As light makes the colors able to affect the eye, so the agent intellect illuminates the potentially intelligible so that it can affect the possible intellect. The possible intellect is like the eye, the agent like the light, and the intelligible species like the color. Just as the eye cannot see without color, so the possible intellect cannot think without its object being present in some way.[42]

It is questionable whether Aristotle intends to say that the color is brought into act by the light or only that the transparent is brought into act so that the color, already in act, can then affect the eye. If he intends the former, the likeness to the agent intellect is more complete, since the intelligibles as they are in the sensible things are only potentially intelligible and are brought into act by the agent intellect. Once actualized, they are able to affect the possible intellect, or, perhaps more accurately, being made actually intelligible, they are actually in the possible intellect, just as the color being made actually visible is its being made present in the eye. For being actually intelligible is the same as being actually understood, and this is being actually in the mind.[43]

The agent intellect, then, does not itself contain the intelligible species. If it did (and we accept that the agent intellect is a power of the human soul, a point we will discuss shortly), we would immediately understand the species, since we would already possess them immaterially. The species must be present in us in some other more material power. We know that the intelligibles are present in sensible things, and also that we can think about things we have already learned whenever we wish to, even in the absence of the sensibles. We depend, for the intelligibles not exclusively on the sensibles as they exist sometimes present and sometimes absent in the exterior world, but on a power that can retain the sensibles. This is the imagination.[44]

Since we can think in the absence of the sensible objects themselves, the phantasms must have within them the intelligible forms, somewhat in the same way, perhaps, as the light has within it color. For that color, derived from the color in the object, is present in light in such a way as to affect the eye, but not in such a way that the light itself sees the color or that the light itself is colored so as to be itself seen. So too, the phantasms convey to the mind the intelligible objects, but the imagination does not itself understand the intelligible objects. We might also think of words: They convey and so contain meaning, but the ear which perceives them does not thereby perceive their meaning. Meaning is present in the words, but is not known to be present by anything except the mind.

We might add that, given that the things we know are the natures of material things, and that such things do not have real existence except in matter, we would be in danger of misunderstanding these natures if we did not recognize that they are the sorts of things which must be in particular, material subjects. This reference to the particular requires sensation or imagination. So the mind's use of the phantasm is necessary if we are not going to fall into the trap of thinking, as Plato did, that the things we think of in a universal way are themselves universal.

And if the mind did not depend on the phantasms, it would be hard to see why the intellect would be affected, sometimes to the extent of madness, by an injury to the imagination. In fact, this shows not only that the intellect needs the phantasms to learn, but even to consider the things it knows, for an injury to the imagination even after learning can cause us to be incapable of considering what we have already learned. But because Aristotle has already argued that the intellect is immaterial, we cannot say that it depends upon the brain or some other organ as upon a body in which it resides. This is not the only way for a power to depend upon something – it can also depend upon it as providing its object, in the way the eye depends upon color, i.e., not as upon an organ but as upon an object. Since the brain houses the imagination in which the phantasms reside, the mind depends upon the brain. We can even turn this argument around to say that, since a power can depend upon a body either as its organ or as its object, and since the mind depends upon the brain, as we know from observing people who have had strokes or other problems with their brains, and we know, further, by the argument of III.4 that the intellect does not depend upon any corporeal organ, it follows that the mind must depend upon the brain for its objects.

Aristotle's most striking claim about the intellect is this one: that it is immaterial and is separable from the body. He argues this about the possible intellect on the ground that it is able to know all things, and about the agent intellect on the ground that it is more actual, and thus less potential and material, than is the possible intellect:

> This [agent] intellect is also separable and impassible and unmixed, being in substance act. For what makes is always more honorable than what suffers, and the principle than the material.[45]

The argument is that, because the possible intellect is separable, impassible, and unmixed (with body),[46] the agent intellect must be so too. The reason is the fourth predicate in the first sentence: that the agent intellect is not in potency, but is actual. Act is "more honorable," that is, better and more complete, than potency, which is, after all, nothing but the ability for act. Both the agent and the possible intellects are, then, powers of the soul and immaterial. Aristotle has finally conclusively answered his question from Book I: Is the soul separable from body? He has shown that the intellect is not merely the form of a body, but has its own operation separate from the body[47] and so is itself separable from body.[48]

Herein lies a world of ink.[49] Many commentators have taken III.4–5 to mean that the intellect, or one of the two intellects, the agent or the possible, is not really a part of the soul at all, but is instead a separate substance, like an angel or a god, one which has some peculiar relation to the human soul. Aristotle does go on to say, "When separated, this alone is that which truly is, and this alone is immortal and eternal,"[50] and the "this" seems possibly to refer to the agent intellect. How plausible is this view? Or the other extreme, namely, that the soul is nothing but the form of a body and that even the intellect is a material power and uses an physical organ, e.g., the brain?

Having studied with Plato for many years, Aristotle had to have been quite familiar with the notion of the soul as an entity separate from the body.[51] Plato's idea of the intellect seems to be that it is a separate being from the body, one that learns best when it separates itself as much as possible from bodily concerns and sensation. It is even conceivable that Aristotle did not think the possibility of the soul existing apart from the body something very controversial; he may have felt rather that its strong connection to body, even in regard to knowing, is what needed emphasis.

The view that the possible intellect, the intellect which *knows*, is a separated substance flies in the face of our obvious experience of knowing. Aristotle begins his discussion of the intellect by referring to the "part of the soul by which the soul both knows and judges (whether that part be separable, or not separable according to magnitude but [only] according to account)," and shortly afterward to "the intellect of the soul."[52] When I know that $2 + 2 = 4$, it is I who know it, I who also eat and drink and walk and talk. I do not just know *that* I do these things, as I might know that someone else does them, but I experience in myself my doing of them and that I who am one do all these many things. There has to be one knowing power which knows all these things, and, again, not as by an inference about another being but as by immediate experience recognized as one's own. Moreover, if the intellect that knows were a separate substance, it would be neither a part nor the whole of man, and so the use of the intellect could not be what makes man perfect – but it is.[53]

That the agent intellect is not a separate being is harder to see, precisely because it is not that which knows but that which brings into actuality the objects of that which knows, the possible intellect.[54] We need not prove we have a possible intellect just insofar as it is an intellect; what we need to do is prove that it is not a sense power or the imagination, that it is in potency to the intelligibles, that it is immaterial, etc.; we do not need to prove that it exists at all.

The agent intellect is more problematic. The argument, as outlined above, is that the object of the possible intellect is an object to the extent that it is immaterial, but the sense objects themselves wherein these intelligible objects exist only contain these objects potentially, so that there must be an agent which makes the intelligible natures of the sensible objects actually intelligible. This is the agent intellect. Because the agent intellect is not the power which knows, we cannot argue, as we did in the case of the possible intellect, that we have immediate experience of the agent intellect. We might argue, still, that we have the experience of abstracting the natures of the things we experience, and that the agent intellect must be a power of our own souls.

Further, if the agent intellect were not a power of our souls, the human soul would be an oddly imperfect thing, a thing which lacked the fundamental natural principles of its own operation, a position in conflict with Aristotle's general claim that nature operates for the best and provides for things what they need to attain it.[55] In the *Posterior Analytics* and the *Metaphysics*, Aristotle describes a process by which, in at least some cases, beginning from sensation, and utilizing memory to gather individual events and some other organizing power to put like memories with like, we are finally able to seize upon what is common to various instances of some nature and see what that thing is. Knowing what it is, we can see that certain predicates necessarily belong to it.[56] This process is described as a human process, and in fact Aristotle ends the discussion in the *Posterior Analytics* with the claim that the first principles of science are neither always present, nor do they come from other more perfect knowledge, but rather they arise from sensation; "...and the soul is such as to be able to undergo this."[57] But how can universal and necessary propositions arise from the flux of the senses? He leaves that further determination for the study of the soul, and the answer provided in the *De Anima* is that the soul has an agent intellect which can illuminate the phantasms in the imagination, once they are well organized,[58] so that they can be seen by the possible intellect. The intellect, then, is both immaterial and a power of the human soul, a soul which, like all others, is the form of an organized body. We ourselves are able to operate in the body and in our minds, and there is one "self" who does this in each of us. Aristotle explains the character of the human soul in a way faithful to our experience, especially our interior experience, avoiding both reductionist materialism and Cartesian dualism. We are not just complex machines, nor are we really two things, a body and a soul; we are each one substance with many powers, some latent, some overt. Aristotle's account of the soul, the body, and the intellect is not only compatible with our common experience of being unified beings but takes its beginnings from these experiences – experiences too well known to be denied.

Endnotes to Appendix 5

1   The word νοῦς may be translated by mind or intellect or thinking power. Aristotle also uses this word to speak of the act of understanding and of the habit by which one grasps first principles.

2   III.3, 427a17–b8.

3   III.3, 427b27–28.

4   Hume, David 1888, pp. 1–7; 155–172; 251–263.

5   *Meta.* IV.5, 1009a22–1011a2.

6   As noted in Appendix 4, knowledge demands that the object itself of the knowing power be present to the latter.

7   II.4, 415a16–22.

8   II.5, 417b22–23.

9   *Meta.* I.1, 981b10–13.

10   II.5, 417b22–26.

11   III.2, 425b24–25.

12   III.3, 427b27–29.

13   III.4, 429a13–18.

14   II.5, 417a21–b16.

15   Some causes do not seem to follow this rule. A hammer produces a house or a table, not a hammer, for example. This is a case of instrumental causality. But even here, the hammer does produce its likeness, a flattened surface or just the motion in a nail caused by its own motion. There are other sorts of apparent exceptions as well, but they all are only apparent. A thing cannot give what it does not have.

16   It can seem like mere word play to say the sense or the intellect receives a "form" or "species" from its object. But the words fit. In the *Physics*, "form" and "species" are the names for what is novel about a thing at the end of a change, the words being extended from their basic meanings of "shape" and "appearance." When fire heats water, the water is first cold and then hot. The new thing about the water, its hotness, is a new "form." The form differentiates two things that have the same matter, here, the hot and the cold water. It is a likeness of the agent and by the action of the agent it comes to be present where it was not before, in the water. So too, the colored object is colored, and, acting as an agent on the eyes, the color comes to be present in the eyes. The color is thus also called a form or species.

17   Cf. Appendix 4, *The Sensing Soul.*

18   III.4, 429a13–21; II.11, 424a7–10.

19   III.4, 429a18.

20   III.4, 429a21–22.

21   *Phys.* I.7, 191a7–15.

22   III.4, 429a18; 429a24–25.

23   See Appendix 4, *The Sensing Soul.*

24   See Appendix 4.

25   It may be objected that this argument fails because it makes a false assumption: Because what is known by an idea, the nature, is known without dimensions or shape or position, that the idea has no such properties. But a representation and a thing which is represented are not the same, so the argument does not follow. The objection overlooks the main fact about awareness: When we know, the intelligible species of the thing we know, not a simulacrum, is what is in our intellects (or senses). See III.8, 431b20–432a3.

26   III.4, 429b10–22.

27   We can define quantities without reference to sensible qualities like hot and cold and if we do so we are within mathematics; but we can also define quantities as connected to sensible qualities, as when we define the meter by reference to a certain sort of metal bar at a certain temperature, etc., and when we do this we are within natural philosophy. For the modes of defining of the sciences, see *Meta.* VI.1, 1025b28–1026a16.

28   Plato *Meno*, 70a–71a; 100b.

29   See *Introduction* and Appendix 4, *The Sensing Soul*.

30   *Po. An.* I.2, 71b26–29.

31   *Po. An.* II.19, 99b17–19; 99b32–100b17.

32   Thomas Aquinas *De Ente et Essentia*, Ch. 3.

33   This does not mean that we know these natures perfectly, only that we know them in some way, perhaps only enough to recognize them as "things."

34   III.4, 429b29–430a2.

35   *Meta.* IX.1049b12–17.

36   III.4, 429b5–9.

37   *Meta.* XII.6–10.

38   *Nic. Eth.* X.7, 1177a12–b26.

39   For example, cf. Plato, *Phaedo*, 100b–e.

40   III.5, 430a10–13.

41   III.5, 430a15–17.

42   III.7, 431a14–b12; III.8, 432a3–10; *De Mem.* 1, 449b3s–450a27.

43   III.7, 431a1–2.

44   III.2, 425b22–25; III.3, 428b10–429a2. The images in the imagination should not be thought of as restricted to visual or audial images; there are also images corresponding to the other senses. If not, we could never remember what a rose smells like.

45   III.5, 430a17–19.

46   These three predicates are said of the possible intellect in III.4, 429b4–5; 429a15; 429a17; 429a24–25.

47   Cf. I.1, 403a10–11.

48   Given the doctrine of the *Phys.* I.7, that things which are generable and corruptible must be composed of matter and form, and that he has just shown that the intellect is not so formed but is immaterial, it follows that he would necessarily conclude that the rational soul is immortal. (*Phys.* I.7, 190b17–20) Aristotle does not explicitly claim that the possible intellect is immortal or deathless. But see *Meta.* XII.3, 1070a24–26, where he suggests that there are forms which come to be but never pass away, and restricts this possibility to intellectual souls.

49   As might be expected in the case of a text so old, terse, and significant, this one has

been debated, if not *ad infinitum*, at least *ad nauseam*. Here I mean to make only some general remarks; more detailed commentary will be found in the endnotes to the relevant passages, the most important of which are: I.1, 403a5–10; I.4, 408b18–32; I.5, 411b14–19; II.1, 413a3–7; II.2, 413b13–29, II.3, 415a7–12; III.3, 427a17–b14; III.4, 429a10–b5, 429b22–26, 429b29–430a2; III.5, 430a10–25; III.7, 431a14–b2, 431b17–19; III.8, 432a3–14. Also important are *Meta.* VI.1 1025b34–1026a6 and XII.3, 1070a24–26. For the various positions concerning III.4–5, see Cohoe 2022, 2014, 2013, Gerson 2004, Caston 1999, Burnyeat 2008 and the notes on the significant passages in Polansky 2007, Shields 2016, Reeves 2017, and Bolotin 2018.

50   III.5, 430a22–23.

51   Cf., e.g, Plato, *Phaedo*, 105c–107a. Anaxagoras, too, may have thought the mind was completely separate. Cf. I.2, 405a13–19, 405b19–23. See also I.3, 407b2–5.

52   III.4, 429a10–12, 23.

53   *Nic. Eth.* I.7, 1177b14–26.

54   The defenders of the view that the agent intellect is a separate intellect would no doubt say it does know, but my point is that it is not the thing doing *our* knowing.

55   *Phys.* II.2, 194a32–33; *MA* 2, 704b12–18; *Gen. An.* V.8, 788b20–25; *De Juv.* 10, 476a11–15; *PA* III.1, 661b28–32.

56   *Po. An.* II.19, 99b32–100b17.

57   *Po. An.* II.19, 100a3–14.

58   The need for organizing the phantasms is not so explicit in the text of the *Posterior Analytics*. But mere memories are not enough: Aristotle compares the sensations to a group of soldiers during a rout: Each one flees away until one takes a stand (which corresponds to being remembered), and then another and another, until they attain a "principle" – the Greek word can also mean command – and thus control the field, as one controls an entire field of study not by seeing every instance of the thing studied but by seizing what is common to all, the universal nature. Just as this control of the field of battle requires organization in the army, so for the mind to attain control of a field of thought requires that the mind come to the universal, which in turn requires that our memories be organized so that we can see what they have in common.

Glossary

This glossary lists the primary translations of each word considered. In the translation itself, there are places where an alternative is given within curved brackets ("{}").

Abstraction – ἀφαιρέσις – Aristotle restricts the use of this word to mathematical abstraction. The English philosophical tradition will also speak of the "abstraction" of the universal. This is not what Aristotle is referring to when he uses this word.

Accident – συμβεβεκός – This may also be translated "incidental attribute." In modern English, the word "accident" usually means an occurrence which comes about by bad luck; in this translation, and most others of the *Physics*, the word means what just happens to be in something but does not belong to the nature of the thing or follow from that nature. Thus, white or black are "accidents" of men. The etymology of "accident" closely mirrors the Greek etymology of συμβεβεκός – the former originally means (in Latin) "what has fallen together," the latter, "what has run together."

According to itself – καθ'αὐτό – often translated by the Latin *per se,* which literally means "through itself;" often incorrectly and misleadingly translated "essentially."

Account – λόγος – This Greek word can be translated in a number of ways. It started out meaning a computation or reckoning. λόγος then comes to mean "word," that by which we gather notions, and "speech," a complex of words, and "argument," a particular sort of speech. It is extended to mean "notion," that which a word signifies, and "reason," the power wherein notions reside. It is also used to mean "ratio." I have translated this word in almost all cases by "account." Other translations (in certain contexts) might be "notion," "definition," "thought," "argument," "reason," "formula," "statement," "expression."

Act (n) – ἐνέργεια – The Greek word ἔργον is cognate with our English word "work" and should sometimes be so translated. Ἐνέργεια means "at work" or "operating" (itself derived from the Latin *opus,* "work"). The verbal form I translate as "is in act." For a more complete explanation of these translations, see Coughlin, 2005, pp. xxv–xxviii.

Act (v.) – ποιεῖν – This is also translated by "make" or "do" at some points. "Make" is in some ways better than "acting," but the English has not been extended as far as the Greek and this makes it difficult always to translate by "make."

Action – ποίησις – The noun formed from the verb ποιεῖν.

Actuality – ἐντελέχεια – coined by Aristotle, it seems, to indicate what is opposed to the potential. It is derived from ἐντελὲς ἔχειν, "having completion." Cf. Chantraine 2009, entry "ἐντελέχεια." See Coughlin, 2005, pp. xxv–xxviii for further discussion of ἐντελέχεια and ἐνέργεια.

Affirmation – φάσις, κατάφασις

Alteration – ἀλλοίωσις – Change in quality, as opposed to change in substance (i.e., in the thing itself, like man or stone or hydrogen), or in amount, or in place. The nature of sensation and intellection cause Aristotle to extend the meaning of this term in II.5, 417a22–b22.

Amount – ποσόν – Also translated "quantity."

Analogy – ἀναλογία

Appetite – ὄρεξις

Appetetive – ὀρεκτικόν

Art – τέχνη – The Greek word was used in a broader sense than we now use the word "art." We tend to mean "fine art" when we say "art." But we still do speak of chairs and tables as "artifacts," i.e., things made by art, and if we note this we might be inclined to call manual skills like carpentry and brick-laying "arts." This is the way the word is used in this translation.

Attribute – κατηγορία – Also translated "predicate" and, when used to name one the ten most universal univocal predicates, translated "category." See "Category."

Beginning – ἀρχή – Also translated by "principle," which is derived from the Latin "principio," "beginning." It can be a beginning in thought or in things.

Belief – ὑπόληψις – Refers not only to the belief which is only opinion or faith, but also to the conviction following upon proof or understanding.

By nature – φύσει – the dative of φύσις, "nature."

Category – κατηγορία – Though the Greek word means literally "accusation" or "predicate" (things said about something), the English has come to mean a group. I have translated the word by "predicate' or "attribute" where the reference is not to one of the ten highest univocal names, i.e., the "categories" of the logical work of that name. Cf. *Cat.* 4, 1b25–2a10.

Cause – αἴτιον – Originally the word means the guilty party, the one responsible. It is then extended to mean any sort of cause. Cf. II, 3, 194b16–195a4.

Change – μεταβολή – This is more general than motion, because, while change in what a thing is most fundamentally, i.e., substantial change, is certainly change, it is not motion. The sorts of motion are change of place, alteration, and growth and diminution.

Choice – προαίρεσις

Color – χρῶμα

Come to be, Become – γίγνεσθαι – "Simple" coming to be is the coming to be of what is simply, i.e., a thing in the radical, unqualified sense of the word. The things of this sort, men, horses, rocks, elements, etc., are "substances," not in the modern chemical sense of the word, but in the sense that they "stand under" (Latin: *sub + stant*) other "things," such as sizes or colors or temperatures. They are called "beings" is the normal sense of the word. Because other things are beings by inhering in these, in the case of "accidents," their coming to be is not "simple," but qualified, or, as Aristotle usually puts it, it is a coming to be *this*. Cf. 190a31–33.

Complete – τέλειος – Also translated "perfect."

Contemplation – θεωρεῖν – Literally, "looking;" might also be translated "consideration" or "speculation." These English words can carry the connotation of tentativeness, as in "I am contemplating buying a new car" or "That's just speculation," but the Greek does not have this shade of meaning. It refers to the actual use of knowledge or, in its first meaning, the actual use of the eyes.

Conviction – πίστις

Definition – ὁρισμός

Demonstration – ἀπόδειξις

' *Desire* – ἐπιθυμία

Discern – κρίνειν

Element – στοιχεῖον

End – τέλος

Ensouled – ἔμψυχον – This could also be translated "animate." I prefer the former because it indicates to the English reader the root of the word, "soul," as does "animate" to the reader familiar with Latin. ("Animate" is from the Latin "anima," "soul." Both the Latin and the Greek words originally mean "breath," and are then extended to mean the principle by which the living thing breathes or, even more generally, is alive.) The word "soul" does not carry the connotations for Aristotle which it does for modern readers. We tend to think of it as implying immateriality, immortality, etc., but for Aristotle, it simply means whatever is the principle by which the living thing is alive.

Eternal – ἀΐδιος

Flavor – χυμός

Form – μορφή – This seems to name the term of a change, like the result of turning a piece of clay into a statue. It has an obvious parentage in Plato's "ideas" or "forms." What both thinkers are looking at is that within a thing in virtue of which it is what it is and remains stable in its being such. It is sometimes used synonymously with "species" (εἶδος) and even "account" (λόγος). Cf. II.1, 412a8; II.3, 414a9.

Genus – γένος – The translation "kind" or even "general name" might be preferable sometimes. I have sometimes translated this by "kind." Where the intention is clearly to speak of the logical genus, not just some "kind" (which in English seems to include the species), I have used "genus."

Growth – αὔξησις

Habit – ἕξις – Can also be translated as "state," "possession, and "condition."

Harmony – ἁρμονία

Hearing – ἀκοή, ἄκουσις

Imagination – φαντασία

Immortal – ἀθάνατος

Impassible – ἀπαθής

Imperfect –ἀτελής – Also translated, "incomplete."

Intellect – νοῦς – See "mind."

Intellectual – νοητικόν

Intelligible – νόημα

Invisible – ἀόρατον

Judge (v) – φρονεῖν

Kind – γένος – See "genus."

Know (v) – γνωρίζειν – Used as a quasi-genus for both intellectual and sensitive knowing.

Light (n. opposed to "dark") – φῶς

Locomotion – φορά – Literally, "carrying" or "bearing." Aristotle extends the usual Greek word for carrying to any kind of change of place.

Material, Matter – ὕλη

Mind – νοῦς – This can and will be translated "intellect" or "understanding." The word poses problems for the translator. I have chosen "mind" because it seems to include the memory and imagination while the other possibilities do not, or do not do so as readily. Until III.3 the question is on the table: Is the mind something other than the imagination and memory? Aristotle will distinguish imagination from intellect in III.3 and discuss intellect in detail in III.4–8. Until intellect and imagination are distinguished in III.3, I translate the word by "mind;" where Aristotle is referring to the intellect as opposed to the mind, mostly in III.4–8, I translate it by "intellect." When he moves on to consider the power of locomotion in III.9–11 I again use "mind," as he is expressly including the imagination at that point. (Cf. III.10, 433a9–10) The same word may also refer to the habit of knowing, and then it is translated by "understanding," and the verbal form of the word by "to understand." The related noun νόησις, since it names the activity of the intellect, is also translated "understanding." The object of this power is called νόημα and is translated by "intelligible." A closely related word, διάνοια, is translated "the power to think things through" and the verbal form is translated, "to think things through."

Mobile – κινητόν

Motion – κίνησις – See the note on "change."

Mover – κινοῦν

Natural science – φυσική – This includes any scientific study of natural beings. For this reason, I have not translated the word by "physics," which has come to be opposed to chemistry and biology. In Aristotle's usage, the study in question includes these and all other studies of natural beings.

Nature – φύσις

Negation – ἀπόφασις

Odor – ὀσφραντός

Opinion – δόξα

Opinion, to form an – δοξάζειν

Organ – ὄργανον – Also translated "tool."

Pain – λύπη

Part – μέρος

Particular – καθ' ἕκαστον – Literally, "according to each thing;" contrasts with "universal" (καθόλου, literally, "according to the whole").

Passion – πάθος – The word could also be translated "undergoing" or "affection" or "suffering." It signifies that which a thing acted upon by another has in virtue of that action.

Perfect – τέλειος – Also translated "complete."

Phantasm – φάντασμα – Could also translated "image."

Pleasure – ἡδονή

Potency – δύναμις – When used in an active sense, translated "power." See next note.

Power – δύναμις – When used in a passive sense, translated "potency." See previous note.

Principle – ἀρχή – This might also be translated "beginning," "source," or "origin."

Prudence – φρόνησις. This might also be translated "judgement."

Quality, such – ποιόν

Ratio – λόγος – See note on "account."

Reason – λόγος – See note on "account."

Receptive – δεκτικός

Science – ἐπιστήμη – This word is used to name the perfection of discursive reasoning as described in the *Posterior Analytics*, but it is also used less strictly to mean knowledge, though not the knowledge afforded by the senses. It is often to be contrasted with opinion (δόξα) and understanding (νοῦς).

Seed – σπέρμα

Sensation (n) – αἴσθησις

Sense (n) – αἴσθησις

Sense (v) – αἰσθάνεσθαι

Sensible – αἰσθητόν

Separable – χωριστός

Separate – χωριστός

Separate (v) – χωρίζειν

Sight – ὄψις

Simply – ἁπλῶς

Smell – ὀσμή – i.e., an odor

Smell – ὄσφρησις – i.e., the sense of smell

Soul – ψυχή – See "ensouled."

Sound – ψόφος

Species – εἶδος – See "genus."

Speech – λόγος – See "account."

State – ἕχις – Can also translated by "habit," "possession," or "condition."

Subject – ὑποκείμενον

Substance – οὐσία – A substance is what exists simply speaking, like a man or a horse or a tree. The word might be translated "thing." It does not mean substance in the modern, chemical sense of the word, i.e., an element or compound, as opposed to a mixture. The word is extended in II.1 to mean not only the thing that exists, but its intrinsic principles, matter and form, as well.

Suffer (v) – πάσχειν

Suffer, able to (adj) – παθητικός

Suffering – πάθησις

Tangible – ἁπτός

Taste (n) – γεῦσις

Term – ὅρος

That for the sake of which – τὸ οὗ ἕνεκα

Think things through – διάνοια – This indicates the power to think things through. The verbal form will be translated by appropriate forms of the infinitive "to think things through."

This something – τόδε τι – Aristotle uses this expression, translated in Latin by "hoc aliquid," to indicate a particular existing substance, this man or this horse, without determining what sort of substance it is. Such a thing is "something," and it is a particular (a "this").

Time – χρόνος

Touch (n) – ἀφή

Touch, able to (adj) – ἁπτικός

Touch (v) – ἅπτεσθαι

Transparent – διαφανής

Underlying – ὑποκείμενον

Universal – καθόλου

Unsouled – ἄψυχος – Cf. note on "ensouled," above. This might also be translated, "inanimate."

Visible – ὁρατόν

What it is – τὸ τί ἔστιν

What it was to be – τὸ τί ἦν εἶναι

Whole – ὅλος

Will – βούλησις – Some argue that this should be translated by "wish," not by "will," on the grounds that the English word "will" is freighted with connotations foreign to Aristotle. I would contend that the everyday use of the word simply indicates intention and the power that intends due to intellectual perception, and this is all we need understand Aristotle to mean.

Work (n) – ἔργον

Bibliography

Greek Texts

Ross, W.D,. ed. 1956 *Aristotelis De Anima*. Oxford: Oxford University Press.

Ross, Sir David, ed. 1961 *De Anima*. Oxford: Oxford University Press.

Siwek, Paul, S.J. 1965 Aristotelis Tractatus de Anima Graece et Latine. Rome: Desclée.

Works Cited

Allen, D.J. 1955 *Aristotelis De Caelo*. Oxford: Oxford University Press.

Bywater, L. 1894 *Aristotelis Ethica Nicomachea*. Oxford: Oxford University Press.

Aquinas, Thomas *De Ente et Essentia*. Sancti Thomae Aquinatis doctoris angelici Opera omnia iussu Leonis XIII, P.M. edita, cura et studio Fratrum Praedicatorum 43. Rome and Paris: Leonine Commission, 1976.

Aquinas, Thomas *Sentencia libri De anima*. Sancti Thomae Aquinatis doctoris angelici Opera omnia iussu Leonis XIII, P.M. edita, cura et studio Fratrum Praedicatorum 45/1. Rome and Paris: Leonine Commission, 1984.

Bolotin, David trans. 2018 *De Anima (On Soul)*. Macon, Georgia: Mercer University Press.

Burnyeat, Myles F. 2008 "Aristotle's Divine Intellect." The Aquinas Lecture. Milwaukee, WI: Marquette University Press.

Cajetanus, Thomas De Vio Cardinalis. 1939 *Commentaria in De Anima Aristotelis*, Vol. II, ed. P.I. Coquelle, O.P. Rome: Angelicum.

Caston, Victor 1999 "Aristotle's Two Intellects: A Modest Proposal." Phronesis 44 (3), pp.199–227.

Chantraine, Pierre 2009 *Dictionnaire Étymologique de la Langue Grecque* . Paris: Klincksieck.

Cohoe, Caleb 2013 "Why the Intellect Cannot Have a Bodily Organ: De Anima III 4." Phronesis 58, pp. 347–377.

Cohoe, Caleb 2014 "Nous in Aristotle's De Anima." Philosophy Compass. Vol. 9, Issue 9, pp. 594–604.

Cohoe, Caleb 2018 "Why the View of Intellect in De Anima I.4 Isn't Aristotle's Own." British Journal for the History of Philosophy. Vol. 26, Issue 2, pp. 241–254.

Cohoe, Caleb 2022 "The Separability of Nous" in Aristotle's *On the Soul: A Critical Guide*. Cambridge University Press. Ed. Caleb Cohoe. Cambridge University Press, pp. 229–246

Coughlin, Glen trans. 2005 *Aristotle: Physics, or Natural Hearing*. South Bend, IN: St. Augustine's Press.

Descartes, René 1967 *Le Monde* in *Oeuvres de Descartes* XI, eds. Adam and Tannery. Paris: Librairie Philosophique J. Vrin.

Descartes, René 1967 *Les Passions de l'Ame* in *Oeuvres de Descartes* XI, eds. Adam and Tannery. Paris: Librairie Philosophique J. Vrin.

Descartes, René 1964 *Meditationes de Prima Philosophia* in *Oeuvres de Descartes* VII, eds. Adam and Tannery. Paris: Librairie Philosophique J. Vrin.

Drossaart Lulofs, H.J. 1965 *Aristotelis De Generatione Animalium*. Oxford: Oxford University Press.

Ernout, Alfred and Meillet, Antoine 2001 *Dictionnaire Étymologique de la Langue Latine*. Paris: Klincksieck.

Euclid, *Elements,* Vol. 1–3. 1956. trans. Heath, Thomas L. London: Dover Publications.

Gerson, Lloyd P. 2004 "The Unity of Intellect in Aristotle's De Anima," *Phronesis* 49 (4), 348–73.

Gould, James and Marler, Peter, 1987. "Learning by Instinct." Scientific American. Vol. 256 (1), pp. 74–85.

Harold, Franklin M. 2001 *The Way of the Cell: Molecules, Organisms and the Order of Life*. New York: Oxford University Press.

Hume, David 1888 Treatise of Human Nature, 2nd ed., ed. Selby-Bigge, L.A. Oxford: Oxford University Press.

Joachim, H.H. 1922 *Aristotle: On Coming-to-Be and Passing-Away: A Revised Text and Commentary.* Oxford: Oxford University Press.

Jonas, Hans 1966 *The Phenomenon of Life: Towards a Philosophical Biology*. Evaston, IL: Northwestern University Press.

Kass, Leon R. 1999 *The Hungry Soul: Eating and the Perfecting of Our Nature*. Chicago: University of Chicago Press.

Kass, Leon R. 2002 "The Permanent Limitations of Biology" in *Life, Liberty and the Defense of Dignity: The Challenge for Bioethics*. New York: Encounter Books, pp. 277–297.

Kirk, G. S., Raven, J.E, and Schofield, M. 1983 *The Presocratic Philosophers,* 2nd ed. New York: Cambridge University Press.

Lucretius, *De Rerum Naturae* 1995 (trans.) Esolen, Anthony M. *On the Nature of Things.* Baltimore: The Johns Hopkins University Press.

Mayr, Ernst 1991 *One Long Argument: Charles Darwin and the Genesis of Modern Evolutionary Thought.* Cambridge, MA: Harvard University Press.

Minio-Paluello, L. 1949 *Aristotelis Categoriae et Liber de Interpretatione.* Oxford: Oxford University Press.

Monod, Jacques 1971 *Chance and Necessity: An Essay on the Natural Philosophy of Modern Biology*, trans. Austryn Wainhouse. London: Collins.

Nussbaum, Martha Craven 1978 *Aristotle's De Motu Animalium.* Princeton: Princeton University Press.

Plato 1997*Complete Works.* ed. by Cooper, John A. Indianapolis, IN: Hackett.

Plato 1901–1903 *Platonis Opera, 4 Vols.* ed. Ioannes Burnet. Oxford: Oxford University Press.

Polansky, Ronald 2007 *Aristotle's De Anima.* New York: Cambridge University Press.

Ptolemy 1998 *Almagest.* ed. Toomer, G.J. Princeton: Princeton University Press.

Reeves, C.D.C. trans. 2017 *De Anima.* Indianapolis: Hackett Publishing Company.

Ross, Sir David ed. 1936 *Aristotle's Physics: a Revised Text with Introduction and Commentary.* Oxford: Oxford University Press.

Ross, Sir David ed. 1949 *Aristotle's Prior and Posterior Analytics: A Revised Text with Introduction and Commentary.* Oxford: Oxford University Press.

Ross, Sir David ed. 1961 *De Anima.* Oxford: Oxford University Press.

Ross, W.D. ed. 1956 *Aristotelis De Anima.* Oxford: Oxford University Press.

Ross, W.D. ed. 1957 *Aristotelis Politica.* Oxford: Oxford University Press.

Ross, W.D. ed. 1959 *Aristotelis Ars Rhetorica.* Oxford: Oxford University Press.

Shields, Christoper 2016 *Aristotle, De Anima.* Oxford: Oxford University Press.

Simplicius 1995, trans. J.O. Urmson *On Aristotle's 'On the Soul 1.1–2.3'.* Ithaka, NY: Cornell University Press.

Simplicius 2000, trans. H.J. Blumenthal *On Aristotle's 'On the Soul 3.1–5'.* Ithaka, NY: Cornell University Press.

Smith, J.A., trans. 1984 "On The Soul" in *The Complete Works of Aristotle*, The Revised Oxford Translation Vol. 1, pp. 641–692. Princeton: Princeton University Press.

Other Works Consulted

Augros, Michael 2017. *The Immortal in You*. San Francisco: Ignatius Press.

De Koninck, Charles 1947 "Introduction à l'étude de l'âme." Laval théologique et philosophique, Volume 3, Number 1, 1947, pp. 9–138.

Hamlyn, D.W., trans. 1968 *Aristotle's De Anima Books II, III*. Oxford: Oxford University Press.

Lawson-Tancred, Hugh, trans. 1986 *Aristotle: De Anima (On the Soul)*. London: Penguin Books.

Ross, G.R.T. 1906 *Aristotle: De Sensu and De Memoria, Text and Translation with Introduction and Commentary*. Cambridge: Cambridge Universitty Press. Reprinted 2014.

Ross W.D. 1995 *Aristotle*, 6th Ed.. London: Routledge.

Ross, W.D. 1924 *Aristotle's Metaphysics: A Revised Text with Introduction and Commentary*. 2 Vols. Oxford: Oxford University Press.

Ross, W.D. 1955 *Aristotle, Parva Naturalia: A Revised Text with Introduction and Commentary*. Oxford: Oxford University Press.

Sachs, Joe, trans. 2001 *Aristotle's "On the Soul" and "On Memory and Recollection."* Santa Fe, NM: Green Lion Press.

Shields, Christopher, trans. 2016 *Aristotle, De Anima*. Oxford: Clarendon Press.

Index